Hoover Institution Studies

The Turkish Straits and NATO

The Turkish Straits and NATO

Ferenc A. Váli

Hoover Institution Press
Stanford University
Stanford, California

Hoover Institution Studies 32
Standard Book Number 8179-3321-2
Library of Congress Card Number 70-170205
Printed in the United States of America
© 1972 by the Board of Trustees of the
  Leland Stanford Junior University

CONTENTS

Preface

The Bosporus and Dardanelles, the waterways between the Black Sea and the Aegean now known as the Turkish Straits, have played an important role in all ages of history. Originally arteries of commercial navigation, they became, with the foundation of Constantinople, access routes to the capital of two universal empires, first the East Roman or Byzantine and later the Ottoman. During the past two centuries they have become a much-sought-after channel of penetration by Russia in her desire to reach out into the Mediterranean, and also a potential route to be used by Russia's opponents in the reverse direction. Napoleon perceived the supreme strategic value of the Straits when he declared his willingness "to abandon mastery over half the world rather than yield Russia those narrow straits."[a]

The problem of the Straits did not end with the dissolution of the Ottoman Empire and the downfall of the Empire of the Tsars. Despite assurances that the foreign policy of the Soviet Union was not a continuation of Tsarist politics, in 1939-40 and again in 1945-46 Moscow attempted to obtain

---

[a] Comte de Las Cases, *Mémorial de Sainte-Helène*, Vol. I (Paris: Ernest Bourdine, 1842), p. 474.

control over the Straits. At the time of this writing, the "umbilical cord" of Soviet naval penetration into the Mediterranean and the Arab Middle East passes through these waterlanes. Sooner or later, it may be expected, Russia will again raise the question of the Straits and attempt to gain unassailable control over the access route to the Mediterranean. Such a venture is already foreshadowed by her claim to be a Mediterranean power.

A policy-oriented examination of the Straits question must be carried out on a three-dimensional basis. Political and strategic considerations are paramount. Since 1936 navigation through the Straits has been regulated by the Convention of Montreux, and insofar as the Convention is applied (or revised, as may be expected), issues relating to the Straits are handled legalistically by the chancelleries concerned. Thus, because political and defense interests are at present embedded in the clauses of Montreux, their provisions and interpretation had to be given ample coverage in this book. But it should never be forgotten that the Russian urge to remove the restrictions imposed on the movement of her warships through the Straits is a strong one, and that power politics might soon replace the presently pertinent legal argumentation.

At no point can problems affecting the Straits be properly evaluated without the experience offered by their history. In fact, the entire evolution of the geopolitical and navigational issues of the Straits presents a continuum which should not be ignored when discussing the contemporary aspects of the problem. After all, it is the chronic discontent of Moscow which creates the major issue concerning the navigation of these maritime arteries.

I have been closely interested in the geostrategic, political, and legal questions of the Straits since my wartime sojourn in Turkey, from 1943 to 1946. Research conducted from 1965 to 1968 and supported by the North Atlantic Treaty Organization and the American Research Institute in Turkey led to the completion of a book entitled *Bridge Across the Bosporus—The Foreign Policy of Turkey,* published in 1971. Pursuant to this study, a fellowship granted by the Hoover Institution on War, Revolution and Peace made it possible for me to prepare the present work, which is focused on the Turkish Straits and their place in the political and military concepts of NATO.

Chapter One is devoted to the examination of the geopolitical significance of the Straits and Chapter Two to the development of the Straits issue prior to the Montreux Convention. Chapter Three endeavors to present an analysis of the provisions of this Convention, and Chapter Four describes Soviet attempts to gain control of the Dardanelles. Chapters Five and Six deal with the Turkish Straits insofar as they affect NATO and the Soviet concentration of forces in the Mediterranean. Finally, in Chapter Seven I have undertaken to submit suggestions concerning a possible revision of the Montreux Convention and concerning policies to be pursued by NATO—or individually by the United States—with regard to the Soviet threat to the Straits. Documents providing background to the questions discussed are assembled in thirty-three Appendixes which follow the text.

As to place names mentioned in the text, I have generally used the present Turkish spelling. Thus, I write Küçük Kaynarca and Hünkâr Iskelesi. In some cases, however, the internationally current version will be used, with the Turkish names in parentheses. I use the terms current in their times to denote Constantinople and Istanbul—the former until the post-World War I period; the latter thereafter. Throughout the text I shall speak of the Dardanelles and Bosporus because the Turkish version of these names is hardly known outside Turkey.

For the assistance which has made possible the writing and publishing of the present volume, I owe thanks principally to the Hoover Institution on War, Revolution and Peace. Thanks are also due to my own institution, the University of Massachusetts, for having given me a faculty research grant which enabled me to avail myself of various services. I am also grateful to the many persons I interviewed in Turkey, in the United States, and in some European capitals.

I also wish to express thanks to Mr. John F. Kikoski, who gave me research assistance, and to Mrs. Doris Holden, who typed the manuscript in its final form.

Amherst, Massachusetts   F.A.V
September 1971

Turkish Spelling and Pronunciation

Turkish spelling and pronunciation is, as a rule, phonetic. Vowels are never diphthongized and their sound values never vary (thus *e* is like the English *e* in "men," *u* like the *u* in "put"). While consonants are generally pronounced as in English, some letters have different sound values in Turkish:

c is pronounced as the *j* in "jar"
ç is pronounced as *ch* in "chair"
ğ is not pronounced but the preceding vowel is lengthened
g always has a hard pronunciation as in "go"
ı, the undotted *i*, is an intermediate neutral sound approximately like the *u* in "measure"
j is pronounced as in French (as the *s* in "measure")
ö is pronounced as in German
ş is pronounced as *sh* in "ship"
ü is pronounced as in German
y is always a consonant as in "yard"
The circumflex, as in French, extends the vowel but also softens the preceding consonants (g, k, or l), as in "Hünkâr" (... *kyar*).

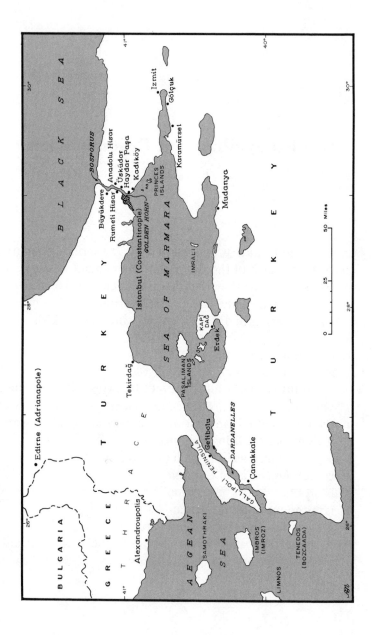

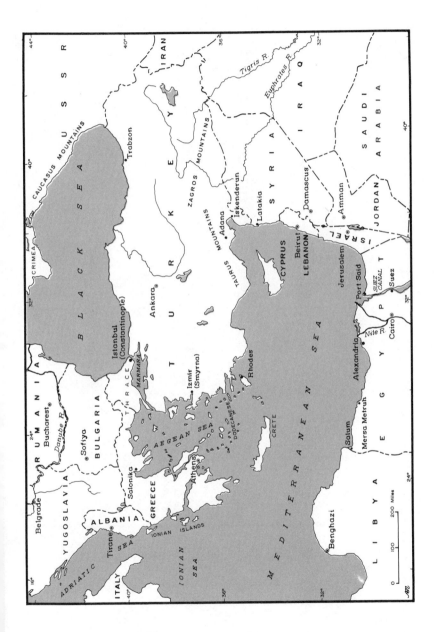

The Turkish Straits and NATO

- 1 -

Geopolitical Significance of the Straits

In a macrocosmic view the Eurasian continent is a single huge land mass whose western extremity is a peninsula called Europe. This peninsula is surrounded on the north and west by the Atlantic, and on the south by the narrow Mediterranean Sea which separates Europe from Africa. From the European peninsula, in turn, several curiously shaped smaller peninsulas protrude: the Scandinavian peninsula in the north and the Iberian, Italian, and Balkan peninsulas in the south. The Balkan one faces yet another peninsula on its eastern flank, which juts out from the main body of the Asian mainland and was named Anatolia ("sunrise" or "the East") by the ancient Greeks and Asia Minor by the Romans. It extends in an east-west direction between the Black Sea and the Mediterranean.

These two Eurasian peninsulas, the Balkans and Anatolia, are divided by two narrow straits and, between these two, by an elliptically shaped basin. The straits were known in the ancient world as the Hellespont and the Bosphorus, and the in-between expansion was called the Propontis.[a] Since the Middle Ages the Straits have been known as the Dardanelles and the Bosporus, and the middle-basin as the Sea of Marmara. [b]

The microcosmic view of the ancient world centered around the Mediterranean, the midland sea. According to the Hellenic and later Roman concepts, this sea was surrounded by a triad of continents: Europe, Asia, and Africa. Europe and Africa were separated by the Mediterranean; Africa and Asia were bound together by a narrow landbridge and were divided in the nineteenth century by an artificial waterway, the Suez Canal. The most crucial boderline of the Hellenic World, and also of later centuries, was that between Europe and Asia, the two rivals or antipodes of the Herodotean confrontation of Hellas and the Persian Empire.

Since the time of the ancient Greeks the border between Asia and Europe has followed the chain of waterways between the southeast corner of the Balkan Peninsula and Asia Minor or Anatolia: the Dardanelles, the Sea of Marmara, and the Bosporus. This was the waterway from the Mediterranean and its northeastern extension, the Aegean Sea, into the Black Sea, the Pontus Euxenus of the ancient world. "Euxenos" means "hospitable" in Greek; thus the Black Sea is occasionally called the Euxine Sea. Thus Europe and Asia were separated by a natural watercourse; the contiguity between the European subcontinent and the larger portion of Eurasia, along the range of low hills called the Ural Mountains, remained unknown to the ancients and was artificially drawn in the wake of the Hellenic dichotomy of Europe and Asia.[1]

---

[a] Hellespont means "Sea of Helles" in Greek and takes its name from a girl who according to mythology killed herself in its waters (another version of the Hero and Leander legend). Bosphorus means "oxenferry" in Greek. Propontis means "fore-sea," or the sea before the Black Sea (when moving away from the epicenter of Greece).

[b] The Dardanelles is named after an ancient city in the Strait which obtained its name from Dardanos, the legendary founder of Troy. The modern spelling of Bosphorus is Bosporus, which will be used here.

GEOGRAPHICAL DESCRIPTION

In the fifth century B.C. the Greek historian Herodotus gave the following description of the Black Sea and the Straits leading to it:

> No sea can equal the Euxine Sea; it is 1380 miles long, and 410 wide in its widest part. Its mouth is half a mile wide, and the length of the Bosphorus, the narrow strait which leads into it . . . is nearly fifteen miles. The Bosphorus joins the Propontis, which is about sixty miles wide and a hundred and seventy long, and runs into the Helles-pont, a narrow strait nearly fifty miles long but less than one mile wide. The Hellespont leads into the broad sea we call the Aegean.[2]

This brief description has hardly lost its pertinence for our present age. Indeed, among all the natural straits of the world the straits connecting the Aegean with the Black Sea are characterized by their relative length and narrowness. They are ideal routes for navigation by power-driven craft. Because of the strong currents flowing from the Black Sea into the Sea of Marmara and again from that sea into the Aegean, they were always less suitable for sailing boats, which had to wait, possibly for months, for a southeastern wind to carry them through the Dardanelles and then, if their destination was the Black Sea, through the Bosporus. Of course, boats driven by oars or pulled by draft animals were independent of the whims of the weather.

The southwestern entrance of the Dardanelles (in Turkish, Çanakkale Boğazi) is between Cape Helles, at the tip of the Gallipoli Peninsula, about 60 miles long and shaped like a tongue.[c] The southeastern coast extends along the mainland of Asia Minor.[3]

---

[c] In the diplomatic conversations concerning the partition of the Ottoman Empire between Napoleon's ambassador Caulaincourt and the Russian Foreign Minister Rumiantsov, the Gallipoli Peninsula was re-ferred to as the "langue de chat" (cat's tongue); Puryear, *Napoleon and the Dardanelles*, p. 282.

The length of the Dardanelles is about 36 nautical miles. About fifteen miles from the entrance are The Narrows, having a general width ranging from one to two miles. At the town of Çanakkale (on the Asian shore) the breadth is only three-quarters of a mile. The passage continues for about sixteen miles with a general width of two miles. At the town of Gelibolu (Gallipoli) there is a second narrow strip, the Gallipoli Strait, with a width of one and three-quarters of a mile. Shortly thereafter the waters join the Sea of Marmara. There is a current from northeast to southwest in the Dardanelles of 2 knots, except in The Narrows where it is 4 knots. The fairway (navigable channel) has a depth of between 25 to 50 fathoms (150 to 300 feet).

The Sea of Marmara, an oval-shaped inland sea, connects the Dardanelles with the Bosporus. Its extreme length is approximately 150 miles and its breadth at its widest part is about 40 miles. It is a relatively deep sea with a current running in the east-west direction at a rate of one-half to one knot. The northern (European) shore of the Sea of Marmara has no deep indentations nor any harbor of importance. The southern (Asian) shoreline is considerably curved: the Kapı Dağ Peninsula juts out into the Marmara forming on its west side the deep Gulf of Erdek (Artaki). Farther east lies the deep Gulf of Mudanya (or Incir Liman) and, finally, at the easternmost extremity of this sea is the deep and narrow Gulf of Izmit, which has a length of 26 miles and whose entrance is only three-and-a-half miles wide.

On the southern side of the Sea of Marmara there are several good harbors: Bandırma at the eastern base of the Kapı Dağ Peninsula; Mudanya and Gemlik in the Gulf of Mudanya; in the Gulf of Izmit we find the principal Turkish naval base and dockyard of Gölçük and the port of Izmit. The Sea of Marmara is dotted with several islands. The largest is the Marmara Island near the northern tip of the Kapı Dağ Peninsula, with the Paşaliman Islands nearby. Imralı is at the entrance to the Bay of Mudanya. The famous Princes Islands lie near the mouth of the Bosporus.

The Bosporus, as already mentioned, connects the Sea of Marmara with the Black Sea. Its Turkish name is Boğaziçi. The length of this waterway is about seventeen miles and at its narrowest point it is only 750 yards wide while its average width varies between one and four-and-a-half miles. Close to the southern mouth of the Bosporus on the western (European) side lies the central section of the city of Istanbul (Constantinople) which is divided by a deep creek known as the Golden Horn which forms the harbor of the city. On the Asian shore, opposite the Golden Horn, is the port of Haydar Paşa; but most of the other parts of the Bosporus may also be used as anchorage.

The Bosporus resembles a river more than a maritime strait; it has sharp bends and a current from north to south which may attain a rate of five knots at the narrows. The narrowest channel lies about five miles north of Istanbul between Rumeli Hisar and the European and Anadolu Hisar on the Asian shore.[d] Farther north the channel widens and forms the Büyükdere Bay on the western shore. Running northeast, the strait narrows again to less than one mile and widens at the Black Sea entrance to about two and a half miles.

There are no islands in the Black Sea facing the mouth of the Bosporus. On the other hand, two small islands lie near the entrance of the Dardanelles in the Aegean: northeast of the tip of the Gallipoli Peninsula is Imbros (in Turkish, Imroz), and south of the mouth of the Dardanelles near the Asian coast is Tenedos (Bozcaada), well known for its role in the Trojan War.

The significance which the Straits area possesses was not bestowed only by nature; human settlements have also contributed to the making of this remarkable region. While there are towns all along the coast of the Dardanelles and the Sea

---

[d] It is at this point that the Ottoman Turks intercepted all traffic through the Bosporus during the year before the fall of Constantinople in 1453.

of Marmara, the Bosporus obtained a much greater importance from the city of Istanbul (formerly Constantinople)
and its surrounding area. This is a very densely populated
area, the city itself having a population of about two million.
Although the capital of Turkey was transferred to inland
Ankara in 1923, Istanbul is still by far the largest city in
Turkey, the center of her industrial and commercial life and
also her principal harbor.

The two narrow straits which connect the Black Sea with
the Mediterranean constitute not only the rather artificial
borderline between Europe and Asia; they are also the
"bridges" between these two continents, connecting the
European "bridgehead" of Turkey with the Asian-Anatolian
bulk of that country. Thus the Straits area has served both as
an important channel for navigation and also as a route for
east-west traffic. Geography and history have combined to
make this region a strategic hub of worldwide significance.

STRATEGIC OBSERVATIONS

Both the Dardanelles and the Bosporus are ideally suited for
defense against conventional surface attack. Like narrow
entrances to harbors, they could in the past be easily defended against intruding warships provided mines and heavy gunnery were available. Natural heights on both banks of these
narrow passages facilitated the construction of fortifications.
Amphibious operations against a well-armed and well-forti-
fied defense force were considered impossible or at least
highly hazardous. In fact, no hostile navy ever managed to
enter the Straits against sustained resistance, neither the Bosporus from the north (as was planned but never attempted by
Tsarist Russia)[4] nor the Dardanelles from the southwest. The
only large-scale amphibious attempt to force the Dardanelles
was the so-called Gallipoli Campaign undertaken by British,
ANZAC (Australian and New Zealand Army Corps) and
French forces in World War I.

In March 1915 the British fleet tried to penetrate in force into the Dardanelles but after a loss of four battleships had to withdraw. In April landings on the Gallipoli Peninsula and on the Asian mainland met determined resistance by the Turks. A half-million Allied troops were unable to achieve the objective of opening up the Dardanelles and capturing Constantinople. In January 1916 the beaches were evacuated.[5]

The Straits are more than barriers against naval and amphibious onslaughts. They may also be traps for warships which are allowed to enter and then prevented from leaving. This happened to the fleet under the orders of the British Admiral John Y. Duckworth in March 1807; he entered the Dardanelles but could withdraw only with great difficulties from the Marmara into the Aegean.[6]

It appears to be axiomatic that the capture of the Straits presupposes naval superiority of the attacker. In World War I, the Allies could not have even attempted to force their way through the Dardanelles without such an overwhelming superiority. Tsarist Russia could never have hoped to storm the Bosporus because she lacked the superior naval strength in the Black Sea which would have made a successful attack possible. Indeed, after the Crimean War the Ottoman Navy held the ascendance over its Russian counterpart in the Black Sea.

But as history has proven, the Straits area is exposed more to the assaults of land forces than to operations from the southeast or the north. European Turkey—Eastern Thrace—is a low-lying land which offers no obstacle to an invader. This triangular-shaped southeastern corner of the Balkan Peninsula forms only 3 per cent of Turkey's entire land surface, but it contains about 8 per cent of the country's population because of the presence of the city of Istanbul.[7]

Istanbul was threatened several times from across the Thracian plain in the nineteenth and early twentieth centuries. In 1828-29 and again in 1877-78 Russians captured Adrianople (Edirne), the gateway to the Golden Horn, the second time even approaching the outskirts of the Ottoman capital. During the Balkan War of 1912-13, Bulgarian forces reached the outer defense girdle of Constantinople.

The Straits area, including Constantinople-Istanbul, is also highly vulnerable to potential attack from the east, from the Anatolian plateau. The highlands of Asia Minor loom over the nodal Straits area like a mountain fortress over a fertile and wealthy river valley. In the past whenever the Straits area and Western Anatolia lived under different political or military control, the master of the Anatolian stronghold eventually was able to extend his mastery over the lowlands of the Dardanelles and the Bosporus. In such a way the ruler of Nicaea recaptured Constantinople from the Latins in 1261, the Ottoman Turks conquered the rump Byzantine state, and more lately the Government of the Grand National Assembly under Mustafa Kemal regained possession of the City of the Sultans in 1923.

The decision to transfer the capital from the Bosporus to Ankara, on the Anatolian plateau, was made only partly for strategic reasons. It did not mean an abandonment of the historical center of Ottoman-Turkish power; but Ankara, some 220 miles from the Bosporus, is strategically better protected than Istanbul, which lies 16 miles from the Black Sea and 80 to 100 miles from the Bulgarian frontier. The other nonstrategic reason for removing the capital from Istanbul was the endeavor to place the center of political life into a purely Turkish ethnic environment, away from the cosmopolitan atmosphere of Istanbul with its memories of the degenerate sultanic past.

There is no doubt that the possibility of aerial attacks greatly weakens the defensive position of the Straits area. Whereas no naval forces and not even a highly superior ground force was needed for the defense of the Straits against naval or amphibious assaults, attacks supported by aerial bombardments could be successfully met only if the defenders possessed an adequate air defense—fighter planes and antiaircraft gunnery. In other words, air superiority or missile superiority could ensure a victorious seaside invasion of the Straits unless the defenders could prevent massive aerial attacks and destroy approaching warships or amphibious craft. But even without the conquest of the area by ground forces, the vulnerability of Istanbul and its vicinity is very high indeed without adequate air protection.[e]

Attacks against Istanbul and the Straits by tactical or strategic nuclear weapons from any direction would destroy people, buildings, and ships, and radioactivity would bar military occupation of the area and transit of ships for some time. Because such an attack would most likely provoke a global exchange of nuclear blows, instead of a limited conflagration, we need not speculate here on its effect concerning the geographically more restricted region of our present scrutiny.

All the natural routes—land, sea, and air, from the Black Sea to the Mediterranean and from the Balkans to the Persian Gulf—lead across Turkey and in most cases, in one way or other, across the Straits area. The Turkish Straits form, without doubt, "one of humanity's most important crossroads."[8] The Bosporus and the Dardanelles primarily serve as waterways for maritime traffic, but their strategic significance far exceeds their original and natural destiny. Control over this area provided the apple of discord between European Great Powers for two and a half centuries. The ominous Eastern Question may be epitomized as follows: Which power should succeed the faltering Ottoman Empire as master of Constantinople and the Straits?

---

[e] The reluctance of Turkey to join the Allies in late 1943 and early 1944 in the war against Germany can be traced to the fear that failing adequate air protection, Istanbul, which consisted largely of wooden houses, would be destroyed by the Luftwaffe. The ensuing panic (people trying to find protection by crossing the Bosporus) would render the defense of Thrace against the invasion of land forces very difficult if not impossible. But Turkey also feared that she would, in the event of a German occupation, be "liberated" by the Red Army. See Váli, *Bridge Across the Bosporus—The Foreign Policy of Turkey*, pp. 32-33.

Russia placed herself first among the pretenders seeking to inherit the Sultan's most precious possession. The only outlet from her Black Sea ports led through the Straits. Commercial, military, political, and ideological expansionism drove the empire of the Tsars toward Constantinople, the gateway to further advancement into the Aegean, the Mediterranean, and beyond. "Geography wills that I have it, because if it goes to another, I would no longer be master in my own house," said Tsar Alexander to the French Ambassador.[9] "Constantinople, Constantinople, never! That is the empire of the world! " was Napoleon's response to the Russian demand.[10] Nor was Britain, until World War I, willing to abandon this priceless treasure to the power which, in her view, threatened to cut the British lifeline to India.

While Russia sought free movement for her own merchant vessels and warships through the Straits and even hoped to obtain physical control over these waterways, from the defensive point of view she objected to the entry of non-Black Sea warships into what she considered a "closed sea." She wanted the Straits to be a one-way revolving door with herself as the doorman. The Soviet state has not abandoned these objectives in the post-World War II years. The legal provisions accepted during the interwar period undertook to find a compromise between the conflicting interests of the interested Great Powers and Turkey, the most closely affected owner of this prize.

The problem of the Straits is heavily burdened by Turkey's vital security interests. They run across Turkey's nerve center: her commercial and industrial hub, her "bridge" toward the West, and last but not least her largest city and harbor. But even if Istanbul-Constantinople were not what it is and where it is, the security of Turkey would be jeopardized if she were to lose control over that crucial area.

When the Ottoman Turks conquered Constantinople, the capital of the Eastern Roman Empire, possession of the city conclusively established them as masters of a multinational empire. From this vantage point, they could conveniently dominate the Black Sea, the Balkans, and even parts of Central Europe, the Aegean, and the Eastern Mediterranean as well as Asia Minor to the confines of Mesopotamia and Arabia. And in the period of Ottoman decadence, the rivalry over the Straits area and Constantinople delayed or even prevented their final downfall. Even today with Ankara as its official capital, Turkey would not be the same without Istanbul and the Straits. Her importance, because of the Straits, is relatively much greater, politically and strategically, than would be the case without the ownership of this all-important area. But her interests in the Straits area are less navigational than imposed by national security considerations.[f]

When Emperor Constantine the Great transferred his capital to Byzantium in 330 A.D., he must have been led by eminent strategic considerations. He hoped to govern the overextended Roman Empire from a place which possessed the advantages of a central location and easy communication with all the endangered borders of his empire. But even before the founding of Constantinople, called "the Second Rome," the Straits played an important role in the historical development of that part of the world. Before examining the effects of Ottoman domination over these waterways, let us briefly trace those early historic precedents which cast the long shadow of their influence across world history.

LESSONS OF EARLY HISTORY

The peculiar geographical formation of the Straits, their uniqueness as waterways to the Black Sea, have impressed navigators since time immemorial. Greek mythology, always

---

[f.] For some contemporary observers the Great Power rivalry over the Straits must have appeared as a mixed blessing for the Sultan. Mohammed Ali, the ruler of Egypt, is said to have objected to the Suez Canal with such an argument: "A canal cut across the Suez Isthmus would become another Bosporus-Dardanelles, coveted by European control." Anshen (ed.), *Mid-East: World Center*, p. 93.

an expression of the interrelation between natural and human phenomena, embellished them with legends which symbolized their navigational hazards and enticing challenges. The dangers of navigating the Straits were symbolized by the story of the Symplegades (clashing rocks) which, standing on both sides of the entrance to the Bosporus from the Black Sea, moved to crush passing ships. The *Argo* of Jason, sailing to Colchis for the Golden Fleece, managed to pass unharmed, whereupon the Symplegades remained fixed.

The profitable trade between points of the Black Sea and ancient Hellas dated back to the earliest times. Many settlements along the Dardanelles, the Sea of Marmara, and the Bosporus, ports such as Lampsakos (Lapseki), Heliopolis (Gelibolu), Cyzicus (Erdek) or Chalcedon (Kadiköy), gave evidence of the importance of this trade route. Near the entrance to the Dardanelles from the Aegean stood the city of Troy. In a way, the Trojan War (probably around 1200 B.C.) was the earliest precursor of the struggle for the control of the Dardanelles and for the freedom of the trade route to the Euxine.[11]

Chalcedon, on the Asian coast at the point where the Bosporus enters the Sea of Marmara, was founded by colonists from the town of Megara in the seventh century B.C. Some years later Byzas, also a Megarian, the eponymic founder of Byzantium, was told by an oracle to settle with his folk across from the "blind ones." The "blind ones" happened to be the colonists of Chalcedon who failed to discover the more suitable site for a harbor along the Golden Horn, where Byzantium, the later Constantinople, was established in 658 B.C.

The double role which the Straits area plays today was well known to the ancient world. The Dardanelles and the Bosporus served, on the one hand, as waterways for the traffic between the Black Sea and the Mediterranean, and on the other hand as connecting points for the land-to-land traffic from Asia to Europe and vice versa. When leading his campaign against the Scythians north of the Black Sea (about 512 B.C.), the Persian King Darius led his army over the Bosporus by means of a bridge which was probably near the spot north of Istanbul where the Bosporus Bridge is being constructed at present. And his son, Xerxes, bridged the Dardanelles when leading his famous campaign for the conquest of Greece in 480 B.C.

It is less widely realized that many of the decisive naval actions of the Peloponnesian War between Athens and Sparta were fought for the control of the Dardanelles, which was of paramount importance to Athens; wheat and other products indispensable to its people were shipped through the Straits from the Euxine region. Alcibiades defeated the Spartan fleet near Cyzicus, but the battle which preceded the fall of Athens by one year was fought between the two navies in the Dardanelles near the mouth of the Aegospotamos (405 B.C.).

When Alexander the Great set out on his triumphant campaign to conquer the Persian Empire, he crossed the Dardanelles with his army in 334 B.C. During his short reign and also during that of the Diadochi (Alexander's Macedonian successors), the Straits area served as the main line for the conveyance of forces frequently moving from Macedonia and Greece to Asia Minor and beyond. When the Romans subdued the entire eastern Mediterranean, they extended their rule over the area around the Dardanelles and the Bosporus. For their armies too these "bridges" between Europe and Asia provided the best land routes between the Balkan possessions and those of Asia Minor. [12]

As may have been observed, during all these centuries the Straits mainly filled the requirements of transit: navigation through their waters or easy transit from west to east and back. No center of power had as yet established itself within that nodal area. Rivalries for its control and battles fought for its conquest moved men, ships, and goods. No internal concentration of power existed; developments were dictated from the outside, by powers external to the Straits area, and the interests of these outsiders determined possible actions which resulted in changes of mastery over the region. But when Emperor Constantine made Byzantium the capital of his realm, the internal interests of those who now controlled the Straits area and, indeed, the Eastern Roman Empire, became the controlling factor of strategy and politics.

The supremacy of the capital, Constantinople, was so preponderant that it was its defense and survival, despite the invasion of the rest of its realm, which secured for the Byzantine Empire its astonishing powers of recuperation and a lifetime of over a millennium. With the establishment of Constantinople the Straits ceased to be primarily a route of transit over water and land; they became rather an area of self-sufficing strength and a center for dominating outside regions.

The frontiers of the Byzantine Empire shifted according to the fortunes of war, both in Europe and in Asia. It was quickly recognized by the foes of the Eastern Roman Empire that a mortal blow could only be imparted to it when directed against Constantinople. Arabs in the eighth century twice attempted to capture the city by sailing into the Marmara and storming its walls. Normans (Varangians) entered the Bosporus from the Black Sea but likewise failed to attain their goal. The powerful walls of Byzantium withstood these onslaughts except on three occasions: the army of the Fourth Crusade took the city in 1204; the Byzantines managed to retake it in 1261; and it finally fell into the hands of the Ottoman Turks in 1453.

Before the advent of firearms the entrance to the Straits could be defended only by a navy more powerful than that of the attacker. And the Byzantine emperors, especially in the latter centuries of the Empire, did not possess such navies and often had to seek assistance from the Italian city states of Venice, Genoa, or Pisa. Today it seems safe to say that the Straits could be protected only by a powerful defense against aerial attacks.

The Ottomans administered their coup de grâce to Constantinople in an excruciatingly slow fashion. After having conquered most of the Asian hinterland of the Straits, they crossed the Dardanelles in 1354 and moved their capital to Adrianople, thus encircling Constantinople from the European side as well. But for various reasons, the rump-Byzantine Empire, almost reduced to the city itself, survived for another century. The Ottomans were unable to prevent navigation and the supply of Constantinople through the Dardanelles or through the Bosporus. Then, with cannons at his disposal, Sultan Mehmet II succeeded in cutting off the city's northern supply route: the year before the final siege of the city he erected Rumeli Hisar, a castle on the Bosporus which blocked enemy shipping.

When Constantinople fell in 1453, besieged from both land and sea, it became the heart and brain of another universal empire. Thenceforth, as in the golden era of the Byzantine Empire, control of the Straits depended solely on the Ottoman Government, known later as the Sublime Porte, and was dictated by internal political and military considerations. The navigational interests of outsiders again became negligible and were disregarded for a number of centuries under the "ancient rule of the Ottoman Empire."

The Ancient Rule of the Ottoman Empire

Some twenty years after the fall of Constantinople the entire coast around the Black Sea came under Ottoman control. The Sultan's writ ruled the Caucasian shore of that sea and in the west Ottoman power extended beyond the mouth of the Danube. The Tartar Khan of the Crimea pledged allegiance to the Sublime Porte. Thus the Black Sea became a "Turkish lake" after 1475.

For the next three hundred years only ships flying the Crescent were permitted to navigate the Black Sea. No foreign vessel, whether merchantman or man-of-war, was allowed to pass through the Straits. Commercial ships of nations having secured treaties (so-called capitulations) to this effect from the Sublime Porte were authorized to sail only to the harbor of Constantinople and not beyond. His uncontested power position enabled the Sultan to exclude from the Straits area all interests save his own.

RUSSIA AND THE OTTOMAN EMPIRE

The descent of Russia to the shores of the Black Sea was primarily responsible for ending Ottoman domination over both navigation in the Black Sea and use of the Straits. Peter the Great had already, albeit unsuccessfully, attempted to eliminate Ottoman rule from the northern shore of the Black Sea.[1] But the war of 1768-74 with Russia under Catherine the Great and the peace treaty of Küçük Kaynarca ended Turkey's monopolistic position. The Sultan had to accept two conditions which could be considered disastrous for the Empire and the beginning of its decay as an international power. One was the abandonment of the Crimea (where the Tartar Khanate was to become independent, but soon was annexed by Russia); the other was the granting of permission to Russian merchant ships to sail not only in the Black Sea but also in both directions through the Straits (see Appendix 1). As a consequence of these two conditions Russia established herself as a Black Sea power—a situation she soon exploited to the point of threatening the very existence of the Ottoman Empire, the "sick man of Europe."

While it has been rightly said that the Straits are the "heart" of Turkey, Russia contended that they were the "keys" to her house or the "door" to her possessions. Tsarist Russia appeared to be driven partly by a mystique, partly by an imperialistic urge to take possession of, or at least to control, the exit to the Mediterranean and the warm waters she sought there, in her drive toward the Middle East and the Persian Gulf as well.

With the control of the Turkish Straits, Russia was seeking three advantages: satisfaction of the religious-historic missionary aim of restoring the City of Constantine to Christianity; the strategic and commercial advantage of securing complete freedom for both her naval and merchant vessels to pass the Straits and reach out into the "open sea" beyond; and with possession of the Straits area to obtain a forward position which would secure her defenses against any aggressor who might threaten her vital industrial-agricultural region in the south. It appears that the Soviet Union has not abandoned these two last objectives which were so ardently sought under the Tsars.

Although Russian policy throughout the century and a half following the Treaty of Küçük Kaynarca aimed at the destruction or partition of the Ottoman Empire, there were periods when the defensive thesis prevailed at the Court of St. Petersburg—when it was thought more favorable to accept the continued existence of a weak Turkey rather than see one of the other Great Powers firmly established on the Bosporus.

After freedom of navigation through the Straits was recognized for Russian merchant ships, this right was extended by the Sublime Porte to the merchant vessels of other flags. However, the Straits remained closed to Russian or other non-Turkish warships. Until 1919 the question of the passage of warships through the Dardanelles and Bosporus remained one of the principal issues in which both Russia and the Ottomans, as well as the main Western naval powers, were vitally interested. The principle applied by Constantinople was to exclude all foreign warships from the Straits in time of peace. This "ancient rule of the Ottoman Empire" was first officially invoked in the so-called Peace of the Dardanelles, concluded between Britain and Turkey on January 5, 1809 (see Appendix 2).

Russian naval interests went far beyond the Straits; it is not generally realized that Russian deployment in the Mediterranean was practiced in the late eighteenth century. During the Russian-Turkish war of 1768-74, Russian warships entered the Mediterranean from the Atlantic and dealt a heavy blow to the Turkish fleet off the port of Çeşme in 1770. Following the French invasion of Egypt, a Russian squadron, with the permission of the Sultan, passed through the Straits in 1799 in order to assist the Turkish Navy against the French.[a] This Russian force expelled the French from the Ionian Islands (formerly a Venetian possession) and only withdrew in 1801. But within two years these islands were again occupied by the Russians and at one time 11,000 Russian soldiers were stationed there.[2] A secret clause in the new Treaty of Defensive Alliance dated 11/23 September 1805 between the Ottoman Empire and Russia again permitted the passage of Russian warships through the Straits (see Appendix 3).

In 1806, however, Turkey shifted her alliance away from Russia and Britain and approached France; this led to a break with St. Petersburg and the abrogation of the Defensive Alliance. At Tilsit, in July 1807, the reconciliation between Napoleon and Tsar Alexander I portended great danger for the Ottoman Empire: a plan to partition the Sultan's realm was weighed between the two sovereigns. During the next year negotiations were conducted in St. Petersburg and Paris for the implementation of this project. Only their inability to reach an agreement concerning the future fate of Constantinople and the Straits prevented the ruin of the Ottoman State,[3] and this disagreement may have been one of the things which persuaded the French Emperor to turn against Russia, somewhat as Hitler did in 1941 (see below, pp. 59-61.)

After 1806 Russian warships again were not permitted to pass through the Straits. Under the Treaty of Tilsit, Russia handed over the Ionian Islands to Napoleon in 1807; the Russian naval forces had to withdraw from the Mediterranean via Gibraltar and they were captured by the British near Lisbon.

For nearly the next three decades the "ancient rule of the Ottoman Empire" prevailed; that is, no foreign warship passed the Straits. But the balance which the Sublime Porte

---

[a] A secret clause in the Treaty of Alliance between Russia and Turkey of January 3, 1799, authorized Russian warships to pass through the Straits for the duration of the war.

was able to maintain during that period was jeopardized again when Mohammed Ali, the Pasha of Egypt, threatened the power of the Sultan. The Sublime Porte felt obliged to seek help from its hereditary foe, Russia. In February 1833 Russian naval forces entered the Bosporus and Russian troops landed north of the Ottoman capital. On July 8, 1833, the Treaty of Hünkâr Iskelesi was signed (see Appendix 4); in the belief of many contemporaries, this established a quasi-Russian protectorate over Turkey and opened the Straits to Russian warships.[4]

GREAT-POWER RIVALRY OVER THE STRAITS

The Hünkâr Iskelesi Treaty provoked protests by the British and French governments and led to protracted negotiations. After a number of years the crisis created by Mohammed Ali was finally disposed of. Then upon the insistence of the Western powers and Austria, which also opposed preponderant Russian influence in Constantinople, the London Convention of July 13, 1841, fully restored the principle "invariably established as the ancient rule of the Empire" which forbade the entry of foreign warships into the waters of the Turkish Straits (see Appendix 5).

Russia thus succeeded three times between 1774 and 1841 in obtaining for the duration of emergency situations the right of passage for her warships into and through the Straits. In all these cases as soon as the particular situation which compelled the Sultan to extend these unusual privileges to the Russians came to an end, the former status forbidding foreign warships of all nations to enter the Straits was restored. These precedents, despite their short-lived and ambiguous character, have subsequently been distorted by Russian historians[b] and were even invoked by Molotov, the Soviet

---

[b]J. C. Hurewitz, in "Russia and the Turkish Straits," *World Politics,* July 1962, pp. 605-32, undertook to refute in particular the distortions of Russian historian Serge M. Goriainov. The French edition of Goriainov's book was published under the title *Le Bosphore et les Dardanelles* (Paris: Plan-Nourrit, 1910).

People's Commissar for Foreign Affairs, at the Potsdam Conference of 1945.[5]

Whatever may have been the extent or interpretation of these pro-Russian concessions, it seems undeniable that they were abrogated by the Convention of London (if not earlier), which was signed and ratified by all the major powers—Great Britain, France, Austria, Prussia, Russia, and the Ottoman Empire. The purpose of this treaty was to confirm, without leaving any doubts, the right and obligation of the Sultan to close the Straits to non-Turkish warships in time of peace except for small craft to be used by embassies.

The prohibition upon warships entering the Straits did not apply to a situation when the Sublime Porte was involved in war. In such an eventuality, it remained the discretionary right of the Sultan's government to allow the entry and passage of men-of-war of allied or friendly powers. This was the case when the Crimean War broke out in 1853.

In 1853 Tsar Nicholas I attempted to extract concessions from the Sublime Porte and his armies invaded Moldavia and Wallachia. With the permission of the Sultan, Britain and France sent their squadrons into the Straits and subsequently into the Black Sea. British and French troops landed in the Crimea and besieged the Russian naval base of Sebastopol, which fell in 1855. The ensuing peace treaty of Paris of March 30, 1856, while providing for the neutralization of the Black Sea and the demilitarization of its Russian coast, confirmed once again the ancient rule of the Ottoman Empire— the closure of the Straits to warships of all nations save the Turkish. In this treaty freedom of navigation for commercial vessels of every nation (not only those with whom the Sublime Porte had concluded a treaty to this effect) was now generally recognized (see Appendix 6).

The Crimean campaign revealed the vulnerability of Russia to foreign warships entering the Black Sea. It confirmed the correctness of the view that it was in the interest of the Tsar's government to uphold the "ancient rule." Although it was explained to the Russian representatives at the peace talks preceding the conclusion of the treaty of Paris that as long as the Black Sea remained closed to warships of non-Black Sea Powers, Russia really needed no navy in those waters. Nevertheless, St. Petersburg strongly resented the demilitarization clause of the Paris peace treaty. During the Franco-Prussian War of 1870-71, Russia denounced these restrictive conditions of the treaty; the Great Powers, meeting once more in London, condoned the act but reconfirmed again the closing of the Straits to all foreign warships (see Appendix 7).

In 1877 Russia invaded the Ottoman Empire for the protection of her co-religionists in the Balkans. In early 1878, Russian forces approached Constantinople and the British cabinet sent its Mediterranean fleet into the Straits, where it laid anchor near the Ottoman capital. The Treaty of St. Stefano, which was forced upon the Sultan on March 3, 1878, and which set up Great Bulgaria, did not win Britain's approval. Under the pressure from other Great Powers, Russia consented that this treaty be discussed by a conference of all interested states which convened in Berlin. As to the Straits, the Berlin congress contented itself with the confirmation of previous agreements. British and Russian interests, however, clashed again when British Foreign Secretary Lord Salisbury declared on July 11 that the closing of the Straits to foreign warships depended on the "independent determination" of the Sultan. On the following day, Count Shuvalov, the Russian representative, retorted that in the opinion of his government "the principle of the closing of the Straits is a European principle" and therefore binding on all the powers including the Ottoman Empire.

Although the interpretation of the "ancient rule" remained controversial, the regime of the Straits as accepted by various conventions remained in force until World War I. In practice, the Sublime Porte occasionally allowed the passage of armed vessels for particular humanitarian or other reasons. But Russian attempts to obtain greater freedom for the movement of her warships remained unsuccessful. Thus during the Russo-Japanese War in 1904-5 only two auxiliary cruisers, disguised as merchantmen, managed to pass the Straits. Otherwise, the closure of the Straits to Russian warships helped the Japanese insofar as the best squadron of the Russian Navy found itself immobilized in the Black Sea, unable to join the fleet of Admiral Rozhestvensky which sailed from the Baltic and around Africa to the Far East.[6]

By the end of the nineteenth century, the attitude of Britain and France on the question of the Straits had undergone a gradual change. The British acquired the Island of Cyprus in 1878 and occupied Egypt with its Suez Canal in 1882. They were thus in physical control of the waterway which vitally connected them with India and other Asian possessions. Furthermore, they began to recognize the shaky foundations of the Ottoman Empire and were wondering whether it was wise to protect Turkey much longer.

After her defeat by Germany in 1870-71, France wished more and more to rely on an alliance with Russia. The shifting of the European balance of power with the rise of a united Germany—which in addition to being the major land power began to build a powerful high-sea navy—also persuaded London and Paris to change their policies concerning the Eastern question. On the other hand, the Ottoman Empire, around the turn of the century, had obtained a new protector: Germany provided military aid to the Sultan and invested heavily in various projects, among them the construction of the Baghdad Railway. While expansionist Germany now appeared as the main danger to the balance of power, Russian expansionism was considered to be the lesser danger by the West. And the Russian Black Sea fleet, even if it could manage to enter the Mediterranean freely, was not regarded as a match for the British fleet in those waters.

The Balkan Wars of 1912-13 had reduced the Ottoman Empire's European possessions to Eastern Thrace. Even the town of Adrianople (Edirne) appeared to have been lost before it was recaptured by the Turks during the second phase of the war. Previously, the Bulgarians had closely approached the Ottoman capital but were cautious enough to keep away from the Dardanelles.

The Peace Treaty of Bucharest of 1913 also assigned to Greece all the islands of the Aegean, except Imbros and Tenedos at the entrance to the Dardanelles. In 1911 the Italians had taken possession of the Dodecanese Islands and the Island of Rhodes. The Ottoman Empire found itself in an exhausted state when its supreme ordeal, World War I, brought the Great Powers of Europe into violent confrontation. At the time of the outbreak of World War I, a spectacular event focused world attention on the status of the Straits; the strategic role of these waterways bore heavily on the military and political developments of this global struggle.

WORLD WAR I

On August 10, 1914, after the outbreak of the war between Germany and Austria-Hungary on the one hand, and Britain, France, and Russia on the other, two German warships stationed in the Mediterranean, the battle-cruiser *Goeben* and the cruiser *Breslau*, fled into the Dardanelles. They were allowed entry by the Turkish government and proceeded to Constantinople. At that time, Turkey had two of her warships in British shipyards; one had been sent there for repairs, the other was nearing completion. The British government requisitioned both warships. Then, in a grandiose gesture, the German Emperor presented the *Goeben* and the *Breslau* to the Sultan, although the German crews continued to man them.[7] The Young Turk group which governed the country was already under German influence and was further impressed by this spectacular gift, which gave Turkey superiority over the Russian Black Sea fleet.

On August 2, 1914, the Ottoman government had already concluded a secret agreement with Germany committing itself to enter the war on the side of the Central Powers. After nearly two months of hesitation, while Britain and France attempted to prevent Turkey from abandoning her neutrality, the *Goeben* and the *Breslau* were given permission to sail out into the Black Sea and bombard Russian harbors. War was then declared by Russia, Britain, and France. It should be observed that Turkey's entry into the war occurred after Germany had lost the Battle of the Marne—that is, at a time when a quick victory or any victory at all had become more questionable than in the early days of World War I.[8]

While the Ottoman Empire's interest in joining the Central Powers was at least controversial and eventually proved to be catastrophic, Germany obtained a considerable advantage by seating Turkey at her side. The Ottoman Army was still exhausted after the Balkan Wars and, except in the defense of the Dardanelles, and temporarily in Mesopotamia, had no outstanding successes. But control of the Straits, which closed them to commercial and naval ships of the Entente Powers, had a major impact on the military and political developments of the war. The geopolitical significance of Turkish territory in general, and that of the Straits in particular, have never been more clearly demonstrated than by the role they played between 1914 and 1918.

With Turkey as an enemy, Russia's most important route of supply was cut off and the Western Entente Powers were largely unable to send her badly needed weaponry and ammunition.[9] The Baltic route was also blocked by the German Navy while the Arctic route was of little use because the port of Archangel was icebound through a major part of the year. The port of Murmansk and the railroad leading to it were constructed only during the course of the war. While Russia could deploy immense manpower, only a fraction of it could be provided with modern weapons, a circumstance which greatly contributed to her eventual collapse.

As mentioned earlier, Britain and France undertook to open up the Straits by military force. But both the initial naval action and subsequent landings failed to defeat the de-

fenses of the Dardanelles and the action had to be called off
by January 1916. In the meantime, Tsarist diplomacy succeeded in persuading the Western powers to agree to the
cession of Constantinople and the Straits. Although the
Russian government welcomed the siege of the Dardanelles, it
became nervous when considering the occupation of Constantinople by Britain and France or even by the Greeks, who
were to be enticed into the war by that prize.

In an exchange of diplomatic notes from February to
April 1915, Britain and France reversed their century-old
policy against the annexation of Constantinople and the
Straits by Russia and agreed that this area should be incorporated into the Russian Empire. The City of Constantinople,
the Western bank of the Bosporus, of the Sea of Marmara,
and of the Dardanelles, southern Thrace to the Enos-Midya
line, and also the Eastern bank of the Bosporus to the
Sakarya River and to a point on the Gulf of Izmit, the islands
of the Marmara, Imbros and Tenedos—all were assigned to
Russia, provided, of course, that the war could be brought to
a successful conclusion (see Appendix 8). Italy subsequently
also agreed to the partition of the Ottoman Empire, receiving
her share along with the other powers.

After two centuries of aggressive actions and diplomatic
pressures, Russia appeared to have obtained Western approval
for the fulfillment of Catherine the Great's dream, the possession of Constantinople, the Second Rome, and the Straits,
the keys to the Mediterranean. It should also be observed
that Britain and France, while agreeing to the annexation of
these territories by Russia, only asked for free transit through
the Straits for their commercial vessels (and a free port for
transit goods in the harbor of Constantinople); under these
agreements Russia would have had the right to prohibit entry
of warships into the Black Sea, thus effectively turning it into
a "Russian lake."

Had the Entente Powers victoriously concluded World War
I with Russia alongside, the above agreement, together with

other secret arrangements between Britain, France, and Italy, would have sounded the death knell for the Ottoman Empire and for an independent Turkish nation. However, the vagaries of history are unpredictable; the Entente Powers won the war, but without Russia. Following the Bolshevik takeover in November 1917, Russia withdrew from the war, an event which made the above agreements a dead letter. They were even vehemently denounced as imperialistic by the Soviet government and made public, causing no little embarrassment to the governments of London, Paris, and Rome.

At first, despite Russia's secession, it appeared that the "sick man of Europe" was doomed. With the collapse of Germany and Austria-Hungary, Turkish resistance also ended. An armistice was signed at Mudros on October 30, 1918, and under its terms Allied warships entered the Straits and dropped anchor before the Ottoman capital. The Allies had also obtained the right to occupy any strategic point in Turkey—a right of which they made ample use. Thus Greek forces occupied Eastern Thrace, except for the area of the Dardanelles which was garrisoned by British troops. In May 1919 the Greek Army was invited to occupy Izmir (Smyrna) and its hinterland. Despite her predicament, Turkey unexpectedly recovered her former stamina.

THE NEW TURKEY
AND THE END OF THE "ANCIENT RULE"

Mustafa Kemal Pasha (later known as Kemal Atatürk), who had served during the World War with outstanding success on many battlefronts but particularly in the defense of the Dardanelles, organized the resistance against the dismemberment of Turkey in Central Anatolia. In November 1919 the Sultan's government, acting under the pressure from the Allies, convoked an elected parliament which, however, turned out to be highly nationalist. Dissolved by the ruler, it assembled as the Grand National Assembly in Ankara and established its

own counter-government under the leadership of Mustafa
Kemal. While in Constantinople the Assembly adopted the
National Pact, a program for a rejuvenated Turkey. Article 4
of the National Pact, dealing with the question of the Straits,
was phrased as follows: "The security of the City of Constantinople (which is the seat of the Khalifate of Islam, the capital of the Sultanate, and the headquarters of the Ottoman
Government), and likewise the security of the Sea of Marmara must be protected from every danger. Provided this
principle is maintained, whatever decision may be arrived at
jointly by us and all other Governments concerned, regarding
the opening of the Bosporus to the commerce and traffic of
the world, shall be valid." [10]

Allied forces formally occupied Constantinople in March
1920 and presented the government there with the draft of
the peace treaty. This instrument, among others, stipulated
that Greece was to receive Eastern Thrace, the European portion of Turkey, except for a narrow piece of territory west of
Constantinople. Izmir and parts of western Anatolia were to
be placed under Greek administration. The Straits area was to
be placed under the control of a body called the Commission
of the Straits, composed of representatives of the Great
Powers, each of whom had two votes, and representatives of
Greece, Rumania, Bulgaria, and Turkey with one vote each.
Navigation through the Straits was to remain open in time of
war and peace to all vessels of commerce and of war. The
Commission, almost a state within the state, was to exercise
extended jurisdiction over the execution of the provisions
in the treaty. On August 10, 1920, the Sultanic government
signed what was known as the Peace Treaty of Sèvres, which
would have sanctioned the dismemberment of Turkey and
left the remaining trunk under foreign tutelage. [11]

But the Greek Army, called to suppress the government of
Ankara, failed in its objective. After having approached the
Kemalist capital, its advance was checked by nationalist
forces. And in August and September of 1922 the new Turk-

ish Army defeated them and expelled them from Anatolia. A Kemalist force now faced British forces stationed at Çanak-kale, along the Dardanelles, which threatened to take Constantinople. The Armistice of Mudanya (October 11) ended hostilities. The Turkish Army entered Eastern Thrace and later Constantinople; the Sultanate was abolished, and a Turkish Republic proclaimed with Mustafa Kemal as its first president.

The Peace Conference of Lausanne was held from November 20, 1922, to February 4, 1923, and again from April 23 to July 24, when the treaty was signed. This treaty essentially fulfilled the demands set forth in the National Pact. Turkey abandoned all Arab lands but retained all Turkish inhabited regions, including Eastern Thrace. The islands of the Aegean were left to Greece, except for Imbros (Imroz) and Tenedos (Bozcaada) at the entrance to the Dardanelles. Italy kept the Dodecanese Islands and Rhodes.

A special Convention Relating to the Regime of the Straits was signed simultaneously with the peace treaty. For the negotiation of this convention, representatives of the Soviet government were also invited. It should be recalled that the Treaty of Friendship concluded on March 16, 1921, between Turkey and Soviet Russia provided that an international agreement on the Straits will be sought by a conference composed of delegates of the Black Sea powers (see Appendix 9). But in view of the international situation, Turkey could not avoid (and was willing to seek) an agreement concerning the navigation through the Straits with the European Great Powers and others, and not only with the littoral states of the Black Sea. In 1946 Turkey was accused by Moscow of having failed to comply with this provision of the Treaty of Friendship.

Although the Treaty of Sèvres remained unratified and was ignored at Lausanne, the international regime planned by it, as well as the principle of free navigation through the Straits, was maintained. It was now generally recognized, even by Turkey, that the "ancient rule of the Ottoman Empire" had become anomalous and outdated. The National Pact had already expressed readiness to cooperate in setting up a system of free navigation which would be compatible with Turkey's security interests.

In Lausanne a common denominator was sought to reconcile the conflicting interests of the Western powers, Soviet Russia, and Turkey. Moscow, following in the footsteps of the Tsars, wished to exclude Black Sea entry to warships of non-riparian powers while securing free exit for its own warships into the Mediterranean.[c] The Western powers, particularly Britain, wished to guarantee complete freedom of navigation for all warships to and from the Black Sea. Turkey was less interested in the navigation of these waterways; she desired to maintain sovereignty over the Straits area and to ensure that passing warships should not jeopardize her security. There was general agreement that merchant vessels should be given unrestricted right of passage.

The Lausanne regime of the Straits accepted a compromise. The maximum force which any power was allowed to send into the Black Sea in time of peace was not to be greater than that of the most powerful navy of the Black Sea powers; however, under all circumstances the powers were permitted to dispatch a force of no more than three ships, the individual ships not to exceed 10,000 tons.

The Straits Convention of Lausanne also set up an International Commission, which had considerably reduced powers compared to the Sèvres Commission. It was to operate under the auspices of the League of Nations. The area on both sides

---

[c] While the Straits were under Allied control (1919-22), the Russian White Armies of Denikin and Wrangel were supplied, primarily by France, through the Straits. After the end of the civil war the Soviet Union possessed no navy in those waters and was more anxious than even before to prevent the entry of foreign warships into the Black Sea. Soviet Russia was prominently represented at Lausanne by the People's Commissar for Foreign Affairs, G. V. Chicherin.

of the Dardanelles and the Bosporus was to be demilitarized (see Appendix 10). The Soviet government signed the convention but, finding many of its provisions unsatisfactory, subsequently refused to ratify it.[d] However, Moscow cooperated with the Straits Commission by furnishing the required data with regard to its naval forces in the Black Sea and by notifying the commission of desired movements through the Straits.

With the Lausanne regime of the Straits, an entirely new page had been opened in the history of these important waterways. The right of the Sultan to close them according to his discretionary judgment had been replaced by a truly international control. The regime of 1923 was, however, imbued with the optimism which pervaded international politics following World War I; it was expected that international rivalries would be checked by the operation of the League of Nations and violent conflicts eliminated altogether. The failure of the world to live up to these expectations and a return to greater realism led the Great Powers to a revision of the regime established in Lausanne and to a system which gave far greater authority to the territorial state, namely Turkey.

---

[d] The most serious objection Moscow raised was the eventuality of a war in which Turkey remained neutral. In that case the peacetime limitations of naval forces entering the Black Sea lapsed, and in a war between Britain and the Soviet Union it would have been legally permissible for the entire British Navy to enter the Black Sea. See Cemil Bilsel, "International Law in Turkey," *American Journal of International Law*, October 1944, pp. 551-52.

- 3 -

The Montreux Regime of the Straits

On April 10, 1936, a diplomatic note was addressed by Turkey to all the signatories of the Lausanne Straits Convention—the British Empire, France, Italy, Japan, Bulgaria, Greece, Rumania, the Soviet government, and Yugoslavia—and to the Secretary-General of the League of Nations; in this note Ankara drew attention to the changed circumstances in Europe since the conclusion of the convention. In 1923 Europe had appeared to be on the road toward disarmament; respect for international agreements was paramount; guarantees under the League of Nations' security system seemed fully realistic. Furthermore, the guarantee given by the four Great Powers (Britain, France, Italy, and Japan) for the security of the demilitarized Straits was deemed to be reassuring.[a]

---

[a] For the text of the Turkish note, see Appendix 11. Previously, the Turkish representative at the conference for the reduction and limitation of armaments in May 1933 already had suggested the remilitarization of the Straits.

But by 1936—so the note explained—navies had been strengthened and uncertainty prevailed, especially in the Mediterranean area (the Spanish Civil War began in that year), and the threat of a "general conflagration" appeared to be close. The guarantees for the security of the Straits and for the freedom of navigation through them, as were offered in Lausanne, seemed unreliable or outrightly unrealistic because the equilibrium of the entire Convention had by then collapsed. One of the guarantors, Japan, had ceased to be a member of the League, and another, Italy, had been subjected to sanctions by the League because of her invasion of Ethiopia. The demilitarized Straits had therefore become a most vulnerable area; in view of this situation the government of Turkey could not expose its own country to sudden foreign aggression without being guilty of negligence toward its own people.

The note proposed the conclusion of a new agreement for the regime of the Straits, one which would take into consideration the new situation and also the requirements of Turkey's security. The note also emphasized that Lausanne recognized only a state of peace or a state of war and failed to provide for the contingency of a particular or general threat of war that would justify Turkey's right to legitimate self-defense.

The Soviet government promptly supported the Turkish bid, hoping that the new regime of the Straits would better suit its interests than the reluctantly accepted and never-ratified Lausanne Convention. Like Turkey, Moscow was at this time very much interested in securing protection for its sensitive Black Sea coastline and the industrial region of the Ukraine against a potential attack by Fascist Italy or Nazi Germany. Furthermore, the Kremlin believed it would be easier to gain further advantages from a regime which restored Turkey's full sovereignty over the Straits and eliminated the uncomfortable International Straits Commission. It should be remembered that it has always been the Russian objective to settle the Straits Question with Turkey and with Turkey alone—as it was undertaken, for instance, at Hünkâr Iskelesi in 1833.

The Turkish initiative was well received by all the interested powers except Italy. There was a fear among the democratic governments that Turkey might resort to some unilateral action, a fait accompli—the Japanese attitude and the Italian and German precedents were much in mind.[b] It therefore seemed evidence of a highly constructive and peaceful attitude when Ankara sought to change this international agreement through strictly legal procedures. The Lausanne powers quickly responded by agreeing to the convocation of a new Straits conference which was to meet on June 22, 1936, at the Swiss town of Montreux, having been invited there by the Swiss Federal Government.[1]

THE MONTREUX CONFERENCE

All the signatories of the Straits Convention of Lausanne were represented at the Montreux Conference except Italy, which let it be known that she considered the meeting of the conference untimely and therefore would not attend it; at the same time, she reserved for herself all rights stemming from the Lausanne Convention.

Since the conclusion of the Lausanne Treaty, the British Empire had become the British Commonwealth and the dominions had become independent states. The government of the United Kingdom of Great Britain and Northern Ireland and the government of Australia were individually represented at Montreux; the governments of Canada, New Zealand, India, and the Irish Free State did not send representatives but informed the conference that they had no objection

---

[b] On March 7, 1936, German forces, in violation of the provisions of the Versailles Treaty and the Locarno Convention, entered the demilitarized Rhineland.

against the revision of the provisions of the Lausanne Convention.

Britain's chief delegate was Lord Stanhope, minister of state, who was later replaced by Lord Stanley, parliamentary secretary for the Admiralty. France was represented by former Prime Minister Joseph Paul-Boncour; Greece, by her ambassador in Paris, Nicolas Politis; Rumania, by Foreign Minister Titulescu. The Union of Soviet Socialist Republics was prominently represented by Maksim Litvinov, people's commissar for foreign affairs. On behalf of Turkey, Foreign Minister Tevfik Rüştü Aras and Numan Menemencioğlu, secretary general of the Ministry of Foreign Affairs, participated.

A Turkish draft convention first served as the basis for the deliberations. Throughout the discussions great differences emerged, as they had at Lausanne, between the British and the Soviet positions. The ending of the demilitarized status of the Straits and their fortification by Turkey were tacitly accepted by all participants as the raison d'être for the holding of the conference[2] (the Turkish draft did not even contain a reference to remilitarization); but considerable differences arose concerning the international legal status of the Black Sea and the entry into that sea by warships of non-Black Sea powers. Inconsistencies between the guarantee to be offered by the League of Nations for the security of the Straits on the one hand, and existing treaties of collective security on the other were additional obstacles faced by the conference. Turkey herself appeared to be mainly interested in the full restoration of her sovereign rights over the Straits area and her security against possible dangers from entering or passing foreign warships.

The Soviet position was essentially the same as the one upheld by the Russian representative at Lausanne: warships of non-Black Sea powers (the so-called non-riparian or non-riverain powers) should be prohibited from entering the Black Sea (except for making courtesy visits or entering for

"humanitarian" reasons). Litvinov did not formally submit
the old-time Russian thesis concerning the Black Sea—
namely, that it is a "closed" sea in the international legal
sense and not a "high sea" open to the warships of all nations. But he referred to the fact—as Chicherin, the chief
Russian delegate, had at Lausanne—that there could be no
acceptable purpose for non-Black Sea states to send their
warships into that sea. The Black Sea, he said, "leads nowhere."[3] The Soviet representative also wished to link the
League's collective security machinery with the collective
security treaties concluded by some powers (such as those
concluded by the Soviet Union with some countries, and the
Balkan Entente) for the purpose of offering guarantees for
the protection of free navigation through the Straits.

The British representative was reluctant to agree to major
changes of the Lausanne regime other than the remilitarization of the Straits area. Lord Stanhope hoped that, as far as
possible, the new convention would retain the accepted principles of international law, such as freedom of navigation for
all ships through the Straits and in the Black Sea. The interests of those powers which did not participate in the conference should also be safeguarded. (He was probably thinking
primarily of Germany.) Mutual assistance pacts should not be
linked up with the regime of the Straits. Out of deference for
Japan (which had withdrawn from the League after its condemnation of her), the Covenant of the League of Nations
should not be mentioned in the new convention unless by
common agreement (that is, with the consent of Japan).

Black Sea riparian states other than Turkey and the Soviet
Union, namely Rumania and Bulgaria, generally supported
the Soviet position with regard to the exclusion of warships
of non-Black Sea powers. France and Rumania favored the
connection of the new convention with all collective security
systems. On the other hand, France rejected the Soviet concept of the Black Sea being a "closed sea."

With regard to the Black Sea, the British and Australian
representatives strongly upheld the view of traditional inter-

national law which chose to consider the Black Sea as part of the high seas, which cannot be closed to the navies of any country. However, Britain was ready to accept some conclusions derived from the peculiar geographical situation of the Black Sea and the Straits which command its outlet. The British recalled that at Lausanne a certain balance had been established between the naval strength of the Black Sea powers and the naval forces of non-Black Sea powers which were to enter the sea. They wished to employ the same method of reciprocity and flexibility which made possible the agreement reached at Lausanne.[4]

The Turkish draft made no reference to an international commission of the Straits; it merely stressed that the sovereignty of the Turkish state should fully extend over the Straits area. There was an attempt on behalf of Britain to have the existing international commission maintained, at least as a body that would carry out certain technical tasks (such as the collection of statistics and the furnishing of relevant information to the signatory powers). But Turkey strongly opposed the continued existence of such an organization and she was able to have her point of view accepted. It was agreed that the Turkish government was to carry out the functions of the existing commission.

After a constructive general debate the plenary conference adjourned on June 25 and reconvened only on July 6. In the interval, a technical committee (on which naval and other experts were included) discussed the disputed details. Two days before the renewed meeting of the plenary session, the British representatives submitted a counter-draft which was a revised text of the original Turkish proposal. Tevfik Rüştü Aras, the chief Turkish delegate, agreed that the new draft should be discussed article by article.

During the second phase of the conference, the main points of controversy were once more at the center of the debate. For instance, an extended argument revolved around alleged humanitarian reasons for warships of non-Black Sea powers to enter the Black Sea.[5] The question of Turkey's remaining neutral in case of war was also hotly debated; was she obliged to admit naval forces into the Straits acting in execution of the League's mandate or acting by virtue of a mutual assistance pact? [6] Finally, on all these and other questions compromise proposals were adopted and a drafting committee was able to produce texts which reconciled conflicting views and were acceptable to all participants.

The Convention Regarding the Regime of the Straits was signed on July 20, 1936 (see Appendix 12). It came into force, after the deposition of the required ratification documents, on November 9, 1936. However, a protocol enclosed to the Convention already authorized the Turkish government to remilitarize the zone of the Straits and also to proceed, as of August 15, 1936, to apply the provisions of the Convention, pending its ratification.

THE MONTREUX STRAITS CONVENTION

The guiding purpose of the Montreux Convention, as expressed in its Preamble, was "to regulate transit and navigation in the Straits . . . within the framework of Turkish security and of the security, in the Black Sea, of the riparian States." The Preamble defined the Straits as comprising the Dardanelles, the Sea of Marmara, and the Bosporus. In Article 1, the Convention once more reiterated the principle of freedom of transit and navigation by sea in the Straits. Although the convention, as we shall see, could be denounced with a two-year notice after a duration of twenty years, Article 28 provided that the principle of free transit and navigation in the Straits shall in any case continue to be observed without time limit; in other words, it is defined as a principle not subject to denunciation.

Notwithstanding the principle of freedom of navigation and transit, their exercise is regulated by the Convention in its various articles. Like its Lausanne predecessor, the Montreux treaty distinguishes between merchant vessels and warships. The former are negatively defined: they are all those ships which do not fall under the description of warships in Section II of the Convention.

Merchant Vessels

1. In time of peace, merchant ships of any nation enjoy complete freedom of transit and navigation in the Straits by day and by night, whatever cargo they may transport. The only formality to which they are subjected is the sanitary control carried out at the entrance of the Dardanelles for ships entering from the Aegean Sea, and at the entrance of the Bosporus for ships entering from the Black Sea. Ships have to stop for this control and if they have a clean bill of health or present a declaration of health they are entitled to proceed and are not required to make any further stop during their passage through the Straits. The convention prescribed that the sanitary control should be performed by day and by night with all possible speed.

Merchant vessels which have on board cases of plague, cholera, yellow fever, exanthematic typhus, smallpox (or which have had such cases on board during the previous seven days), or have left an infected port within less than five days, have to accept sanitary guards on board during the transit through the Straits as directed by the Turkish authorities.

Taxes and charges which may be levied by Turkey on passing merchant ships are listed by Annex 1 of the Convention and are not to be higher than necessary to cover the cost of maintaining the services in question. These taxes cannot be raised (but may be reduced on a nondiscriminatory basis). Ships which not only pass the Straits but are also calling at Turkish ports in the Straits area may be required to pay further taxes.

Merchant ships when stopping at the two entrance stations are to communicate to the officials their name, nationality (flag), tonnage, destination, and last port of call. The Convention leaves pilotage and towage optional in time of peace. If ships avail themselves of such services, however, additional taxes and charges are levied.

2. In time of war:

a. If Turkey is not a belligerent[c] the same provisions apply as in time of peace; that is, merchant ships of any flag and of any cargo enjoy freedom of passage under the same rules as apply in peacetime.

b. If Turkey is one of the belligerents, merchant vessels which do not belong to a country at war with Turkey continue to enjoy full freedom of transit through the Straits provided "they do not in any way assist the enemy." Evidently, it is for Turkey to interpret the meaning of the words "assisting the enemy."[d] When Turkey is a belligerent, all merchant vessels must enter the Straits at daytime and the route they have to follow will be prescribed by the Turkish authorities.

c. Should Turkey consider herself threatened with imminent danger of war, she may require merchant vessels to enter the Straits only by day and to follow the route indicated in each case by the Turkish authorities, such as is the case when Turkey is already at war. The wording of the Convention leaves no doubt that it remains Turkey's discretionary decision to consider herself to be threatened by the

---

[c] The Montreux Conference, after some deliberation, adopted the terms "belligerent" and "nonbelligerent" instead of speaking of "Turkey at war" as originally suggested in the Turkish draft.

[d] The Greek delegate, Nicolas Politis, an eminent international lawyer, expressed the view at the conference that any act contrary to the obligations of a neutral is to be interpreted as "assisting the enemy" in the meaning of the Convention. Such acts may include the transport of "contraband" or of persons likely to enroll in the army of the enemy.

danger of imminent war. In this eventuality, Turkey may make pilotage obligatory without, however, levying charges for it.[e]

Warships

On principle, and in accordance with general international law, the Montreux regime of the Straits grants freedom of transit and navigation to vessels of war (Article 10). But only on principle; the rules laid down in Montreux (as previously in Lausanne) contain so many qualifications and exceptions that the freedom of passage for warships is considerably restricted. Furthermore, there is a distinction—indeed a discrimination—in favor of the navies of Black Sea powers, although the principle of a "closed sea" was not accepted. The Montreux Convention accorded a somewhat more favorable treatment to the Russian contention which aimed at excluding altogether warships of non-riparian states from the Black Sea. Naturally, no restrictions whatsoever apply to Turkish warships.

The various categories of warships as well as the means of calculating their displacement (tonnage) are to be found in Annex II of the Convention. The classification of warships was taken over verbatim from the Treaty for the Limitation of Naval Armaments, concluded in London on March 25, 1936.[f] Thus, distinction is made between capital ships, air-

---

[e] There seems to be some inconsistency in the text of the Convention when it authorizes Turkey to make pilotage obligatory under Article 6 (imminent danger of war) while not making it obligatory when Turkey is actually a belligerent (Article 5). But the right of Turkish authorities to indicate the route a vessel has to follow would, in any case, render the use of pilots indispensable. During World War II pilots had to be employed in order to lead ships through the minefields and nets placed by Turkey at the entrance of both the Bosporus and the Dardanelles.

[f] See *Documents on International Affairs, 1936* (London: Oxford University Press, 1937), pp. 616-32. Simple reference to this treaty in the Montreux Convention was objected against because Japan had not been a signatory of the London treaty.

craft carriers, light surface vessels, submarines, minor war
vessels, auxiliary vessels, and small craft. For reasons unknown, the last category (small craft) was omitted from
Annex II of the Montreux Convention, which caused controversies during World War II (see Chapter Four).

The characterization and categorization of vessels of war is
based on displacement (tonnage) and the calibration of gunnery, or in other cases on some other criteria (aircraft carriers, submarines, auxiliary vessels). Subsequent innovations
and technological changes in naval construction and armaments have to some extent rendered obsolete the above classification of warships and have placed before the Turkish
government the necessity of making delicate decisions in
doubtful cases.

Although warships are not to be visited by Turkish officials when entering the Straits, sanitary rules also apply to
them. If they have on board cases of plague, cholera, yellow
fever, exanthematic typhus, or smallpox, or if they have left
infected ports, they too must pass the Straits in quarantine
and apply such prophylactic measures as needed to prevent
the Straits area from being infected (Article 22).

In regard to the passage of warships, the Montreux Convention, like its Lausanne predecessor, distinguishes between
situations when there is no war, when there is one in progress
with Turkey as a nonbelligerent, or when Turkey also partici-
pates in a war. Furthermore—and this was a novelty introduced by Montreux—the eventuality of Turkey being threatened by war is also provided for.

1. In time of peace:

a. Warships of non-Black Sea powers may enter and
pass the Straits only when their maximum aggregate tonnage
does not exceed 15,000 tons (Article 14). Their number cannot comprise more than nine vessels. Furthermore, the displacement of individual warships cannot exceed 10,000 tons
and they cannot carry guns with a caliber exceeding 8 inches
(203 mm) (Article 10).

The above provision practically excludes from the Straits those modern capital ships and aircraft carriers which belong to non-Black Sea states. An exception, however, exists for such warships, even if they exceed the 10,000-ton limit, when they pay courtesy visits of limited duration to a port in the Straits (such as Istanbul) at the request of the government of Turkey. This exception renders possible customary visits of American capital ships and aircraft carriers and of large warships of other nations.

The entry and transit of war vessels must be preceded by a notification given to the Turkish government through diplomatic channels. The Convention prescribes eight days as the "normal period" for such notification but proclaims it desirable that in the case of non-Black Sea powers this period be extended to fifteen days. The notification has to specify the destination, name, type, and number of vessels and also the date of entry and, if pertinent, the date of return. Notification of any changes in these dates must be given three days before the entry of the respective warship. These ships are under no obligation to stop at the entrance of the Dardanelles or the Bosporus; nevertheless, their commanders must communicate to the signal stations at these entrances the exact composition of the force under their orders (Article 13).

Article 9 was inserted in the Convention at the request of the French government. It exempts naval auxiliary vessels (tankers) specifically designed for the carriage of fuel, liquid or nonliquid, from the duty of notification. These are also exempted from the tonnage limitation provided they pass through the Straits singly. (If they accompany other warships, their tonnage is not to be calculated in their aggregate tonnage.) Otherwise, they are to be handled on the same footing as other war vessels.[g]

---

[g] In order to qualify for the exemption, these ships cannot carry more than two guns of a maximum caliber of 105 millimeters against floating targets, and no more than two guns against aerial targets of a maximum caliber of 75 millimeters.

The French government in the pre-World War II period imported crude and refined oil from the Soviet Black Sea port of Batum, and for this reason representatives of France insisted on the inclusion of this special provision in the convention. Because of the expansion of the Soviet Navy into the Mediterranean and other seas since the mid-1960s, the Soviet government has availed itself of the privileges granted under Article 9 to naval tankers.

Vessels of war in transit through the Straits are not allowed, except in the event of damage or peril at sea, to remain there longer than necessary for passage through these waters (Article 16). When vessels have suffered damage and are obliged to stay within the Straits, their tonnage will not be included in the calculation of tonnage of other warships entering thereafter. But ships under repair must obey special provisions relating to security as laid down by the Turkish government (last paragraph of Article 14).

Submarines of non-Black Sea powers are not permitted entry and transit through the Straits. Vessels of war in transit (whether those of non-Black Sea powers or Black Sea powers) shall never make use of any aircraft which they may be carrying.

b. Warships of Black Sea powers wishing to enter and pass the Straits are generally subject to the same restrictions as those of non-Black Sea powers. However, in some important respects the former enjoy a more favorable status. Thus capital ships of Black Sea riparian countries may enter and navigate through the Straits in both directions even if their tonnage exceeds 10,000 tons, on the condition that they pass singly and are escorted by no more than two destroyers (Article 11).[h]

---

[h] The Montreux Convention mentions only "capital ships" in this context. Annex II, while establishing the categories of warships, differentiates between "capital ships" and "aircraft carriers." It may thus be maintained that in the meaning of the Convention capital ships do *not* include aircraft carriers. Should, therefore, the Soviet Union construct aircraft carriers with a displacement exceeding 10,000 tons, these ships

Another exception in favor of the Black Sea riparian states concerns submarines. These states have the right to send through the Straits submarines which have been constructed in or purchased from countries outside the Black Sea provided that adequate notice of the construction or purchase of such submarines has been given to Turkey. Also, if submarines of Black Sea powers require repair in dockyards outside that sea, they may pass through the Straits for such purpose and later return to their base, all this under the condition that detailed information on the matter is given to the Turkish government (Article 12).

Submarines proceeding through the Straits must travel by day and on the surface; furthermore, they are obliged to pass singly.

Accordingly, with certain restrictions, freedom of passage is accorded by the convention to surface warships of Black Sea powers; however, the Convention also compels these powers (and the Soviet Union is the paramount Black Sea naval power) to keep Turkey fully informed of their naval construction program and movements of their units through the Straits, their only outlet into the seven seas. The notification clause extends to the entry and passage of warships of Black Sea powers as well as to those of non-Black Sea powers, but the period of notice is shortened for them to eight days.

c. Entry into the Black Sea by warships of non-riparian states was restricted in terms of aggregate tonnage, by the general limitations governing transit through the Straits; thus, individual warships exceeding 10,000 tons or carrying guns of a caliber exceeding 8 inches were already excluded from the Straits and were barred from reaching the Black Sea.

---

may be barred from passing through the Straits. The two helicopter carriers (*Moskva* and *Leningrad*) which the Soviets possess at the time of this writing and which are frequently seen to move from the Black Sea (where their base is) to the Mediterranean have a displacement of 24,500 tons and are evidently not considered by Ankara to be "aircraft carriers" but capital ships in the meaning of the Convention.

The Montreux Convention further specifically restricted warships of non-Black Sea powers from stationing in the Black Sea. The maximum aggregate tonnage which non-Black Sea states may assemble in that sea in time of peace shall not exceed 30,000 tons. This limitation was calculated on the basis of the strength of the strongest Black Sea navy (the Soviet Union's) at the time of the conclusion of the Montreux Convention. The Convention stipulated, however, that if the strongest Black Sea fleet was to exceed by at least 10,000 tons the status quo at the time of the signature of the Montreux instrument, the permissible tonnage of non-Black Sea powers allowed to enter the Black Sea would be increased in the same proportion up to a maximum of 45,000 tons. Since the end of World War II, the Black Sea navy of the Soviet Union has increased its 1936 tonnage by much more than 10,000 tons; non-Black Sea powers, therefore, are entitled to enter the Black Sea with warships having an aggregate of 45,000 tons.

Each Black Sea power is obliged to inform the Turkish government twice a year (on January 1 and July 1) of the total tonnage of their vessels of war in the Black Sea. Ankara then passes this information to the signatory powers of the Montreux Convention (Article 18, par. 1).

In addition to this global limitation of warships of non-Black Sea powers entering the Black Sea, the Convention provides that any individual non-Black Sea power may have at one time no more than two-thirds of the permissible aggregate tonnage in the Black Sea. Thus, if the permissible maximum tonnage of outside warships is 45,000 tons, the United States, for example, may have warships of no more than 30,000 tons total displacement in the Black Sea at any given time. It should, furthermore, be remembered that these warships may not pass the Straits except in two groups (15,000 tons each) and individual warships may not have a displacement larger than 10,000 tons with guns not exceeding 8 inches (203 mm).

Exceptional rules prevail in the case of non-Black Sea powers wishing to send naval forces into the Black Sea for humanitarian purposes. If these naval forces do not exceed a displacement of 8,000 tons all together, they will be allowed to enter the Straits without the notification required by Article 13. Nevertheless, even in this case, authorization must be obtained from the Turkish government. Turkey is to inform all other Black Sea powers of the intended entry into that sea, and if there is no objection she will reply within forty-eight hours at the latest to the government having made the request.

The Soviet representative at Montreux gave only reluctant approval to this exceptional entry of outside warships. He was unable to foresee contingencies that would necessitate the dispatch of naval forces for "humanitarian" reasons. His opponents at the conference table referred to such cases as earthquakes or other natural disasters, epidemics, and so forth.

Whatever their reason for entering the Black Sea may be, warships of non-Black Sea powers are prohibited from remaining in that sea for a period longer than twenty-one days (Article 18, para. 2).

2. In time of war:

a. When Turkey is not a belligerent. In principle, freedom of passage to warships through the Straits, with the restrictions applicable to peacetime, is to be maintained, but only in favor of warships of countries which are not belligerents. For warships of belligerent nations, prohibitive restrictions are in force.

Accordingly, vessels of war belonging to belligerent powers are not permitted to enter and pass the Straits. An exception, however, was made in the Convention in favor of warships of such belligerents when they wish to enter the Straits under the collective security provisions (sanctions) of the League of Nations or "in cases of assistance rendered to a state victim of aggression in virtue of a treaty of mutual assistance, binding Turkey, concluded within the framework of the Covenant of the League of Nations" (Article 19).

The above provision was the result of much heated argument. The key words eventually agreed upon were: "binding Turkey." Thus, only in case of collective security measures accepted by Turkey or otherwise binding her may belligerent naval forces pass through the Straits.

Compliance with international "police actions" or the implementation of mutual assistance pacts was given such prominence in the Montreux Convention that under its Article 19 all restrictions on tonnage and armament were lifted for warships en route to carry out these assistance missions. The text reflects the insistence of Soviet, French, and Rumanian representatives at the conference and was adopted despite the reluctant attitude of Britain and the opposition of Japan.[i] These provisions are of particular importance today, when it might be possible to construe the Convention in such a manner as to replace the League of Nations with the United Nations and the sanction provisions of the League with those found in the U.N. Charter (see Chapter Seven).

Article 19 also provides that warships of belligerent powers which become separated from their bases as a result of an outbreak of hostilities are permitted to return to their bases by passing through the Straits. This exceptional provision applied to Black Sea and non-Black Sea powers.

It is further provided in the Convention that belligerent rights under the law of war on the seas, such as visit and

---

[i] Japan signed the Montreux Convention with the reservation (the only reservation added to the signatures) that provisions of the Convention do not in any sense modify her position as a state not a member of the League of Nations with regard to the Covenant or mutual assistance pacts concluded within its framework, and that she reserves full liberty of interpretation as regards those articles of the Convention which mention the Covenant or treaties concluded under its aegis.

search, and capture, may not be exercised in the Straits. Nor are any hostile acts to be performed in those waters (should warships of hostile powers meet there). All the above regulations and exceptions refer, of course, to a situation in which Turkey herself is not one of the belligerent powers.

b. When Turkey is a belligerent. In the eventuality that Turkey herself becomes a belligerent all peacetime provisions for the passage of warships through the Straits become inapplicable, as do those which were to apply in a case of a war in which Turkey remained neutral.

When Turkey is at war, the entry and passage of warships of other nations is left to the discretion of the Turkish government. This government is entitled to allow navigation in the Straits for certain ships of certain powers and may freely prohibit passage of others. In fact, the "ancient rule of the Ottoman Empire" as applied by the Sublime Porte in time of war would be restored in such an eventuality. Turkish sovereign rights over the Straits area may unrestrictedly and even in a discriminatory manner be exercised when Turkey becomes involved in a war (Article 20).

c. Threat of a danger of war. Should Turkey consider herself threatened with imminent danger of war, she has the right to apply the provisions of Article 20—that is, those which apply to a situation in which she is actually a belligerent. In other words, when Turkey deems that there is an imminent peril of war which is likely to jeopardize her safety, she may—by unilateral decision—close the Straits to the warships of any or all nations.

Should Turkey make use of this prerogative conferred on her by the Convention, warships which have passed the Straits in either direction before she closed these waterlanes, and thus may find themselves separated from their bases (home ports), may still return to these bases. But Turkey may, notwithstanding this exception, refuse entry and passage to warships into and through the Straits if they belong to that nation or to those nations whose attitude had given rise to the measure taken; in other words, warships of such states which threaten Turkey may be prevented from returning to their bases (Article 21).

Turkey, however, is obliged to notify all the other signatory powers of the Montreux Convention (and the Secretary-General of the League of Nations) of this extraordinary measure. The text further provides that, if the Council of the League by a majority of two-thirds decides that the measure of closing the Straits was not justified, and the measure was also considered unjustified by the majority of the signatory powers of the Montreux Convention, the Turkish government would have to discontinue the closure of the Straits under the alleged threat of imminent war—that is, it would have to open them to warships as generally prescribed by the Convention.

Aircraft

Turkey was expected to fortify the Straits following the conclusion of the Montreux Conference, and she did. Questions were voiced by the future signatories of the Convention concerning the passage of aircraft over that area. There was some apprehension that in the absence of provisions to the contrary Turkey might forbid overflight of the Straits, which are generally considered a crossroads for aerial as well as maritime traffic.

Accordingly, Article 23 provides that Turkey must assure passage of civil aircraft between the Mediterranean and the Black Sea by indicating the air routes available for this purpose, with such routes to be outside any fortified zones established in the Straits. But Turkey must receive, as regards occasional flights, notification three days before a flight occurs and a general notification of regular air schedules. The same article also guarantees freedom of flights in the west-east direction across the Straits. Notwithstanding the remilitarization of the Straits, Turkey was to give authorization for flights over her territory between Europe and Asia. Air routes were to be set up by the Turkish government for occasional and scheduled flights.

Duration, Revision, and Denunciation of the Convention

The Montreux Convention, as foreseen by Article 28, was to remain in force for twenty years from the date of its entry into force (except for the "principle" of freedom of transit and navigation, announced in Article 1, which was to continue in force indefinitely). If two years prior to the expiration of the twenty-year period no signatory power has given notice of denunciation, the Convention is to continue in force until at any time later a two-year notice is given. Notification of the Convention's denunciation must be made to the French government, which is to inform the other signatories.

In case of the denunciation of the Convention, the signatories agreed that they would be represented at a conference to be convoked for the conclusion of a new convention. The Montreux Convention went into force on November 9, 1936, and became liable to denunciation after November 9, 1954. No signatory has yet availed itself of the right of denunciation and so the Convention has remained operative and in force.

The Convention also foresaw that one or several of the signatories might press for a revision of some of its provisions. As long as the Convention is in force, at the expiration of each period of five years from the date of its entry into force, each signatory power is entitled to initiate a procedure for the amendment of one or more of its provisions. This request for modification, if it should relate to Articles 14 or 18 (which deal with the limitation of the tonnage of warships entering the Straits or the Black Sea) must be supported by yet another signatory (i.e., two signatory powers must support the request). If the request for modification relates to any other article of the convention, it must be submitted by

one signatory power and supported by two further signatories (three signatory powers all together). All parties must be
notified of such a request for the revision of the Convention
three months prior to the end of the five-year period mentioned above.

The notification for revision must contain the details of
the proposed amendment as well as the reasons for the initiative. If diplomatic exchanges (notes) do not result in an
agreement on the question thus raised, the signatories agree
that a conference should be convoked for this purpose. The
conference can make decisions concerning the revision of
parts of the Convention only by unanimous agreement,
except concerning Articles 14 and 18 for which a favorable
majority of three-quarters of the participating powers is sufficient to effect a decision. But even this majority has to include three-quarters of the powers which are riparians of the
Black Sea. Turkey, the Soviet Union, Bulgaria, and Rumania
are the Black Sea signatory powers. Therefore, three of them
in addition to other powers have to support any revision of
the convention which aims at a change of the displacement
and armament requirements for warships wishing to enter
the Straits and the Black Sea (Article 29).

No formal request for the revision of any of the provisions
of the Convention has so far been submitted. The question of
revision was discussed at the Yalta and Potsdam summit conferences and in diplomatic notes exchanged subsequently
(see Chapter Four).

AFTER THE MONTREUX CONFERENCE

From the date of its entry into force, the Convention of
Montreux was open to accession by those powers which had
in 1923 signed the Peace Treaty of Lausanne. Italy, which
did not participate in the Montreux Conference, subsequently changed her mind and acceded to the Convention in April
1938.

Nazi Germany, having reached an agreement with Britain concerning the increase of her naval strength, put out feelers in 1937 with the aim of possibly reaching agreement with Turkey through which she would be granted the rights enjoyed by the signatories of the Montreux Convention. She was particularly interested in obtaining assurances that the provisions of Montreux concerning the passage of warships sent in fulfillment of obligations under the League of Nations Covenant, or to render assistance to a victim of aggression under a mutual assistance pact, were not to be applied against her interests. In other words, she wanted to protect herself by the same reservation which Japan had added to her signature of the Montreux Convention.

Turkey, however, hesitated to discuss the Straits question bilaterally with Germany and thus create a precedent which would affect her relations with Moscow and could possibly be exploited later by the Kremlin. Ankara was ready to give verbal assurances to Germany that she would never enter into a treaty of mutual assistance which would oblige her to allow passage of warships to victims of aggression, and also to promise that as soon as an opportunity for the revision of the Convention offered itself she would support the issuance of an invitation to Germany to participate in the revised Convention. German Foreign Minister Ribbentrop thereupon complained that because of "legal subtleties" no agreement could be reached.[7]

Many of the provisions of the Montreux Convention reflect the problems facing the powers at the time of its conclusion. It was a period when both Turkey and the Soviet Union were apprehensive over the possibility that an Italian or German coup would upset the security and balance of power in the Mediterranean region and that these aggressive nations might even obtain control over the strategic area of the Straits. It was at that time that Italy conquered Ethiopia, an event which permitted an exaggerated estimation of its military and naval capabilities.

More than ever since the Bolshevik takeover, Moscow was on the defensive and the potential threat of "capitalist" collaboration, uniting Britain, Germany, and Italy to destroy the only socialist state, loomed large over her foreign policy concerns. Evidently, collective security as envisaged under the Covenant of the League of Nations had collapsed and even the value of bilateral or multilateral assistance pacts appeared questionable. But the Soviet and Turkish community of interest, at least in regard to the Straits, seemed to be assured. During the years of Atatürk's leadership, Ankara had gained the goodwill of most nations; to place the guardianship of the Straits in her hands was not opposed by Britain, by the Soviet Union, or by any other power participating in the Montreux Conference.

Accordingly, the powers of the International Straits Commission were transferred to the Turkish government (Article 24); Turkey was thus authorized to collect statistical data on behalf of the signatories (including the reports of Black Sea powers concerning the status of their navies). The Convention empowered Ankara "to supervise the execution of all the provisions" of the Convention, a role which made her the arbiter over any controversy that might arise with regard to the application or interpretation of the Convention.

As we have seen, in certain crucial situations, Turkey was expressly given discretionary powers to admit or refuse entry of foreign warships into the Straits. This included the right to prevent warships from entering the Black Sea or to prevent those already there from leaving.

The political and strategic objective of the Soviet Union, as it had been for Russia in the past, was to forbid entrance into the Black Sea, in war or peace, of non-Black Sea navies. Considerable satisfaction was given to this aspiration by the Montreux Convention. No large fleet of any non-Black Sea power was to move into the sea in time of peace. On the other hand, in time of war when Turkey was a belligerent, or when Ankara considered itself endangered, it was left to the discretion of the Turkish government to allow or disallow the passage through the Straits and into the Black Sea of warships of any size and any number. It was important for Moscow, then, to gain the friendship of Turkey and to prevent the emergence of any situation which Turkey might consider to be endangering her security.

The Montreux Convention permits Moscow to send its surface warships through the Straits into the Mediterranean. This enables Russia to transfer portions of her navy from the Black Sea into the Baltic or Arctic or even the Pacific and vice versa, but only when Turkey and she are not belligerents and when Turkey does not feel endangered.[8]

For Turkey, in Montreux her own security was the paramount concern. She was able to increase this greatly by the conclusion of the Convention. She was authorized to fortify the area of the Straits (as she was permitted to do with any other part of her territory). And the control which she exercised over the interpretation, application, and implementation of the Convention, over the supervision of movements of ships in the Straits, and over the strength of Soviet and other Black Sea naval forces gave her added authority and prestige.

The United States (unlike Japan) did not participate actively in the proceedings of Montreux. Washington was not a signatory of the Lausanne Treaty and therefore was not automatically invited to the conference. And in view of the isolationist principles which prevailed in her foreign policy, no effort was made to secure American participation. In 1936 Washington was, in the face of the "gathering storm" in Europe, more eager than ever to remain aloof of "entanglements" in the affairs of Europe. The question of the Straits as it was discussed at Montreux was considered a European issue. Since the passage of merchant vessels of all flags was guaranteed by the Montreux Convention and this essentially commercial concern of the United States was satisfied, no further American interest appeared to be involved. World War II had to explode in order to bring the United States to the shores of the Eastern Mediterranean and arouse its interest in the problem of the Turkish Straits.

- 4 -

World War II and Soviet
Attempts to Seize the Straits

Italian and German aggressions in the late 1930s persuaded
Turkey to abandon the nonalignment policy it had pursued
during Atatürk's lifetime. In the spring of 1939, following
the German entry into Prague, the British government began
seeking allies among the East European countries to forestall
further territorial expansion by Hitler and Mussolini. British
guarantees were extended to Poland, Rumania, and Greece;
Turkey was also invited to join this system of alliances. In
May and June of 1939 Anglo-Turkish and Franco-Turkish
declarations of mutual assistance were announced and were
followed later by a formal treaty of alliance.

In the summer of 1939 diplomatic and military negotiations were conducted by Britain and France with the Soviet
government in order to bring the Soviet Union into the anti-
Nazi and anti-Fascist camp. At the same time, Moscow put
out feelers to Ankara for the conclusion of a treaty of mutual

assistance. But the unexpected announcement of the Hitler-Stalin pact of August 23, 1939, created an entirely new situation for Ankara; it placed Turkey, as the defender of the Straits on the horns of a difficult dilemma.

THE HITLER-STALIN PACT AND THE STRAITS

At the time of the German invasion of Poland and the subsequent participation of Moscow in this act of aggression, the Anglo-French-Turkish tripartite assistance treaty was ready for signature. It also contained a clause which exempted Turkey from the obligation of assistance if an armed conflict broke out between her two Western allies and the Soviet Union. However, before signing the draft treaty, the Turkish government agreed to send Foreign Minister Şükrü Saracoğlu to Moscow to seek a clarification of Soviet intentions.

In Moscow Saracoğlu was invited by Stalin and Molotov not only to modify the tripartite treaty but to do so in such a way as to deprive it of any Turkish obligation to come to the aid of Britain and France should the war extend into the Mediterranean. Moreover, the Soviet leaders, with an even greater insistence, urged Turkey to ignore the provisions of the Montreux Convention by refusing permission of passage through the Straits to warships belonging to non-Black Sea powers, unless with the consent of the Soviet government. Later Molotov hinted at the idea of a "joint defense" of the Straits by Turkey and the Soviet Union.

Saracoğlu refused to accept terms which would result in a rupture between Turkey and the two Western powers and make Turkey a tool of German-Russian ambitions. As to the Straits, the Turkish foreign minister categorically refused to be drawn into a bilateral relationship with Moscow which would set aside the Montreux Convention. After three weeks of abortive negotiations, Saracoğlu returned to Ankara where, on October 19, 1939, the Tripartite Treaty of Alliance was signed.[1]

Turkey and the Straits figured prominently in the discussions which German Foreign Minister Ribbentrop conducted with the Soviet leaders during his two visits in Moscow in August and September 1939. Further negotiations between Nazi Germany and Moscow in November 1940 centered largely around intended Soviet penetration "south of the national territory of the Soviet Union in the direction of the Indian Ocean."[2] The draft of a secret protocol prepared by the German Foreign Office and handed to Soviet Foreign Commissar Vyacheslav M. Molotov at the time of his visit to Berlin (November 12-13, 1940) foresaw the replacement of the Montreux Convention by another convention (see Appendix 13). The new regime of the Straits would prohibit the entry of all warships of non-Black Sea countries but would permit unrestricted exit of units of the Soviet Navy into the Mediterranean.[3]

The Soviet government, however, was not satisfied with the German draft and insisted that the other signatories (Germany and Italy) recognize "the focal point of the aspirations of the Soviet Union south of Batum and Baku in the general direction of the Persian Gulf." With regard to the change in the status of the Straits, the Soviet counter-draft asked for "a base for light naval and land forces of the U.S.S.R. on the Bosporus and the Dardanelles by means of a long term lease." Molotov also suggested that if Turkey refused to comply with this plan, Germany, Italy, and the Soviet Union should agree on the required military and diplomatic measures to be carried out. This counter-draft was passed on by the German ambassador to Ribbentrop on November 26 (see Appendix 14).

These Soviet-German talks concerning the Straits and the territorial integrity and political independence of Turkey were conducted at a time when Ankara appeared isolated in a hostile environment. France collapsed in the summer of 1940 and Britain, threatened by German invasion, stood alone. By invoking the Soviet clause in her treaty of alliance with Britain and France, Turkey remained neutral despite Italy's entry into the war. But Berlin refused to go along with the Soviet design; in fact, in December 1940 Hitler decided to invade Russia.

The attack against the Soviet Union, however, was delayed by the German advance into the Balkans; in April and May 1941 Yugoslavia and Greece became victims of German aggression. The German war machine moved into the Aegean and Eastern Mediterranean by occupying Crete and the Greek Islands in the Aegean. The entry of ships of the Western Allies into the Straits thus became impossible until late 1944.[4]

Turkey endeavored to apply the Montreux Convention as best she could during the difficult wartime years. When most of the Black Sea was controlled by the Germans, after the occupation of the Crimea and the Aegean, attempts were made by the Axis powers to send auxiliary war vessels through the Straits disguised as merchantmen. Despite the pressures exerted on Ankara by Berlin (and counter-pressures by Moscow and the Western Allies), the Turkish government managed to prevent the passage of forbidden craft through the Straits; when misled by camouflage, it prohibited renewed entry of each ship as soon as its real character was discovered.

After the outbreak of German-Russian hostilities, both Moscow and London pledged to abide by the provisions of the Montreux Convention. While the Soviets were pressed hard by the Germans, the Turkish government was praised for its strictly neutral attitude. But when the tide turned and Soviet armies reconquered the lost ground in Russia, and particularly along the Black Sea, Moscow began raising objections to Turkish neutrality.

THE STRAITS QUESTION AT YALTA AND POTSDAM

In October 1944 Stalin raised the question of the Straits in his conversations with Churchill in Moscow. President Roosevelt was also informed that revision of the Montreux Convention would be on the agenda of the forthcoming summit conference to be held at Yalta. A briefing paper prepared by the State Department and submitted to President Roosevelt expressed hope that the question regarding the Straits would not be discussed at Yalta (see Appendix 15).

At Yalta Stalin raised the Straits question on February 10, 1945. He said that the Montreux treaty was outmoded. He complained that the Japanese Emperor had played a large part in the treaty, greater than that of the Soviet Union. Montreux was linked with the League of Nations, which no longer existed. Under the Montreux Convention the Turks could close the Straits not only in time of war but if they felt there was a threat of war. There was no longer any reason for Great Britain to try to strangle the Soviet Union with the help of the Japanese. It was impossible to accept a situation in which Turkey had "a hand on Russia's throat." The treaty should be revised, Stalin said, and he proposed that the first conference of the three foreign ministers (American, British, and Soviet) should consider this question. Both President Roosevelt and Prime Minister Churchill agreed that the question of the revision of the Montreux Convention should be placed on the agenda of the foreign ministers conference. (For the relevant discussion at Yalta, see Appendix 16).

The Soviet war of nerves against Turkey gathered full steam after the Yalta conference of February 1945. In March 1945 Molotov refused to extend the Turkish-Soviet Treaty of Neutrality of December 17, 1925, with the argument that it no longer corresponded to actual circumstances and the changes brought about by the war. In June, Molotov told the Turkish ambassador in Moscow (Selim Sarper) that to regain Soviet friendship, a price had to be paid. He demanded the return of two Turkish provinces along the Caucasian border which had been given back to Turkey at the end of World War I. Furthermore, the Soviet foreign commissar claimed that Turkey was unable to defend the Straits by herself, that she should agree to the establishment of Soviet bases on

Turkish territory and also come to an agreement with Moscow concerning the revision of the Montreux Convention. The Turkish ambassador, on instructions from his government, categorically refused to consider these demands on the grounds that they were incompatible with the territorial integrity and sovereign rights of Turkey.[5]

The meeting of the three foreign ministers did not advance the Straits question; they agreed only to place it on the agenda of the forthcoming summit conference of Berlin-Potsdam. In Potsdam, on July 22, Churchill unveiled the tension between Moscow and Ankara. Molotov explained the situation as arising from a Turkish request to conclude a treaty of alliance; the Soviet government let Turkey know what the conditions for such a treaty would be. These conditions included territorial demands and also a new arrangement with regard to the Straits.

Churchill opposed the Soviet approach to a bilateral agreement with Turkey and the establishment of a Russian base in the Straits. In a later discussion he pointed out the discrepancy between the Russian proposal to have the Montreux Convention revised, the demand for a bilateral agreement with Turkey, and the proposed establishment of a base—conditions to which the Turks would not submit.

On July 23, Stalin stated that Montreux had created an "impossible situation" when it allowed Turkey to block the Straits while she was at war or felt threatened: "a small state supported by Great Britain," he declared, "held a great state by the throat and gave it no outlet." He referred to the Suez Canal, the Straits of Gibraltar, and the Panama Canal, stating that a similar situation in regard to these waterways would be intolerable to Britain or the United States.

President Truman agreed that the Montreux Convention should be revised. He submitted a paper to the conference on the free and unrestricted navigation of inland waterways. The territorial dispute between Russia and Turkey should be settled by them, but the waterways were of interest to the

whole world. The U.S. president's paper also suggested that
international agencies be set up for all these "inland waterways," among which he included the Danube, the Rhine, the
Kiel Canal, and the Turkish Straits. Molotov also submitted a
paper setting out the Soviet position on the question. Under
his plan the Straits question would be settled between the
Black Sea powers and Turkey.

Churchill remarked that these suggestions wholly differed
from those which aimed at revision of the Montreux Convention. There was also a discussion concerning the threat by
Soviet and Bulgarian troop concentrations along the border
of Turkey; Stalin denied that there was such a concentration
of forces.

After the meeting Stalin suddenly exclaimed to Churchill,
"If you find it impossible to give a fortified position in the
Marmara, could we not have a base at Dedeagatch? "[a]
Churchill replied, over a glass of brandy, "I will always sup-
port Russia in her claim to freedom of the seas all the year
round."[6]

On July 24 it became clear that no agreement between the
three heads of government could be reached in regard to the
Straits. Truman now supported Churchill. Both he and the
British prime minister were in favor of a revision of the Montreux Convention. Stalin then said that the Soviet Union
would continue its negotiations with Turkey. (For the proceedings at Potsdam on the Straits question, see Appendix
17.)

Finally, the three governments agreed on a resolution
which stated that the Montreux Convention should be revised, "as failing to meet present-day conditions." They also
agreed that "as a next step" the matter should be the subject
of direct conversations between each of the three governments and Turkey. But the Soviet version omitted the words

---

[a] Dedeagatch, now known as Alexandroupolis, is a seaport in Greek
Western Thrace, not far distant from the entrance of the Dardanelles.

"as a next step," attempting to avoid the impression that these conversations would be only the preliminaries to an international conference for revision of the convention as prescribed by the Montreux treaty itself.[7]

The exchange of notes which followed the Potsdam conference was initiated by the American note dated November 2, 1945 (see Appendix 18). Before the contents of this note are analyzed, the official views of the United States on the question of the Turkish Straits should be examined.

THE UNITED STATES AND THE STRAITS

The Treaty of Commerce and Navigation of May 1830, concluded between the United States and the Ottoman Empire, accorded the right of most favored nation to merchant vessels sailing under the American flag for the navigation through the Straits.[8] The treaty made no mention of the passage of warships.

The United States was not a party to any of the treaties concluded between the European powers and Turkey in regard to the Straits. It has thus never given approval to the "ancient rule of the Ottoman Empire," the right of the Porte to close the Straits to all non-Ottoman warships.[9] The American position as expressed by Hamilton Fish (U.S. secretary of state from 1869 to 1877) was based on the principles of general international law. The Dardanelles, the Sea of Marmara, and the Bosporus were, according to this view, straits connecting two parts of the high seas; therefore navigation by merchant and war vessels through these waters was to be free in time of peace. The existing restrictions on the movement of warships were not recognized by the United States, although Washington refrained from formally protesting against this "usage." Entry into the Straits by American warships was attempted a few times, but was denied by the Ottoman government.

The American government always viewed the principle of "freedom of the seas" as the mainstay of its foreign policy.

The Turkish Straits were not to be distinguished from other straits, such as the Danish Sound at the entrance to the Baltic Sea, and for a long time the peculiar political significance of the Straits was overlooked or ignored by American leaders. The attitude of the American leaders did not give due consideration to the mastery over the Turkish Straits and the possession of Constantinople, which together epitomized the Eastern Question which preoccupied European policy-makers for more than two centuries.

President Wilson in his Fourteen Points, announced on January 8, 1918, proposed that "the Dardanelles should be permanently opened as a free passage to the ships and commerce of all nations under international guarantees" (twelfth point). In general, the Wilson administration advocated international control of the Straits; an American mandate over all of Turkey was even under consideration. However, the withdrawal of the United States from the League of Nations and all other European commitments prevented any American involvement in the affairs of the Near East. The United States sent only an observer to the Lausanne Peace Conference, and the separate treaty which Washington signed with Turkey on August 6, 1923, was rejected by the U.S. Senate. Only the American-Turkish Treaty of Commerce and Navigation of October 1, 1929, secured for U.S. vessels the most-favored treatment in Turkish waters. Washington also did not participate in the Montreux Convention, but its provisions which permitted freedom of passage for commercial vessels and more restricted rights for warships automatically extended to ships sailing under the American flag.

At the end of World War II, the United States government initially displayed a lack of understanding of the complexities of the Straits question and its concomitant political and strategic implications. The paper submitted by President Truman to the Potsdam conference concerning "free and unrestricted navigation of international inland waterways" combined such vastly different questions as navigation on the rivers of the

Rhine and the Danube, and passage through the Kiel Canal, with the much more delicate and politically explosive question of the Turkish Straits.

The leaders of Turkey were even more disturbed by the American note of November 2, 1945. This note proposed that the revision of the Montreux Convention be undertaken with the observance of the following principles:

(1) The Straits to be open to the merchant vessels of all nations at all times;

(2) The Straits to be open to the transit of the warships of Black Sea powers *at all times*;

(3) Save for an agreed limited tonnage in time of peace, passage through the Straits to be denied to the warships of non-Black Sea powers *at all times*, except with the *specific consent of the Black Sea powers* or except when acting under the authority of the United Nations; and

(4) Certain changes to modernize the Montreux Convention; such as the substitution of the United Nations system for that of the League of Nations and the elimination of Japan as a signatory.[b]

The freedom of transit of merchant vessels was already an accepted principle under the Lausanne and Montreux regimes. But the right for Black Sea powers (that is, the Soviet Union) to pass freely through the Straits even in time of war appeared to be incompatible with the requirements of Turkish security. It meant that when the Soviet Union was at war and Turkey neutral, Moscow could freely send its warships into the Mediterranean and withdraw them when pursued by superior enemy forces. The sanctuary which the Black Sea, with its entrances guarded by Turkey, would thus offer to the Soviets would jeopardize Ankara's neutrality and could involve Turkey in the hostilities. Furthermore, movements of powerful Soviet naval and possibly troop-transport vessels

---

[b] Italics added.

through the vulnerable Straits area would expose Turkey to the danger of invasion. The prohibition against non-Black Sea naval forces entering the Straits and the Black Sea in full strength, even in time of war and with the consent of Turkey, could have deprived Ankara of much-needed assistance in the event that she was threatened or attacked by the Soviet Union. The consent of Black Sea powers to such an entry by non-Black Sea naval forces would, evidently, not be available in the above contingency. On November 21, the British government handed a note to the Turkish government indicating that it sympathized with the American proposals but adding that the matter did not require urgent attention.

Turkish diplomacy was immediately set in motion to explain to Washington why its proposals were replete with dangers and disregarded the delicate balance established after prolonged considerations at Lausanne and Montreux. [10] Not wishing to appear intransigent, however, the Turkish government expressed its readiness to accept the American proposals as "a basis of discussion." It also offered to participate in a new international conference on the Straits and to endorse its resolutions provided that "Turkey's independence, sovereignty, and territorial integrity are not infringed."

It is to be recalled that during the Potsdam conference President Truman expressed the view that he was not interested in the territorial disputes between Russia and Turkey and that such a dispute should be settled between the two powers concerned. Evidently, such a remark was considered by Moscow as proof that Turkey, isolated because of her wartime neutrality, could not count on the support of the United States. The Soviet leaders, therefore, were little interested in an international conference on the Straits and wished instead to settle both the territorial and Straits questions bilaterally with Turkey. As to the Straits, they hoped to achieve their long-cherished goal of placing the Straits area under their control. Their abiding desire to maintain a "base" in the Straits could have no other meaning for the Turks, and we can safely assume that after his phenomenal success in pushing Soviet domination far into the heart of Central Europe and over all the Balkans (except Greece), Stalin desired to excel the Tsars in regard to Constantinople as well.

THE SOVIET-TURKISH CONFRONTATION

At the end of 1945 and early in 1946, Soviet pressures to demoralize and intimidate Turkey grew in intensity. On December 20, 1945, an article was published simultaneously in *Pravda* and *Izvestia* by two members of the Academy of the Georgian Soviet Socialist Republic claiming "historic rights" even beyond the Kars and Ardahan districts to areas which included a considerable portion of the Turkish Black Sea coast. [11] At that time Communist rebels threatened to take over Greece, and along Turkey's eastern borders, in Iranian Azerbaijan and Kurdistan, Soviet puppet governments were set up. And in the first part of 1946 Stalin was able to strengthen Soviet control in Poland, Rumania, Bulgaria, and the Soviet Zone of Germany. The Soviet war of nerves was orchestrated with the help of radio broadcasts and underscored by troop concentrations along the Bulgarian and Caucasian borderlands of Turkey. These threatening noises alternated with seductive suggestions that if Turkey would only exchange her leaders for others more friendly to the Soviet Union, Turkish-Soviet relations could be raised "to the level of Soviet-Polish friendship."

The reluctance of Moscow to withdraw its forces from Iran, the beginning struggle for the control of Germany, and the consistent extension of Soviet-Communist domination among the countries of East-Central Europe heralded the opening of the Cold War. Within a year after Yalta, Washington appeared to have realized that appeasement of Moscow did not pay. The strategic key position of Turkey and the significance of the Straits came to be recognized not only by a few experts (who earlier had provided the president and his advisers with excellent briefings) but by President Truman and the leaders of the Senate.

To demonstrate American interest in the independence of Turkey, the battleship *Missouri* (on which the instrument of Japan's unconditional surrender had been signed) was sent to the Straits and Istanbul in June 1946, accompanied by two destroyers. The formal aim of this "courtesy visit" was to return the remains of Münir Ertegün. Turkish Ambassador to Washington, who died in November 1944. However, the visit of these American warships, whose crews received an enthusiastic welcome, strengthened Turkish morale and its purpose was duly understood in Moscow. Earlier, in February 1946, British Foreign Secretary Ernest Bevin, while addressing the House of Commons, had reminded the world that Britain had a treaty of alliance with Turkey; he observed that the Straits were under an international regime which must be maintained. [12]

At Potsdam Stalin did receive the approval of both President Truman and Prime Minister Churchill for a revision of the Montreux Convention. Although a Soviet base in the Straits was not found acceptable at that time, it appears that both the United States and Britain were ready to agree to an internationalization of the Straits (that is, to deprive Turkey of the control she exercised by virtue of Montreux), to allow complete freedom in peace or war for Russia to move her navy across the Straits. They also seemed to be willing to accede to a virtual prohibition against non-Black Sea navies entering the Straits and the Black Sea, whether in peace or in war. All the discretionary powers which Turkey was entitled to exercise under the Convention of Montreux (such as the right to close the Straits in time of war or when she felt threatened) would thus have been eliminated.

It is still inexplicable why Stalin did not take quick advantage of this atmosphere so favorable to him and press for a quick conference of powers to have the Montreux Convention revised. Apparently his aim was the establishment of a

Soviet naval-military base at the nodal area of the Straits and the subjection of Turkey, through the medium of this military force (as practiced in the countries of East-Central Europe), to the status of a satellite. He went for the highest stake—and finally obtained nothing.

Evidently realizing that Turkey could not be frightened into submission and that she was likely to receive support from both Britain and the United States, Stalin's choice was whether to resort to force or return to diplomatic methods. The next five-year period for demanding a revision of the Montreux Convention under Article 29 was to expire in the fall of 1946; the Soviet Union, as a signatory, had the right to initiate such a revision when supported by one or two other signatories. Rumania and Bulgaria would no doubt have supported such a request. Therefore, the long-awaited Soviet note which was delivered in Ankara on August 7, 1946, was considered the first step toward initiating the procedure for revision of the Montreux Convention, a revision which was, in principle, agreed upon at Potsdam.

The Soviet note referred to certain events which were adduced to prove that the Montreux Convention "does not meet the interests of the safety of the Black Sea Powers." (See Appendix 19.) It proposed the following principles for a new regime to govern the Straits:

(1) The Straits should be always open to the passage of merchant ships of all countries.

(2) The Straits should be *always open* to the passage of warships of the Black Sea powers.

(3) Passage through the Straits for warships not belonging to the Black Sea powers shall not be permitted except in cases specially provided for.

(4) The establishment of a regime of the Straits, as the sole sea passage leading from the Black Sea and to the Black Sea, should come under the competence of Turkey and other Black Sea powers.

(5) Turkey and the Soviet Union, as the powers most interested and capable of guaranteeing freedom of commercial navigation and security in the Straits, shall organize *joint means of defense* of the Straits for the prevention of the utilization of the Straits by other countries for aims hostile to the Black Sea powers.[c]

Moscow thus reverted once more to its *idée fixe* that the Straits regime should be established between the Black Sea powers only, a plan which would be antithetical to the concept on which the Montreux Convention rested. The reference to "joint means of defense" of the Straits was nothing more than a concealed reiteration of the Soviet claim to bases in the Straits area.

The Soviet note was also delivered to Washington and London. The United States replied on August 19, 1946, and opposed the contention that navigation through the Straits should be the exclusive concern of the Black Sea powers. This American note expressly declared that the defense of the Straits should be the primary task of Turkey. In Washington's view the regime of the Straits should be brought into an appropriate relationship with the United Nations (see Appendix 20). The British reply essentially expressed views similar to those stated by Washington (see Appendix 21).

Turkey replied on August 22, 1946. In her note she undertook to refute one by one the Soviet charges against her handling of the incidents when a few German and Italian small vessels passed through the Straits during World War II (see Appendix 22). The Turkish government, nevertheless, admitted that the Montreux Convention required adaptation to "technical progress and present conditions." It declared itself ready to attend an international conference for a revision of the Convention (which the Soviet note failed to propose) with the participation of its signatories and the United States. Ankara refused to agree to points four and five of the Soviet note. Defense of the Straits undertaken jointly

---

[c] Italics added.

with the Soviet Union was "not compatible with the inalienable rights of sovereignty of Turkey nor with its security,
which brooks no restriction."

The Soviet government delivered its rejoinder on September 25, 1946, to the Ministry of Foreign Affairs in Ankara
(see Appendix 23). Moscow reiterated its charges that the
Straits Convention did not prevent enemy powers "from
using the Straits for purposes of the war against the Allied
States." Moscow once again argued that the "closed" nature
of the Black Sea made it necessary "to establish such a regime
of the Straits which above all would meet the special situation and the security of Turkey, the U.S.S.R., and the other
Black Sea powers." Turkey was also reminded that the
Turkish-Soviet Treaty of 1921 recognized the necessity "of
confiding the drafting of the international status of the Black
Sea and Straits to a conference composed only of the representatives of riverain countries." As to "joint defense" of the
Straits, the Soviet note deplored Ankara's refusal to accept
even the possibility of a joint study of this problem with the
Soviet Union.

Before the Turkish government answered the last of the
Soviet notes, the United States recalled in a note dated
October 9, 1946, that the Potsdam agreement of the Three
Powers foresaw an international conference for the revision
of the Montreux Convention; only a preliminary exchange
with the Turkish government was expected to precede the
conference (see Appendix 24). The British Foreign Office
also delivered a note to Moscow on October 9 insisting that
the exchange of views with the Turkish government, the
"next step" agreed to in Potsdam, had been completed and
that the British government was now ready to attend the
projected conference (see Appendix 25).

The Turkish government sent its last reply on October 18,
1946, to Moscow (see Appendix 26). Here Ankara stressed
once more that the difficulties in differentiating between
warships and commercial vessels during World War II "rested

on the imperfections of Annex II" of the Convention (where the definition of "small" warships was omitted). [13]

The Turkish note invoked the almost unanimously held thesis that the Black Sea is an "open" sea. During the nineteenth century the passage of ships through the Straits was considered an exceptional right agreed to by the Sublime Porte, and the Tsarist government supported this rule as part of European public law. When Turkey accepted the Montreux Convention, it was always clear to her and to the other signatories that the Convention could be modified only by another conference of the contracting powers; any other procedure would be a violation of international law. The essence of Turkey's position was explained thus:

> Turkey has a clear consciousness of her status as a power of the Black Sea. But she cannot forget that she is also a Mediterranean country. Charged by a particularly delicate geographic situation with assuring the liaison between two worlds separated by the restricted space of the Straits, she is conscious of the obligation which this situation imposes on her with respect to the two seas which bathe her shores. The Turkish government can, therefore, not consider the question of the Black Sea and of the Straits as a problem interesting the riverain powers of this sea only.

The note also pointed out that the closing of the Black Sea to the warships of the non-Black Sea powers "would put the other riparian States at the mercy of the maritime power which possessed the strongest land forces, in other words, at the mercy of the U.S.S.R. itself."

Ankara reminded Moscow that the question of "joint defense" of the Straits had already been discussed—namely in 1939, when Turkish Foreign Minister Saracoğlu visited the Soviet capital. Accordingly, Turkey had already examined such Soviet proposals and found them incompatible with the sovereignty and security of Turkey.

The Turkish rebuttal also stated that the original Turkish-Soviet understanding of 1921 concerning the meeting of

Black Sea powers to discuss the Straits question was superseded by the participation of both Turkey and the Soviet
Union in the negotiations at Lausanne, where it was agreed
that the regime of the Straits had to be established within a
"considerably enlarged international framework." Ankara,
like the American and British governments in their last notes,
concluded that the exchange of views preliminary to an international conference for the revision of the Montreux Convention had now been completed.

The international conference as envisaged at Potsdam
never met. After the last Turkish note no further initiative
was taken by the Soviet Union. One can only speculate on
the reasons why Moscow refrained from urging the convocation of the conference. Evidently the Soviet leadership was
not interested in a revised convention that would leave Turkey in her role as the sole guardian of the Straits and substitute the United Nations for the League of Nations. If the
majority of the powers together with the United States were
to have agreed on a revised convention of the Straits that did
not meet the essential Soviet demands, Moscow would have
been faced with the alternative of either withdrawing from
the circle of signatories (which would have meant it would
have been unable to secure some of the advantages of this
instrument) or setting its signature to a treaty which it dis-
liked. In any case, Turkey, now in the hostile camp, would
have continued to exercise control over the passage of ships
through the Straits and would also have been empowered to
close them to Soviet warships in certain contingencies. For
Moscow, to wait for a more appropriate time to take up the
question of the Straits, and take it up only withTurkey, must
have appeared the expedient road to follow. Stalin had
evidently overplayed his hand and lost; to pursue further a
path which led nowhere was not his custom.

For Turkey and the Western powers, a revision of the
Montreux Convention was never a matter of priority. Turkey,
as a result of Soviet threats, had become a trusted ally of the

West. She was in effective control of the Straits and was to apply the outmoded Convention in a manner not incompatible with her interests and that of her friends and allies. It seemed, in any case, unwise to urge the revision of the Montreux Convention in the midst of the cold war which existed between the West and the East after 1946.

The Montreux Convention was, nevertheless, revised in a certain direction. In the Treaty of Peace concluded with her in San Francisco on September 8, 1951, Japan renounced the rights and interests which she derived as a signatory of the Straits Agreement of Montreux. Japan thus ceased to be considered a partaker in the Convention, and thus was excluded from any further presence at a new conference on that question.

DEADLOCK AND RELAXATION

In March 1945 the Soviet Union refused to renew the Treaty of Neutrality and Non-Aggression which it had concluded with Turkey in 1925. The tone of the Soviet demands, accompanied by a menacing military posture, made it clear that Moscow's ultimate aim was not only revision of the Montreux regime of the Straits but the submission of Turkey to satellite status.

Turkey, in this precarious situation, had no other alternative than to seek protection from the West. In view of her European orientation and the economic and military assistance which she needed, her inclusion into the alliance system of the West became Ankara's main foreign policy objective. Before Stalin's death, Turkey became a member of the North Atlantic Treaty Organization and several other European organizations. In February 1953 she concluded the Balkan Pact with Greece and Yugoslavia, an alliance to protect the participant countries against potential aggression by the Soviet Union and its East European satellites.

Turkey thus became one of the most militant antagonists

of the Soviet Union. She was warned by Moscow before and after entering NATO. Ankara replied in a note pointing out that Turkey had to join NATO as a measure to protect her independence, a step made necessary by the Soviet menace. [14] The Soviet attitude after World War II revealed that the foreign policy of the Soviet Union toward Turkey had become a replica of that practiced for two hundred years by the Tsars. The Bulgarian border of Turkey (where Soviet forces were stationed until 1954) and the border with Soviet Transcaucasia were among the most inhospitable and dangerous frontier regions in the world. The extreme tension in these areas dissipated only after Stalin's death in March 1953.

The new Soviet leadership under Malenkov undertook a reexamination of the Soviet Union's foreign relations, which were in a confused state with most of the countries on the other side of the Iron Curtain. Relations could not have been worse with Turkey, after the overweaning attitude of Stalin, the territorial claims, and the demand for a base on the Straits. Turkey's intransigent stance dictated a complete reversal of previous positions. On May 30, 1953, the Soviet government issued the following declaration (italics added):

The Soviet government has recently discussed questions of relations of the U.S.S.R. with its neighbors, and among these turned its attention to the state of Soviet-Turkish relations. As is known in connection with the expiration of the period of the Soviet-Turkish Treaty of 1925, the question of regulating Soviet-Turkish relations was touched upon in official talks of representatives of both states some years ago.

In these talks there figured certain territorial claims of the Armenian Republic and the Georgian Republic on Turkey, and also considerations of the Soviet government relative to the removal of the possible threats to the security of the U.S.S.R. from the side of the Black Sea Straits. *This was accepted badly* by the government and public circles in Turkey, which could not but in certain degree be reflected in Soviet-Turkish relations. In the name of preserving good neighborly relations and strengthening peace and security, the governments of Armenia and Georgia *have found it possible to renounce their territorial claims on Turkey.*

 Concerning the question of the Straits the Soviet government *has reconsidered its former opinion* on this question and considers possible the provision of security for the U.S.S.R. from the side of the Straits on conditions acceptable alike to the U.S.S.R. and to Turkey. Thus the Soviet government declares that the Soviet Union has no kind of territorial claims on Turkey. [15]

This document, despite its awkward and evasive language, constituted a public retraction of demands whose wanton nature could hardly be hidden by semantic cosmetics. It was certainly an unusual declaration to be made by a great power as self-righteous as the Soviet Union. Although the renunciation of territorial claims appeared to be unconditional, the remarks concerning the Straits were considered in Turkey to have been equivocal.

The purposely delayed Turkish reply (July 18, 1953) was frosty, formal, and laconic (italics added):

 The government of the Turkish Republic notes with satisfaction the declaration in which the government of the U.S.S.R. declares that the U.S.S.R. has no territorial claims against Turkey whatsoever. The government of the Turkish Republic declares that the concern for maintenance of good neighborly relations and strengthening the peace and security to which reference was made in this declaration fully corresponds to the concern which Turkey has always manifested and will manifest. The government of the Republic considers it necessary to emphasize in this connection that *the question of the Straits*, as is known to the Soviet government, *is regulated by the clauses of the Montreux Convention.* [16]

Almost simultaneously with the rather humiliating disavowal of previously raised claims, the Soviet government gave public notice that it was still closely concerned with the potential threat to its security attributed to the entry of warships of non-Black Sea powers into the Straits. On July 20, the Soviet Ministry of Foreign Affairs handed a note to the Turkish ambassador in Moscow inquiring about visits of American and British naval units to Istanbul (see Appendix 27). The Turkish note of reply called the Soviet inquiry a "pretext" and one "which could be viewed as a kind of intervention." (See Appendix 28). The Soviet Foreign Ministry, however, upheld its view that it had a legitimate interest in seeking information beyond that regularly provided by Ankara under the terms of the Montreux Convention (see Appendix 29).

For the next ten years Turkish-Soviet relations remained cool. Moscow refused to express further interest in a rapprochement and Turkey maintained her frosty distrust. Occasionally Moscow staged new crises of nerves by leveling various accusations against Turkey. But the real stumbling block in the eyes of the Soviet leaders was Turkey's membership in NATO. With this membership Turkey openly joined the ranks of Russia's potential enemies; she provided bases for the "encirclement" of the Fatherland of Socialism which could threaten the Soviet Union's "soft underbelly," the steel mills of the Donets Basin, the oil wells of the Caucasus and of the Volga region, and the breadbasket of the Ukraine. While the Soviet Union since World War II had greatly advanced its defensive glacis into Central Europe and neutralized its northern flank of Finland, the southern flank of European Russia remained as it was prior to the war, with unchanged borders facing Turkey, previously a benevolent neutral, now a determined opponent. But the worst part of the situation was the fact that through maladroit handling of relations with Turkey, that country, the gatekeeper of the Straits which guard the lifeline of Russia, had become sharply antagonized.

Since there seemed no possibility of forcing Turkey into client status without provoking a third world war, the only realistic aim for Soviet diplomacy was to convert Turkey into a neutral country, to persuade her to leave the anti-Soviet camp. For years Moscow had emphasized that genuine cordiality, even normality, in Soviet-Turkish relations could be established only if Turkey were to decide to quit NATO. The military coup of May 27, 1960, which overthrew the Menderes government of Turkey and established the rule of a military junta, was seized upon by the Soviet leader Khrushchev as an opportunity to send a trial balloon to Ankara in an attempt to induce the new Turkish leadership to embark on the road of neutrality.

Khrushchev's letter dated June 28, 1960, was addressed to the prime minister, General Cemal Gürsel (see Appendix 30). He expressed a desire to turn Soviet-Turkish relations toward "close cooperation." He "frankly" invited Turkey to become a neutral and thus stop "squandering" her resources on military expenditures. The Soviet leader emphasized that this was not a condition for beginning the improvement of relations between the two countries. He stated that "irrespective of the past, the time has now come to start ridding our relations of the burden of prejudices of various kinds."

General Gürsel replied on July 8, 1960, and expressed satisfaction that the Soviet Union wished to establish better relations with Turkey (see Appendix 31). He wrote that the defensive alliances to which Turkey was a party left her "enough leeway" for arriving at such an improvement of relations. He explained that without a system of international disarmament which would ensure security to all countries in the world, whether large or small, Turkey had to remain loyal to her policy of membership in collective security systems.

This exchange of letters may be considered as the preliminary to the subsequent normalization of the Turkish-Soviet relations, which was for Turkey prompted by a desire to abandon a one-sided cold war policy and loosen its excessive dependence on the United States.

Atatürk's foreign policy was essentially to pursue friendly relations with all of Turkey's neighbors. [17] Turkey, the guardian of the Straits, was to be at peace with all the countries of the world. Particular emphasis was placed on good relations with the most powerful close neighbor, the Soviet

Union. It was hoped that the Bolshevik leadership of Russia had given up the imperialist dreams of the Tsars concerning Constantinople and the Straits. The realization that these aggressive policy aims had by no means been abandoned had led Turkey to throw herself wholeheartedly into the arms of the Western Alliance, and in particular to call upon the West's most powerful leader, the United States. However, after a honeymoon that had lasted nearly ten years, a new reappraisal of Ankara's foreign policy was inevitable. Relations with Moscow had been improved and greater flexibility in foreign relations was established.

But by the late 1960s Turkey was faced with the dramatic political and military involvement of the Soviet Union in the affairs of the Middle East, and a momentous Soviet naval expansion into the Mediterranean and beyond. Turkey's geographical location and her possession of the waterways between the Russian colossus and the Mediterranean created far-reaching problems for her as well as for her allies in NATO, particularly the United States. The impact of these developments on the Straits question, which is an important element of the balance of power in the Mediterranean area, will be examined in the following chapters.

- 5 -

Turkey in NATO and the Straits

Geography has endowed Turkey with a particular strategic significance; her possession of the Straits is the single most important segment of the overall Turkish geostrategical complex. This significance, though somewhat modified by the more recent developments in the art of warfare, found recognition in Turkey's admission into the North Atlantic Treaty Organization.

Turkey sought admission not only because of the threatening posture of the Soviet Union, which vividly recalled her nearly three centuries of struggle against the giant of the north. After the end of World War II, it appeared to her that the globe was split between the East and the West; the Turkish urge, prominent since Atatürk's time, to belong to the European or Western family of nations had made her choice in the face of this Manichean cleavage a foregone conclusion. For Turkey in the postwar period the West meant not only, as before, the world of Western Europe; it also meant primarily the United States, the most powerful member of the Atlantic Alliance.

TURKEY JOINS NATO

The NATO treaty was originally signed on April 4, 1949, by only twelve countries. Among the strictly Mediterranean states only Italy was an original signatory.[1] Turkey applied for admission into NATO in August 1950. In October of that year both Turkey and Greece were invited by the NATO Council to cooperate with the agencies of the organization in Mediterranean defense planning. But it took yet another year before the member states of the alliance were ready to act in a positive manner upon the requests for admission by Turkey and Greece.

Strategic and ideological objections were voiced against the membership of these two countries, since they had no territorial links with the other European participants. It was even pointed out that Greece and Turkey were connected with one another only by a narrow landbridge in Thrace. Arguments were raised against Turkey's membership because of her eastward extension deep into the Middle East and to the Caucasian border of the Soviet Union. Nor could Greece or Turkey be considered "Atlantic" powers, although this criterion had already been abandoned to admit Italy. Finally, while the Greeks were Orthodox Christians, the Turks professed the Islamic faith and were often regarded as Asians.

However, overwhelming strategic reasons militated for the inclusion of both Turkey and Greece in the alliance. Among those which weighed most heavily in favor of an affirmative decision was the fact that, as the guardian of the Straits, Turkey could close the only maritime outlet of the Soviet Union to the Mediterranean in a case of danger or the outbreak of hostilities. Both Turkey and Greece protected the northeastern and eastern shores of the Mediterranean. Turkey could muster a considerable land army, though its forces would require modernization. Ultimately, it was believed, the advantages of admitting these two countries largely outweighed the possible disadvantages.[2]

In London on October 22, 1951, Turkey and Greece signed the Protocol of Accession, which became effective on February 18, 1952. The Protocol of Accession had to redefine the territorial limits of the alliance, that is, the area that was to be mutually defended against an armed attack. The new Article 6 explicitly included the entire (not only European) territory of Turkey, the forces, vessels, and aircraft of the member states not only in or over their territories and in the North Atlantic area north of the Tropic of Cancer, but also those in or over the Mediterranean Sea. The alliance thus became not only an Atlantic but also a Mediterranean alliance. (In 1955 NATO was further extended by the admission of the Federal Republic of Germany.)

With Turkey and Greece in the alliance, the command structure of the organization had to be broadened so that it would reach out into the eastern Mediterranean and to the eastern borders of Turkey. Ankara thus became the southeastern cornerstone of NATO, the linchpin between the Atlantic Alliance and the Central Treaty Organization (successor to the Baghdad Pact). The northern tier countries (Turkey, Iran, and Pakistan) which form CENTO were—with the intermediary of Turkey—territorially connected with NATO.

Turkey's territory belongs under the European Command of NATO, which is headed by the Supreme Commander Europe (SACEUR). The headquarters for this group, known as the Supreme Headquarters Allied Powers Europe (SHAPE), since 1967 has been located near Brussels in Belgium. The land, air, and sea area of Turkey is divided between two commands: the Commander-in-Chief Allied Forces southern Europe (CINCSOUTH) in Naples, Italy, with a further subcommand (Commander Allied Land forces Southeastern Europe) in Izmir, Turkey; and the Commander-in-Chief Allied

Forces Mediterranean (CINCAFMED), with a subcommand (Commander Eastern Mediterranean) in Ankara. The defense of the Straits by land and air forces would thus be the immediate concern of the NATO subcommand in Izmir, and their naval defense would fall under the authority of the Mediterranean subcommand in Ankara.

All the member states of NATO (except Iceland, which maintains no armed forces) keep military representatives at SHAPE. These, and other representatives stationed at other NATO command posts, form the ordinary channel of communication between these headquarters and the national commanders in the respective countries. In Turkey the national commander is the chief of staff of the Turkish Armed Forces.[a]

Under the existing agreements, Turkey has "assigned" fifteen of her seventeen divisions to NATO. But these forces remain, at least in time of peace, under the direct command of the Turkish military authorities. It is understood that the NATO command would exercise operational authority only in a war in which, because of an outside aggression, the NATO alliance would be directly involved.

Turkey is not, on principle, opposed to military integration within NATO, as was the France of General de Gaulle. Even so, integration, as far as Turkey is concerned, would extend to the higher command levels but not to the troop level. Integration, in the Turkish interpretation, signifies such measures as would ensure a joint and coordinated command of all allied forces in time of war.[3] Notwithstanding the NATO arrangements, Turkey would prefer that in case of war her armed forces be led by her own chief of staff. When during the two crises over Cyprus (in 1964 and 1967) Turkey

---

[a] According to the Turkish Constitution of 1961, the supreme commander of the armed forces is the president of the Republic, exercising the sovereign powers of the Grand National Assembly (Article 110). The chief of the General Staff, however, is the executive commander.

prepared for an invasion of the island, it was evident that the government and the military leadership had not abandoned supreme command over Turkish forces.[b]

TURKEY'S ARMED FORCES AND THE STRAITS

The Turkish Army is the largest land force "assigned" to NATO and also the largest in the Middle East. Among the members of the Atlantic Alliance, Turkey maintains the third largest military force, in terms of numbers, following the United States and France. The Turkish armed forces number around 480,000 men. By calling up reserves, this number can be tripled.

Turkey's land frontiers extend over 1,910 miles. In Europe, her frontier with Bulgaria is 125 miles long and the border with Greece is of the same approximate length. The Turkish-Soviet border in eastern Anatolia is 300 miles long; the frontier with Iran, 290 miles; with Iraq, 235 miles; and with Syria, 835 miles. But she also has a 955-mile maritime frontier on the Black Sea, facing the Soviet Union. The Aegean and Mediterranean maritime border is 1,230 miles long.

The potentially most threatened borders are those which Turkey has with Bulgaria and the Soviet Union. Any direct attack from the land side that would jeopardize her control of the Straits would come from the Bulgarian frontier. But an attack need not come only across the border between Bulgaria and Turkey; it might also be carried out by an advance into Greek Western Thrace. The easternmost panhandle of mainland Greece extends northward between Bulgarian and Turkish territory to form what is known as the Pithion quad-

---

[b] The possible inconsistency between NATO supreme command in time of war and the Turkish constitutional requirement that the president (or the chief of the General Staff, acting on the president's behalf) be the supreme commander of Turkish armed forces has so far not been officially raised.

rangle. At one point Bulgaria is just 25 miles across Greek territory from the Aegean. This sensitive Thracian Turkish-Greek border region has given many headaches to NATO strategic planners. It has been argued that in case of an attack from Bulgarian territory, contact between Turkish and Greek forces could not be maintained and most of Eastern Thrace would even have to be abandoned; Turkish forces would have to retire to defend Istanbul and the Straits.[4]

The distribution of Turkish land forces in time of peace has taken account of the strategic needs of the Straits. The Turkish First Army, the largest of the three, is stationed in Thrace and around Istanbul garrisoning different strategic points in the Straits area. The First Army is expected to cooperate with the First Hellenic Army stationed in Western Thrace. The tensions with Greece over Cyprus, however, have led Turkish generals to watch not only the Bulgarians across the border but also the First Hellenic Army. Had Turkey invaded Cyprus in the 1964 or 1967 crises, an armed clash between the "allied" Greek and Turkish armies in Thrace could hardly have been avoided.

The Turkish Third Army is to cover the Soviet border toward the Caucasus while the Second Army, the weakest of them, is placed along the Syrian and Iraqi borders. The land forces also include a training corps, three Communications Commands (West, Central, and East), and several base commands.

The Turkish Air Force contains 27 squadrons. A considerable portion of the air force is concentrated in the region around Istanbul and the Straits. Six batteries of Nike-Hercules and Nike-Ajax anti-aircraft missile units defending Istanbul are also attached to the air force, which is 53,000 men strong and is considered up-to-date. On the other hand, although modernization has greatly increased their capabilities since World War II, the Turkish land and naval forces are still considered inferior in terms of equipment when compared to the Soviet forces they are expected to oppose.[5]

The Turkish Navy is composed of the North and South Area Commands and several training commands. The commanding admiral of the navy resides at Gölçük, the naval base in Izmit Bay. The headquarters of the Northern Command are in Istanbul and those of the Southern Command in Izmir. The subcommand in charge of operations in the Straits is likewise established in Istanbul. The entire Turkish Navy is "integrated" into the NATO command structure. Its commanding admiral is the NATO commander of the North-East Mediterranean Command (COMEDNOREAST) under the authority of the NATO Eastern Mediterranean Subcommand.

The Turkish Navy (70,000 tons of combat force) consists of 4 modernized American destroyers, 8 older destroyers, 10 1,500-ton submarines, 21 minesweeper-escorts, 25 coastal minesweepers, 7 minelayers, 10 patrol vessels, 11 missile-launching modern patrolboats, more than 20 landing craft, and 30 coastguard boats. The navy is slated to receive additional modern vessels which are under construction in German, Danish, and French shipyards. The naval personnel consists of 37,000 men and 3,000 officers.[6]

Among the tasks of the Turkish Navy, the control of the Straits and surveillance over the navigation through it are of primary importance. The stations at both ends of the Straits, at the entrances of the Bosporus and the Dardanelles, are maintained by the navy, and these stations receive instructions with regard to warships which have given due notice of their intention to pass through. Questions of quarantine as well as of pilotage are also handled or supervised by naval authorities.

The role of the navy and the land forces in the defense of the Straits is now somewhat diminished by air power and rocketry. Partly because of the technological developments of the past twenty years and partly because of the lack of natural obstacles in Thrace, it is maintained by military writers that "Turkey's strength is not equal to her importance," and that "Turkish pride rather than pragmatic strategy dictates the maintenance of large forces in European Turkey."[7] There can be little doubt that the bombing of Istanbul and its crowded environs would create utter confusion and would disrupt the connections between the European and Asian shores. The Bosporus bridge, when completed, would be an easy target for enemy bombers. Of course it is believed that Turkish forces could cope with Bulgarian-Rumanian troops, but by themselves they would be unable to hold the Thracian front or even the Straits area against a major Soviet attack by land, air, and sea.

On the other hand, the terrain is considerably more suitable for defense in depth along the Caucasian border toward Russia. On the whole, the Anatolian "fortress" is considered defensible; the Taurus-Zagros mountain-line is often cited as the main allied defense line against a Soviet assault directed toward the Mediterranean and the Middle East.[8]

There is undoubtedly some discrepancy between Turkey's strategic needs, as seen by Turkey, and the NATO strategy of "flexible response." There is a sustained anxiety in Turkey that her territory might be traded against time. According to press reports, in the event of a major Soviet attack NATO planners envisage the abandonment not only of large areas in Eastern Anatolia (the Taurus-Zagros chains lie in the southeast of Turkey), but also of Thrace with Istanbul and the northern Straits area as well; defense would be concentrated on the Anatolian plateau and the Gallipoli Peninsula. But the official view upheld by the Turkish government emphasizes that the defense line will start at the borders of Turkey.[9]

Another source of uneasiness among Turks is the widespread belief that in the eventuality of a war NATO would exert all its strength to defend the center, that is, the area of Central Europe (Germany), and neglect the defense of the two flanks of the alliance, Norway in the north and Turkey in the south. However, it is sometimes maintained by experts, both in Turkey and outside, that potential Soviet military inroads would focus on the flanks of NATO rather than the central section of its defense perimeter, where the likelihood of escalation into an all-out nuclear exchange is considered greater. [10] This writer is of the opinion that while the space-time equation, relying on a graduated response, would suit the geographical conditions of Eastern Anatolia, the value, both strategic and political (as far as Turkey is concerned), of the Straits area would render the application of a flexible response inadvisable.

The defense of the Straits, and of Turkey as a whole, is an object of considerable concern. Various plans have been developed to meet this problem and to allay Turkish anxieties. In the mid-fifties not only were Intermediate Range Ballistic Missile (IRBM) sites installed in Turkey and supplied with U.S. Jupiter missiles, but tactical nuclear devices were delivered under the so-called "double key" system. These nuclear bombs remained in the custody of the United States forces, but in case of war they would be launched by Turkish crews. The consent of both the American and Turkish governments is required for their use.

The use of ground-to-ground missiles with tactical nuclear warheads, even against a conventional attack, is regarded with some misgivings in Turkey. While they could be usefully deployed in the sparsely inhabited mountain districts of Eastern Anatolia, the densely populated region of Thrace and the Straits (with Istanbul) is just as unsuitable for such weaponry as are the crowded urban areas of Central Europe.

After the Cuban missile crisis in 1962, the Jupiter missiles with their nuclear warheads were withdrawn from the territory of Turkey.[c] These missiles formed a nuclear deterrent

---

[c] At one moment during the Cuban crisis, Soviet Premier Khrushchev attempted to trade the withdrawal of Soviet missiles from Cuba for the withdrawal of the Jupiter missiles from Turkey. But President Kennedy refused such a deal. Washington had already suggested their withdrawal a year before the Cuban dispute, but they had been left in Turkey because of Turkish insistence. For an account of the episode, see Robert F. Kennedy, *Thirteen Days: A Memoir of the Cuban Missile Crisis*, especially pp. 196-201.

that was rendered obsolete by the deployment of submarines equipped with Polaris missiles cruising in the Mediterranean. Moreover, they might fail to be useful if only Turkey's territory were invaded and no nuclear retaliation attempted. But NATO was sufficiently solicitous to calm Turkish fears by providing yet another nuclear device in case of a sudden conventional attack against her territory.

Turkey's defenses, along both her Thracian and Caucasian borders were to be bolstered by the emplacement of atomic mines, officially called Atomic Demolition Munitions (ADM). A similar plan had been suggested earlier for the defense of West Germany against possible Soviet aggression, but it was abandoned because of the dense population of the area and because all the access routes could not be protected because of the flat terrain.

Although the placing of atomic mines was seriously weighed, many objections were raised against it. If such mines were to be used in Thrace for the protection of Istanbul and the Straits, the military would have to deal with a problem similar to that of Germany: this area also possesses rather flat countryside with a considerable population and such urban centers as the historic city of Edirne (Adrianople). On the other hand, the Eastern Turkish border region is extremely mountainous and sparsely populated.

There was yet another question to be considered: custody of the "demolition munitions" would remain, in time of peace, in the hands of American personnel and the "double key" method would be applied. Because under existing United States law the authority to detonate the mines could not be permanently delegated to Turkish commanders on the spot, such a decision could not be reached in time to prevent the enemy from overrunning the forward border areas. The mines were considered purely defensive and nonprovocative; their detonation would be underground and would not release nuclear fallout. Still, in Turkish circles it was feared that even such defensive nuclear weapons might elicit a nuclear response from Moscow; in any case, the escalating effect of the use of such weaponry was thought to be unquestionable. Finally the nuclear-mines plan was quietly dropped. [11]

In 1960 the "mobile force" idea was adopted by NATO to provide speedy assistance from naval and army units to Turkey and Greece, on the southern flank of NATO, or to Norway, on its northern flank. The Allied Mobile Force (AMF) consists of an air and a ground arm: Allied Mobile Force Air (AMFA) and Allied Mobile Force Land (AMFL). Both forces are under the direct command of SACEUR; the air element comprises six squadrons of reconnaissance and fighter-bomber planes, and the land element six battalions available on call. Belgium, the Netherlands, West Germany, the United States, Britain, and Italy participate in the air arm, and the same countries together with Turkey and Greece, and to a limited extent, Canada, cooperate in the land force. [12]

The Mobile Forces may be promptly dispatched to the war areas to provide for the support of local forces already in combat. They may also be sent before the outbreak of hostilities "to show the flag," or demonstrate that the attacker will not be faced by the victim of direct aggression alone. This emergency force is particularly suitable to deal with crises arising in the Straits area. In late 1962 mobile forces exercises were held in Northern Greece when air transports brought to the scene Belgian and German infantry and American armored cars. A similar exercise to be held in the Straits area had to be postponed because of the strained relations between Turkey and Greece. Landing exercises were, however, practiced on the coast of Sardinia, where the terrain is somewhat similar to that near or around the Dardanelles.[d]

---

[d] In the fall of 1970 the Mobile Forces held exercises in Thrace. They were sent to Turkish Thrace and United States marines were landed nearby in Greek Thrace. The "enemy," it was anticipated, advanced from the north with the aim of reaching the sea and splitting Greek and Turkish defenses northwest of the Dardanelles; *New York Times*, December 13, 1970.

The Mobile Forces, however, are considered insufficient by Turkish military experts. They believe that the assistance to be provided to Turkey, in an exposed situation at the far end of the Mediterranean, should be more massive and more "credible." [13] For many realistic Turks the presence of U.S. forces, although coupled with problems and misgivings, provides a much greater assurance that Turkey will not be left alone in the case of an aggression against her borders or shores.

TURKEY AND THE UNITED STATES

The first military assistance treaty between Washington and Ankara was signed on July 12, 1947. The United States supplied military equipment together with the personnel for instruction; road, harbor, and other strategic installations were constructed under American aid and advice. Economic aid was also provided under the Marshall Plan and subsequent programs.

Turkey sent a brigade-size force to Korea (the second largest contingent after that of the United States) which distinguished itself and established a "comradeship-in-arms" with the Americans. Soon after the admission of Turkey into NATO, that country was regarded as America's "most reliable ally." [14]

The "honeymoon" in the relations between Washington and Ankara lasted throughout the Menderes administration and even after the military coup of 1960.[e] Turkey invariably supported the American position in international forums; in return, Washington did not fail to assure Ankara of its unfailing assistance against Soviet threats. Turkey cooperated with the United States when American forces, partly using Turkish

---

[e] The broadcast by the military leadership which administered the coup of May 27, 1960, affirmed: "We are loyal to all our alliances and undertakings. We believe in NATO and CENTO and are loyal to them." *Documents on International Affairs, 1960*, pp. 418-19.

bases, landed in Lebanon in 1958. The Cuban missile crisis of 1962 also gave evidence of the "blind" loyalty of the Turkish leadership for the United States; with this event many in Turkey began to realize the dependence of Turkey's security on policies set in Washington.

The Cyprus crisis of 1964 developed into a watershed in American-Turkish relations. The specific event which triggered the reaction, after long-simmering discontent, was President Lyndon B. Johnson's letter of June 5, 1964, addressed to the Turkish Premier Ismet Inönü (see Appendix 32).

The letter was prompted by a warning passed on to Washington that the government of Ankara planned a military intervention in Cyprus because of the widespread disturbances on the island which threatened the life and property of Turkish Cypriots. President Johnson expressed deep concern over the projected action, which could have resulted in a Turkish-Greek armed conflict (not only on Cyprus), and warned Turkey that in the event of a Soviet aggression following a Turkish action, NATO (and United States) assistance might not be forthcoming. Turkey was also told that, under the existing agreements, military equipment provided by Washington could be used only for the purposes for which it was delivered (that is, against the Soviet Union and its allies) and not against Greece, another NATO ally.

Under this pressure, Turkey abandoned her plan to intervene militarily in Cyprus. However, on June 14, 1964, Prime Minister Inönü dispatched a reply which strongly objected to the American suggestion that, in the event foreseen in the Johnson letter, no assistance would be available against a Soviet aggression (see Appendix 33).

While the objective of the Johnson letter may have been correct, the sending of an ultimatum-like message on such a sensitive topic should have been avoided. In any case, it glaringly revealed Turkey's abject dependence on the United States and made it clear that assistance under the existing alliance agreements depended on the willingness of the

United States. The event demonstrated that such assistance was far from automatically forthcoming, and confidence in American commitments was severely shaken. Turkey was thereby led to reevaluate her ties with the United States and to begin to pursue an independent foreign policy line, though without abandoning her membership in NATO and CENTO. In practice, this induced her to seek an improvement in relations with the Soviet Union and its allies as well as with the countries of the Third World, the "uncommitted" nations of Asia and Africa. Within a few years Turkish diplomacy was able to extricate the country from the relative isolation in which it had found itself as well as from what had come to be considered blind obedience to United States policies. [15]

The emancipation from strict dependence on America did not end Turkey's military cooperation with Washington. The presence of American military forces was to continue, although U.S. contingents were successively reduced in strength by Washington. American military personnel in Turkey in 1970 numbered fewer than 10,000. American units operate as the Sixth Allied Tactical Air Force (SIXATAF) and as training units to the First and Third Turkish Air Forces, all of which are committed to NATO in case of war.

Members of American forces are mostly stationed in or around bases officially called "joint installations," some of which have been partly or fully handed over to the Turkish military in recent years. Among these bases the most important are the Karamürsel air base (near the town of Izmit), which may serve to protect against any threat to the Straits area; the Incirlik base near Adana; and the Pirincilik base near the town of Diyarbakır. Other airfields or installations manned or managed by American contingents are along the Black Sea coast, in the northwest or southeast of the country, and around Ankara.

Attached to the United States Air Force in Turkey is the United States Logistics Group (TUSLOG), which has its headquarters in Ankara. It provides logistical support for all the American forces in the area of the Eastern Mediterranean and the Middle East. Also in Ankara are a Joint United States Military Mission for Aid to Turkey (JUSMMAT) and other American units and agencies. The American military forces enjoy the privileges generally accorded to "visiting forces" under international law and under the NATO Status of Forces Agreement signed by Turkey in 1956.

The presence of large American troop contingents, with their weaponry, their movements, and supply required the conclusion of fifty-five agreements from 1954 through to 1964. Most of these "bilateral agreements" (so called to distinguish them from the multilateral NATO agreements) concluded between Turkey and the United States were "executive" agreements, and most of them were never submitted for approval to the Turkish Parliament. After 1964 there was a rising tide of anti-American sentiment, and the opposition parties began to demand publication, cancellation, or revision of these instruments which they alleged violated Turkish sovereignty. Negotiations for the revision of the agreements began in 1966 and lasted until 1969 when, on July 3, the Cooperation Agreement Concerning Joint Defense was signed in Ankara by the Turkish Foreign Minister Çağlayangil and United States Ambassador William J. Handley.

The new comprehensive agreement clarified many doubtful points and underlined the rights of Turkey in cases where the previous arrangements gave rise to ambiguities. Thus it was stipulated that American military installations can only be established in Turkey with the express approval of the Turkish government; that Turkey retains property rights to the land allotted to joint defense installations; and that joint management and utilization will be practiced in such areas. The new arrangements are likely to clear the air with regard to the American uses of Turkish soil for the purposes of joint defense and to remove the causes of accusations or complaints by those Turks who otherwise accept the necessity and usefulness of the American military presence. The great debate over whether NATO membership serves Turkey's security interests continues to occupy many minds in Turkey (see Chapter Six) but so far as the government is concerned the question has been decided in the affirmative.

However, leftist agitation, mostly of the irrational and emotional variety, continues to plague American-Turkish relations. It is admitted that these anti-American demonstrations, writings, and acts of violence originate among a tiny but extremely vocal minority—primarily intellectuals, students, or members of the extreme leftist Turkish Labor Party (this party received less than 3 per cent of the popular vote at the general elections held in 1969). Anti-Americanism is fostered by xenophobia, a nationalism which conceives of the American alliance and aid as an instrument of oppression. American economic assistance which, in the past more than at present has been vital for the dynamic modernization and industrialization of Turkey's economy, is also often represented as serving the United States interests by exploiting Turks. How far the anti-American feeling is due to Communist or Soviet influences is difficult to assess. It must be admitted, however, that communism now possesses a conscious and partly unconscious fifth column which had been absent in the past, and that this factor now constitutes a less negligible element in Turkish domestic and foreign politics. [16]

The centers of open demonstration against the American presence are located in the university cities of Istanbul, Ankara, and Izmir. In Istanbul and also in Izmir these agitations have disturbed or even frustrated customary visits of the United States naval forces stationed in the Mediterranean. The Sixth Fleet of the United States is an important element in the defense of Turkey and the Turkish Straits. Its main task is to secure the long supply route from the Atlantic and Western Mediterranean to the shores of Turkey and Greece.

The Sixth Fleet was formed in January 1946, a few weeks before the dispatch of the battleship *Missouri* to Istanbul was announced. During the next two decades the Sixth Fleet was generally strengthened until it consisted of about fifty combat ships, among them two aircraft carriers and a varying number of cruisers, destroyers, submarines, frigates, patrol

vessels, and attack transports. The American warships enjoy
harbor facilities in the ports of various NATO or otherwise
allied countries situated along the Mediterranean; Gibraltar,
Naples, Barcelona, and Athens (Piraeus) are among the most
important. [17]

Units of the Sixth Fleet make regular visits to harbors of
allied nations and also courtesy calls to ports of neutral
powers, such as Yugoslavia. Visits to places in Turkey, to
Istanbul, Izmir, and Iskenderun, also were regularly scheduled in the past. However, in recent years calls in Istanbul
and Izmir have so frequently been marred by demonstrations
of leftist students that the American naval command has preferred to discontinue these visits.

In view of the Soviet naval concentration in the Mediterranean Sea, steps have been taken to effect closer cooperation between allied navies and to establish a new integrated
naval command with the participation of the United States,
Britain, and Italy. Greece and Turkey have been asked to
assign vessels from time to time, but cooperation on a larger
scale cannot be expected from these two countries unless
greater financial assistance can be provided or more warships
transferred to strengthen their navies. A force including four
or five aircraft carriers, five or six cruisers, and 30 to 40
destroyers could in any case be formed. Whether the United
States Sixth Fleet will have to yield some of its vessels to this
mixed NATO fleet appears as yet uncertain. [18]

Against the threat posed by the presence of many Soviet
submarines in the Mediterranean, the NATO Council in 1968
decided to set up a new allied naval air command, the Maritime Air Forces Mediterranean (MARAIRMED) with the
participation of the United States, Britain, Italy, and, possibly, France.[f] The air forces thus earmarked would operate

---

[f] France, in a limited way, has continued to cooperate with the other
allied navies in the Mediterranean despite her general withdrawal from
NATO's integrated command.

from bases in Spain, Sicily, Malta, Cyprus, and Turkey. The new command's principal task in peacetime is to patrol the Mediterranean for the searching out and screening of submarines. The Aegean Sea, however, cannot be satisfactorily patrolled without the participation of Greece; the frictions between Turkey and Greece over Cyprus and over control of the narrow waters between the islands of Greece and the Turkish mainland have rendered useful cooperation most difficult. And these waters lead to the entrance of the Dardanelles, an area where emergency measures might one day be called for.

The possibilities for entry into the Black Sea by the Sixth Fleet or units of the mixed NATO fleets are limited by the Convention of Montreux. To show the flag in full strength in the Euxine is barred by the limitations imposed on all non-Black Sea powers. While the Soviet Navy may gradually send all its units, after the required notification, in either direction through the Turkish Straits, non-riparian powers possess no such options in time of peace. Turkey, though a member of the Atlantic Alliance, endeavors to implement fully and impartially the provisions of the Montreux Convention, insofar as they are compatible with the changed technological facts of our present era.

THE MONTREUX CONVENTION IN PRACTICE

The application of the regime of the Turkish Straits, as laid down by the Convention of Montreux, met no objection during the last phase of World War II. When Germany invaded the Soviet Union, the critical questions about how to apply the Convention arose. Both Britain and Moscow vowed to abide by its provisions. Most of the Russian Black Sea coast was soon occupied by the Germans; the Greek islands of the Aegean were also under German control. Thus only Axis ships passed through the Straits (in addition to Turkish ships) and supplies to the Soviet Union could not be transported through these waterways, as had been the case with Russia during World War I. Following the liberation of Greece, ships of the Western powers could reach the Soviet Union after January 1945. We recalled earlier the objections which Moscow raised concerning the passage of some German and Italian armed vessels posing as commercial craft.

After the unsuccessful attempts by Moscow in1945 and 1946 to change the status quo of the Straits, the provisions of the Montreux Convention remained unchanged. The accession of Turkey to the North Atlantic Treaty Organization by no means affected the validity of the international instrument controlling the regime of the Straits, nor did it affect the manner in which Turkey continued to apply the pertinent regulations established for shipping through these waterlanes.

Since 1946 no proposal has been made by any of the signatories of the Convention for its revision, nor has it been denounced by any of them. Evidently, as long as the Soviet Union does not prefer to make a move for an alteration of the present regime of the Straits, the non-Communist powers as well as Turkey will refrain from any such initiative.[g]

The passage of merchant vessels has given rise to no particular difficulty or demands; indeed, this has been so since the acceptance of their freedom to passage through the Straits in Lausanne, and even before that time. It is the question of navigation for warships in the Straits which poses a problem and which often places the Turkish government in a difficult position. Turkey has to apply the Convention of 1936 to the changed international conditions of the 1970s. She has to interpret and apply its various and complicated provisions to warships carrying weapons undreamed of in 1936.

---

[g] However, the Turkish press reported that the Assembly of the Western European Union (Britian, France, West Germany, and the Benelux states), in its session held in December 1967, demanded revisions of the Montreux Convention to cover modern ships and arms; *Cumhuriyet*, December 6, 1967.

In 1936 the backbone of the Great Power navies was the battleship. With the rapid development of air power battleships have become largely obsolete and are no longer commissioned. In the post-World War II period, large aircraft carriers have been the mainstay of navies. However, with the introduction of missiles with ranges from a few to many thousand miles, even the huge aircraft carriers may one day become outmoded. The potential uses of nuclear weaponry (tactical or strategic), the conveyance of such arms by ships passing the Straits or the passage of warships equipped with nuclear devices, are novelties for which no provisions could have been made in Montreux.

During the entire postwar period, Ankara has attempted to be an impartial arbitrator of all questions relating to shipping in the Straits. While doing so, it has been closely watched by all maritime powers, and particularly by the leaders of the two antagonistic camps, the Soviet Union on the one hand and the United States and Britain on the other.

Since 1945 the League of Nations has been replaced by the United Nations and its Covenant by the U.N. Charter. At the time of this writing, there has been no indication of how the articles of the Charter relating to collective police actions could be substituted for the "sanctions" under the Covenant, and Turkey has been spared the trial of having to make a decision on such a critical and sensitive point. In 1936 Turkey was nonaligned and on friendly terms with the Soviet Union. Since World War II, she has become a member of the Western alliance system and also of CENTO. Any operations requiring the application of the mutual assistance clauses of these collective defense alliances are "binding" on Turkey (see Article 19 of the Montreux Convention), and even the possibility of Turkey's compliance with these obligations must be alarming to Moscow.

The articles of the Montreux Convention which differentiate between situations of war and those of peace have also become largely outdated by international developments in the last two decades. During the Korean War, when Turkey was a "belligerent," no prohibitions whatsoever were applied by Ankara to the passage of warships. The wisdom of Montreux in leaving any such measures to be taken to the discretion of Ankara has thus been confirmed.

In time of war, when Turkey is not one of the belligerents, warships of belligerent powers are barred from passage through the Straits (Article 19, para. 2). However, neither in the Arab-Israeli conflict (including the three periods of active belligerency) nor in the Vietnam War, did Turkey close the Straits to any of the participants in those conflicts. When Turkish Foreign Minister Çağlayangil was told that because of the United States involvement in Vietnam American warships should not be permitted to pass the Straits, he replied: "The United States is not in a state of war in Vietnam; it only supports one side." The minister also recalled that warships of Egypt (the United Arab Republic), which has considered herself in a state of war with Israel, have passed through the Straits and visited Black Sea ports. Neither Egypt nor Israel, and not even the Soviet Union, has shown any sensitivity over this matter. [19] The former clear distinctions between a state of war and a state of peace became blurred because of the Cold War, because of ideological confrontations, and not the least because of the growing prevalence of subversive and guerrilla operations ("wars of national liberation").

The military and technological innovations adopted since the end of World War II have given rise to some difficulties in the application of the Montreux Convention. Almost all of the controversies concerning such questions have arisen when units of the United States Sixth Fleet have entered the Black Sea. Over the past ten years or more, it has become customary for American warships not only to pay courtesy calls to Turkish ports, including Istanbul in the Straits, but also to enter the Euxine every six months. The reason for these movements is to affirm the right of non-Black Sea war vessels to ply those waters, as permitted by the Convention.

In December 1968, for instance, the United States destroyers *Dyess* and *Turner* passed through the Straits (they entered the Dardanelles in daylight, as prescribed in the Convention) and cruised for five days in the Black Sea. Thereafter they rejoined the Sixth Fleet in the Mediterranean. Although such American ship movements had occurred every six months, the Soviet press this time called the event a "provocation" and a violation of the Montreux Convention. Both of the U.S. warships have a displacement of 10,000 tons (below the maximum of 15,000 tons as limited by the Convention) and their guns were of a caliber not exceeding 8 inches, or 203 mm. However, the *Dyess* was also equipped with an eight-missile ASROC (anti-submarine rocket launcher) which has a perimeter of 305 mm. *Pravda* accused both Washington and Turkey of having breached the Convention which limits the passage through the Straits of nonriparian warships to those not carrying guns of a larger caliber than 203 mm. [20]

The Turkish leftist press took up the charge and accused the United States of wishing to disrupt the "good neighbor" relations and rapprochement atmosphere between Turkey and the Soviet Union. [21] It was also pointed out that in September 1966 Ankara, acting upon objections raised by the Soviet government, prevented the passage of the U.S. destroyer *William V. Pratt* through the Straits. [22]

The Turkish Ministry of Foreign Affairs revealed that both the Soviet and the Bulgarian embassies had orally protested against the movements of the *Dyess* and the *Turner*. In its reply, the Turkish government emphasized: "New arms have been developed since the Montreux Convention. These weapons were not listed in the Convention because they did not exist at the time of its signature. The Turkish government takes the view that carrying such weapons is not conflicting with the Convention if they are not of an aggressive nature." [23]

It was also pointed out that Turkey was authorized to

interpret the Convention and that she established that the rocket launcher in question was to serve against submarine attack and therefore was of a defensive character. The Foreign Ministry also explained that in 1966 the Soviet government had protested against the entry of the *William V. Pratt* and that the Americans then withdrew their notification of passage during the fifteen-day period while it was being examined by Ankara. [24]

Thereafter, destroyers of the Sixth Fleet continued their regularly scheduled visits into the Black Sea. Thus it was noted that in September 1969 the destroyers *N. K. Perry* and *Norris* cruised for four days in the Black Sea; in March 1970 it was the turn of the *Samuel B. Roberts* and the *Strong*. In November 1970 the *N. K. Perry* and *Allen M. Sumner* cruised in that sea. It is not known whether these visits also elicited protests from the Soviet government.

In cases not clearly foreseen by the Montreux Convention, the Turkish government has to establish precedents and follow a practice which conforms with the spirit if not the letter of the Convention. For instance, the statement that defensive anti-submarine rockets are permissible, even if their calibration exceeds the permissible limits established in Montreux, was intended to interpret logically the international treaty in question. No practice, however, has evolved with regard to nuclear weapons which warships may carry. Since warships entering the Straits are not bound to make any declarations with regard to weapons not listed in the Montreux Convention, they never disclose whether nuclear warheads are on board the vessels. Moscow has expressed no concern over this. Evidently Soviet warships of moderate to large size pass the Straits in numbers greater than those of all other countries; and it would be unprofitable for the Soviets to help create precedents which might backfire on them.

The practice of interpreting and applying the Montreux Convention in our time is not a routine matter. It requires a great deal of vigilance and a line of consistent interpretation.

Whenever the letter of the Convention fails to provide a clear-cut answer, precedents have to be deduced by a search to discover the proven or assumed intentions of the signatories. Some of the novel problems which come before the Ministry of Foreign Affairs in Ankara require urgent decisions. The use of helicopters on board warships presented such a question.

Under no circumstances are vessels of war in transit through the Straits allowed to use the aircraft which they may be carrying (Article 15). In February 1969 the United States aircraft carrier *Enterprise* was visiting Istanbul (thus technically she was not "in transit" through the Straits). Students were demonstrating along the quay, and so the admiral in command was taken by a ship's helicopter over the heads of the demonstrators to the palace of the governor of Istanbul for a courtesy visit. In addition to the question of whether the *Enterprise* might be considered "in transit," it could be asked whether a helicopter is an "aircraft" in the meaning of the draftsmen of Montreux.[h]

The requirement of notification of warships intending to enter or pass through the Straits is strictly enforced by Ankara. Without such notification, vessels of war are not allowed to pass beyond the entry stations at the northern point of the Bosporus or the southeastern point of the Dardanelles. If warships proceed farther into the Straits, they will be forced to stop. Thus far it has not been necessary for Turkish naval vessels or shore batteries to use force, but some unlawfully entering foreign warships have been obliged to wait for the required eight days before receiving permission to proceed.[i]

---

[h] In this case, the Turkish Ministry of Foreign Affairs denied having knowledge of a helicopter taking off from the visiting American ship; *Akşam*, February 19, 1969.

[i] Turkish authorities handle such incidents discreetly lest they create a major international conflict. In the early 1960s two destroyers of the

With the tremendous increase of Soviet shipping through the Straits since the late 1960s, the daily problem of passing Soviet warships faces the Turkish authorities. For Moscow, the concentration of a sizable navy in the Mediterranean, most of whose surface vessels have their home base in the Soviet Black Sea ports, has prompted concern for providing timely notice of passage through the Straits. There is a constant movement of Soviet supply ships (tankers and others) in full view of Istanbul in both directions through the Bosporus and the Dardanelles; even a casual observer would gain the impression that the waters of the Straits serve to a very large extent for the transit of Soviet bottoms.[j] But while commercial vessels (including those which transport war supplies) may freely enter and pass the Straits without any restriction in numbers or simultaneous presence in the Straits, warships, even those of the Soviet Union (a Black Sea power) may pass only with certain restrictions, including the obligation of previous notification.

The restrictions imposed by the Montreux Convention on the movement of Soviet warships through the Straits do meaningfully slow down their operational capacity to proceed to and from their Black Sea bases. It should be recalled that no foreign naval forces with a maximum aggregate tonnage exceeding 15,000 tons shall simultaneously be in the course of transit through the Straits (Article 14). The Soviet

---

United Arab Republic, having failed to give the notification required, had to spend eight days in the Marmara before they were permitted to proceed into the Black Sea (private information obtained by this writer). In July 1968 Turkish coastguard vessels stopped a Soviet destroyer at the entrance of the Straits because naval authorities did not receive notice of its passage. The warship was held back with threats to use force for 24 hours until the affair was cleared up in Ankara. Evidently the notification had been misplaced and the Straits stations were not informed of the arrival of the vessel; *Yeni Gazete*, July 7, 1968.

[j] In 1967 commercial vessels totaling 59.5 million tons passed through the Straits. Soviet ships had a tonnage of 26.6 million, that is, somewhat less than half of the total. *Cumhuriyet*, May 14, 1968.

Union, as a Black Sea power, may send through the Straits warships of a tonnage larger than 15,000 tons, but these must pass singly and can be escorted by only two destroyers (Article 11). Accordingly, a sudden massive reinforcement of the Soviet Mediterranean Fleet from Black Sea bases is legally impossible.

As to the notification clause, the passage of any warship must be preceded by at least eight days by notification of the intention to pass. Because such plans may not always be made well in advance, it has, since the Arab-Israeli War of 1967, become the customary practice of the Soviet Union to flood the Turkish Foreign Ministry with stand-by applications for transit and to obtain permissions whether they are effectively made use of or not. [25]

Submarines, even if they belong to Black Sea powers, may not pass through the Straits (except for repairs or delivery after purchase—cases which have no application to the Soviet Union). Because of the large number of Soviet submarines in the Mediterranean, persistent rumors in Istanbul as well as in the American press have accused Turkey of allowing Soviet submarines illicit passage through the Straits, an accusation strongly denied by the Foreign Ministry in Ankara. The ministry has insisted that Soviet submarines in the Mediterranean must have entered via Gilbraltar. [26]

The enhanced Soviet interest in the Middle East, active involvement in the Arab-Israeli conflict, and the presence of a considerable naval force in the Mediterranean have necessarily increased the significance of the Turkish Straits for Moscow. The fact that Turkey, a member of NATO, is close to being clutched in a vise between the Soviet Union and the concentration of Soviet power south of her borders, in the Eastern Mediterranean, has become, whether admitted by Ankara or not, the main topic of foreign policy concern for her as well as for her allies in the West.

- 6 -

Soviet Russia in the Middle East
and the Straits

The rapid, unprecedented growth of the Soviet Navy and the Soviet merchant marine in the post-World War II period, and especially during the 1960s, undoubtedly modified the global naval balance. This development also marked an important change in the naval strategy of the Soviets and enhanced the role of naval power when compared to Moscow's land forces, which have played a largely preponderant role in the past. In fact, it appears that the erstwhile ancillary function of the navy, to assist the operations of the land armies, has been replaced by an independent role of projecting Soviet influence into areas beyond the reach of the Red Army. Simultaneously, Soviet naval activities have acquired an offensive rather than a defensive character; to what extent they have become offensive must remain a matter of conjecture for the time being. Soviet naval strength, its deployment into more distant waters, and the already visible changes in the strategic

108

role of the Soviet Navy cannot but affect the status of the Turkish Straits.

EXPANSION AND DEPLOYMENT OF THE SOVIET NAVY

In the war against Hitler's Germany the Soviet Navy fulfilled a rather auxiliary role, although a few years before the outbreak of World War II Moscow had embarked upon an ambitious shipbuilding program. Most of the larger ships were on the way to completion when the Germans struck in June 1941. At that time the Soviet Union maintained one battleship and several cruisers in the Black Sea, and a number of smaller units. Most of these warships were sunk or heavily damaged by German air attacks. However, they distinguished themselves insofar as German landings behind the Russian lines were successfully prevented.[1]

After the war Moscow resumed construction of its navy— this time from scratch. The obsolescence of battleships, as experienced during the war, was taken into account; nevertheless, a class of light and heavy "cruisers" were to be built, the first with a displacement of 20,000 tons (the *Sverdlov* class); the second with a contemplated displacement of 44,000 tons (the *Stalingrad* class). After Stalin's death, construction of the *Stalingrad* class ships was discontinued.

Moscow also planned to build aircraft carriers, the backbone of the United States Navy in the post war era. But after 1954 such plans were also abandoned, and up to now Moscow has refrained from competing with the United States in respect to large attack carriers. However, the Soviet Union did complete two helicopter carriers (the *Moskva* and the *Leningrad*) in the 1960s. After 1956, under Khrushchev, surface expansion was focused on smaller craft equipped with guided missiles. Among units of the new-built surface fleet, large guided missile destroyers of the *Kashin* and *Kynda* classes are to be mentioned. Patrol boats provided with missiles (such as the *Komar* and *Osa* classes) also were added to the Soviet Navy.

Even under Stalin the construction of many submarines of various sizes was the paramount Soviet maritime ambition. Submarines equipped with ballistic missiles made their debut after 1958. The Soviet Navy presently possesses about 50 nuclear-powered submarines out of a total underwater fleet of about 400 vessels. About 300 submarines have long-range capabilities. Although Russian efforts since Stalin's death have been bent toward the creation of more balanced surface-underwater capabilities, the current real strength of the Soviet Navy remains vested in submarines.[2]

Geography is not favorable to the exercise of Russian naval power beyond coastal defense. The Baltic and the Black seas—those nearest Soviet population and economic centers—are connected only by narrow channels with the high seas. The Arctic Ocean coast, except for Murmansk and its environs, is icebound through the major part of the winter. The Pacific coast of the Soviet Union is far distant from the main demographic and economic areas of the country. Furthermore, communication by sea between these Soviet coastlines is impeded by geographical and climatic factors. Since Tsarist times Russian fleets have had to be based in four different parts of the world with slow and difficult possibilities of interchange. These four fleets are stationed in the Baltic Sea, the Black Sea, the Arctic (the Northern Fleet), and the Pacific.

Until the end of the "ancient rule of the Ottoman Empire," the Black Sea Fleet was completely locked inside the Euxine. Since the Lausanne and Montreux regimes, the closure of the Straits to warships has ended, but the mobility of the Black Sea Fleet is still hampered by the restrictions imposed under the Montreux Convention. Since submarines are prohibited from passing the Straits, the number of Soviet submarines in the Black Sea amounts to only about forty and these include no ocean-going types.[a] On the other hand, the

---

[a] The Baltic Fleet includes about 70 submarines of all types; the Arctic Fleet about 150; and the Pacific Fleet also 150 units.

two helicopter carriers are based in the Black Sea, and the greatest concentration of destroyers, frigates, and escort vessels is with the Black Sea Fleet (more than 70 destroyers and over 200 missile or torpedo-carrying patrol boats). The complement of minesweepers (220) is also larger than that attached to any of the other three fleets. The Soviet Black Sea Fleet Air Arm has no medium bombers but an oversize number (150) of reconnaissance planes.[3]

The isolation of the Black Sea Fleet has been ended since the early 1920s by the right to limited use of the Turkish Straits for surface craft; in the past twenty years, the Soviet inland canal system also has developed to the extent that ships and barges of up to 5,000 tons displacement may move between the five "inland" seas of European Russia (the Baltic, the White Sea, the Black Sea, the Sea of Azov, and the Caspian Sea). Small naval vessels may thus pass from the Baltic or the White Sea via the Volga-Baltic canal, the Volga River, the Volga-Don canal, and the Don River to the Azov and the Black Sea, and in the reverse direction. Such a voyage generally requires fifteen days; but submarines may be moved along this route into or out of the Black Sea, and other small craft are able to avoid circumnavigating Europe—a distance of over 4,000 miles.[4]

The Soviet leadership has evidently come to the conclusion that they possess a navy strong enough and sufficiently well balanced to compete with that of the United States in terms of long-range operations in practically all the seas of the world. As the British did in the heyday of their imperial power, and the Americans when they took over from them in the postwar period, the Soviet Navy feels capable of exploiting the principle of freedom of the seas by making appearances—often in strength—in the various corners of the oceans and in the vastnesses of the oceans themselves, "showing the flag" and demonstrating their power potential.

This naval development ran side by side with the expansion of the Soviet merchant marine. The commercial fleet of the Soviet Union is still inferior to that of Britain or the

United States, but it is slowly edging up toward their strength.[b] The Soviets also have an oceanographic survey fleet, as well as a huge fishing fleet with factory ships that carry 14 fifty-ton vessels capable of being used as landing craft for amphibious operations.

There is no doubt that the Soviet Navy has become an instrument of global strategic activity, in Admiral Mahan's words a "fleet in being," which by its mere actual or potential presence may influence political developments and persuade friends and foes of the reality of Soviet global power. At the same time, the navy may protect the routes followed by the merchant or fishing vessels and give encouragement to distant countries in their struggle against "imperialists" or enemies of Moscow.

Among Western naval experts there is controversy as to whether the meaningful expansion of Soviet naval strength and its deployment not only over neighboring "inland" seas, such as the Mediterranean, the Baltic, or the North Sea, but also into the Atlantic and Indian oceans, signifies the abandonment of a defensive posture for offensive goals. The Soviet Navy undeniably has stepped out of its pre-World War II role and is contesting for mastery of the high seas with the United States naval forces.[5]

It appears correct to assess the strategic goals of Soviet maritime expansion in light of the overall political generalship of the Soviet Union. Since the death of Stalin, the policy of expansion into areas contiguous to the U.S.S.R. has changed into a more versatile and territorially nondiscriminating expansionism. Under Khrushchev attempts were made (and not always unsuccessfully) to gain footholds in areas of

---

[b] In 1968 the Soviet merchant marine was estimated to possess 4,206 vessels with a total displacement of over 12 million tons; the merchant marine of the United Kingdom disposed of 22 million and that of the United States, 19.7 million tonnage; see William M. Newton, "Soviet Aims and Weaknesses," *Atlantic Community Quarterly*, Vol. 6, no. 3 (Fall 1968), pp. 321-30.

the Western Hemisphere, the Middle East, Africa, and Asia. The Congo proved to be unmanageable, but Cuba (although without missile bases) was not. And the Middle East, after several relapses, seems to have developed into a Soviet success story. Still, it has happened that a lack of adequate naval strength has prohibited activities from being carried out successfully in areas separated from the Soviet Union by the sea.[6]

In 1948 Stalin complained that he could not bring the Greek uprising to a successful end because "we have no navy."[7] And the Cuban missile venture of Khrushchev could not be effectively supported because of the absence of a "high-seas fleet." The policy of support for the "national liberation wars" of the Third World was unrealistic as long as the Soviet Union failed to possess the maritime and naval capabilities to provide supplies to these peoples and to reach out to them with powerful warships. The Soviet ambition to "rule the waves" is somewhat reminiscent of the desire of the Kaiser's Germany in the late nineteenth and early twentieth centuries to embark on a Weltpolitik and challenge the British Navy on the seven seas. It seems, however, that the Soviet strategy is more systematic and circumspect; it has to contend with even greater geographical and technological disadvantages than the Imperial German Navy.

The naval concentration of the Soviets in the Mediterranean began in 1963 and was dramatically speeded up after the Arab-Israeli Six-Day War of 1967. While it is only a part, it is a most significant part of the all-out Soviet naval effort. It must be considered in both its geostrategic and strictly political contexts.

THE SOVIET NAVY IN THE MEDITERRANEAN

The naval combat force of the Soviet Union stationed in the waters of the Mediterranean consists of a squadron of fluctuating strength; during the last few years it has varied in size between 30 and 60 units. The Mediterranean Soviet fleet includes the *Moskva*, occasionally joined by her sister ship, the *Leningrad*. These ships are equipped to conduct antisubmarine warfare and to support land operations; they are guided missile cruisers forward and helicopter carriers aft. They were built in the Nikolaevsk naval shipyards and ordinarily carry 20 helicopters each. No jets could be launched from their decks.[8]

The Mediterranean squadron further consists of two to four *Sverdlov* class cruisers which have a displacement of 15,450 tons (some of them are guided-missile cruisers); 8 to 10 *Kynda, Kotlin, Kashin,* and *Krupny* class destroyers, many of them with missile-launching capability; 2 to 5 *Riga* and *Mirka* class destroyer escorts; 3 to 4 minesweepers; and 12 to 15 submarines, some of them nuclear-powered. The fleet also includes 4 amphibious vessels (one of 4,000-ton displacement) which may land 500 marine infantrymen (the Americans call them "black berets") and light tanks. Generally 10 to 20 auxiliary vessels, including tankers and intelligence trawlers, survey vessels, and tenders, accompany these units.[9] Since late 1968 a dredger also has been added, showing how much Moscow is interested in clearing the Suez Canal when an agreement is reached to this effect.

The units of the Soviet Navy are moving into both the eastern and western sections of the Mediterranean; some of them follow the units of the Sixth Fleet or participate in various exercises. For refueling and repair the fleet uses certain anchorages, such as before the Isles of Galite (north of the Tunisian coast), the Gulf of Hammamet (on the east coast of Tunisia), in the Libyan Gulf of Sidra, or near the island of Kythera at the southernmost tip of the Greek mainland. Fuel and other supplies are transported to the Soviet vessels mostly from the Soviet Black Sea ports and through the Turkish Straits. At certain periods the Soviet warships return to their bases (mostly in the Black Sea), thereby reducing their Mediterranean complement to about 30 units.

Although the Soviet Union does not have any port under its sovereign control and does not seem to have any territorially segregated leased areas in any harbor, the Soviet fleet enjoys port facilities in the Egyptian harbors of Alexandria and Port Said, in the Syrian harbor of Latakia, and presumably in the former French naval base of Mers-el-Kebir in Algeria. An air and naval base is being constructed for Soviet use at Mersa Matruh, 150 miles west of Alexandria, and the harbor of Salum, farther west on the Libyan border, is being dredged by the Russians. The Soviet submarine base on the Albanian island Saseno (off the port of Vlona) had to be abandoned by Moscow in 1962 following the Sino-Soviet split and Albania's secession from the Soviet bloc.

The lack of a sovereign or leased harbor area may be a disadvantage to the Soviet naval command in the Mediterranean, where the British possess not only sovereignty over Gibraltar and the sovereign base areas of Akrotiri and Dhekalia on Cyprus, but also permanent harbor, dockyard, airfield, staging, and communications facilities in their former island possession of Malta.[c] These rights are also available to other members of NATO. Accordingly, the warships of the Sixth Fleet, after due notification, also may use these facilities. In addition, Italian as well as other NATO harbors are open to units of the Sixth Fleet but are being visited only with certain reservations to avoid unpleasant domestic reactions, such as those generated by leftist forces in Turkey. The United States enjoys full user's rights in the leased area of the port of Rota in Spain.

Attempts by the Soviet Union to obtain harbor facilities in countries other than Syria, the Arab Republic of Egypt, and Algeria have so far met with little success. Approaches to Malta and Morocco achieved no results and despite the Soviet

---

[c] Under Article 5 of the Agreement on Mutual Defense and Assistance between the United Kingdom and Malta, which came into force on September 21, 1964, and is to run for ten years, and may be extended.

Union's avowed cordial relationship with Turkey, Turkey's NATO membership precludes the presence of Soviet warships in her harbors.

The mobility of the Soviet Mediterranean fleet has also been hampered by the restrictions established by the Montreux Convention for the passage of the Bosporus and the Dardanelles. Technically, the Soviet squadron could receive reinforcements from the main Black Sea Fleet within three to four days if the units in question were allowed to pass these waterways without restraint. But under the Convention not only is a minimum notice of eight days required, but the bigger warships must pass the Straits singly with their smaller escorts; that is, such new units may enter only when their predecessors have exited at the other end of the Dardanelles or the Bosporus. For the bulk of the Soviet Black Sea Fleet to pass the Straits, 30 to 40 days would be needed—and a quick withdrawal from the Mediterranean into the Black Sea is just as unfeasible as egress from that sea into the Mediterranean, at least as long as Turkey insists on observing the Montreux rules. At present it is still unlikely that Ankara would be willing to depart from the international convention which was concluded primarily for its own security.

The Article of the Montreux Convention which prohibits the passage of submarines was mentioned earlier. This category of Soviet warships therefore is completely barred from moving through the Straits. In the event of an emergency, Soviet submarines seeking to leave the narrow Mediterranean, where they could be easily detected, could do so only via Gibraltar.

In view of these impediments to their movements to and from their nearest and natural bases in the Black Sea, the concentration of Soviet naval forces in the Mediterranean proves to be even more remarkable. It can only be explained in light of the overall Soviet naval expansion and the role the Soviet Union wishes to play in the Middle East.

As we have observed earlier, the all-out expansion of Soviet naval power is being pursued for the combined reasons of gaining worldwide prestige and recognition, to provide tangible support and encouragement on many continents to nations fighting "colonialism" and "imperialism," and also to protect the ubiquitous Soviet merchant and fishing fleets in many seas. The Mediterranean presence of Russian warships epitomizes all these aims and efforts. It is the naval component in the Soviet strategy which favors extending Russia's influence in the Middle East; by cruising along its shores, by calling at its ports, the Soviet fleet psychologically strengthens the war machine put at the disposal of the Arab Republic of Egypt and Syria in their fight against Israel. The presence of these warships is also a constant reminder to the Arab core-states as well as to Libya, Algeria, and others of the potential assistance they might gain from friendship with Moscow. There can be no doubt that among the waters affected by the Soviet naval advance, the Mediterranean remains the principal area, because of its geographical location and outstanding strategic significance.

Soviet naval interest in the Mediterranean has been given a much more pronounced emphasis by Moscow than has its navy's presence on the seven seas. The leading Soviet military paper even went so far as to declare the Soviet Union a "Mediterranean power." Thus we read: "Our state, which is, as is known, a Black Sea and consequently also a Mediterranean power, could not remain indifferent to the intrigues of those fond of military ventures organized directly adjacent to the borders of the U.S.S.R. and other socialist countries. No one can be allowed to turn the Mediterranean into a breeding ground of a war that could plunge mankind into the abyss of a worldwide nuclear-missile catastrophe. The presence of Soviet vessels in the Mediterranean serves this lofty, noble aim." [10]

The centuries-old Muscovite ambition to establish Russian influence and power in the Near and Middle East and also over the waters adjacent to these territories appears to be on its way to being satisfied by Soviet political and military penetration into these areas. It is, of course, a novel type of extension of power which is not accompanied by formal annexations or military occupations; its stability is therefore more questionable than that of earlier political and military takeovers. It is largely dependent on the cooperation of the local Arab states, primarily the Arab Republic of Egypt. It was the Arab-Israeli conflict which provided the golden opportunity for Moscow to extend its protecting hand over large parts of the Arab Middle East. While the Soviet naval presence in the Mediterranean is independent of Moscow's military presence in Egypt, these two expansions mutually reinforce each other.

Before the stationing of Soviet Air Force units in the valley of the Nile, the Russian naval units in the Mediterranean lacked essential air support. On the other hand, the military and air base in Egypt guarantees for the Soviet Union all necessary facilities in the harbors of the Arab Republic of Egypt. However, Moscow's air communications with its Egyptian base, like those for its navy, are largely maintained across the territory of Turkey. Although Ankara discourages stops of Soviet military aircraft at Turkish airports, it has not always opposed them, nor has it objected to the overflight of its territory by Soviet planes en route to and from Egypt.

NATO was to contain Soviet expansionism, an endeavor which until the early 1960s was successfully accomplished along the demarcation line set by the Atlantic Alliance. But the massive Soviet build-up in the Near and Middle East now exists behind the line of the Northern Tier. In that corner of NATO defenses the protecting barrier has been pierced; this feat was carried out without the use of violence but in reliance on the rights established by the Montreux regime of the Straits, on the welcome proffered by the Arab states seeking assistance against Israel, and on alleged threats by Western "imperialists." The successful descent of Soviet power into the Middle East and the Mediterranean changed the balance of power prevailing in that part of the world and also tested the stability of the southeast bastion of NATO, both from the military and the political points of view.[d]

CONFRONTATION OR COEXISTENCE IN THE MEDITERRANEAN

For nearly twenty years the Mediterranean was a "NATO lake" and within its waters the Sixth Fleet's superiority remained unchallenged. When Turkey and Greece joined NATO, no Soviet power base existed in the Eastern Mediterranean. With the new situation, however, the strategic equation established between the forces of the Atlantic Alliance and the potential enemy along the northern borders of Turkey and Greece underwent a meaningful change. As Turkish publicists have pointed out, by 1970 Turkey's geopolitical status differed from what it had been twenty years before. [11] Simultaneously, the role of the Straits has changed and must be considered from a different angle. The five questions to be envisaged in view of these new strategic developments may be summarized as follows:

1. First, the power potentials of the rival forces around the southeast corner of NATO defenses and in the Mediterranean have to be considered. It seems clear that the Soviet Union regards the Mediterranean as the direct continuation of the Black Sea, not only in a geographical but in a geostrategic sense. The presence of the Soviet Navy not only is motivated by political-psychological considerations; it also constitutes an actual military threat. [12]

---

[d]Leonid I. Brezhnev, the Soviet party leader, hinted in an election speech that an "equal bargain" might be struck between his country and the United States by mutual withdrawal of both navies from the Mediterranean. He also said that although "U.S. politicians consider it normal and natural for the Sixth Fleet to be constantly stationed in the Mediterranean, hard by the side of the Soviet Union," they see a threat in Russian warships appearing in that sea. *New York Times,* June 12, 1971.

The strength of the Mediterranean squadron of the U.S.S.R. has already been described. The main force which may potentially oppose this presence or thwart its activities is the U.S. Sixth Fleet, a force which is still regarded as superior to its rival. Like the Soviet fleet, the Attack Carrier Striking Force, as the Sixth Fleet is officially referred to, is variable in its strength. Ordinarily, the Sixth Fleet consists of about fifty combat ships, including two large attack carriers, two heavy cruisers, and a number of frigates and destroyers. Also included are an amphibious force with amphibious ships to transport and land a reinforced Marine battalion (about 1,800 men) with tanks, artillery, trucks, and helicopters; and a service force consisting of underway replenishing ships, tenders, and repair ships. Also assigned to the Sixth Fleet are several attack submarines and fleet ballistic missile submarine forces.[e]

The main thrust of the United States Mediterranean naval force lies in its attack carriers with about 200 aircraft (mostly F-4 Phantom jet interceptors) which outmatch anything the Soviet squadron may offer. The Russian ships are equipped with surface-to-surface missiles with a range of more than 400 miles, but those cannot equal the American carrier-based jets in tactical radius or destructive capability.

Periodically—not unlike the Soviet fleet—the Sixth Fleet is augmented by other units from the Second (Atlantic) Fleet, units such as an anti-submarine force with one or two carriers

---

[e] This task of the Sixth Fleet is thus described by Admiral Arthur W. Radford: "The Sixth Fleet is a powerful military force with the dual mission of protecting the rights and safety of U.S. citizens and of supporting the land forces of the North Atlantic Treaty Organization against possible threats on its southern flank. It must be kept in mind that those missions cannot be successfully carried out without due regard to the diplomatic, political, and psychological implications surrounding all aspects of fleet operations in time of tension. The purpose of all our military forces is to deter attacks from possible enemies, and the Sixth Fleet exists to support that purpose." *New York Times*, February 16, 1971.

and screening destroyers. Such an augmentation occurred in October 1970 at the time of the Jordanian civil war. All the ships of the Sixth Fleet are based in the United States and are deployed overseas for specific periods in rotation with vessels and aircraft squadrons of the Second Fleet. Accordingly, reinforcements from the Atlantic and landing teams air-transported from European bases can reach the Mediterranean within periods ranging from a few hours to four to five days. The limitations upon reinforcing the Soviet Mediterranean units from bases in the Black Sea have already been noted.

While the Sixth Fleet alone has a preponderance of about three to one over the Mediterranean naval forces of the Soviets, [13] most of the American ships are overaged or nearing that status, whereas the Soviet ships are mostly brand new. Nevertheless, experts believe that the Soviet fleet could be sunk within a few minutes. [14] However, the lack of air cover by land-based aircraft has to some extent been overcome by the operational possibilities of Soviet planes based on Egyptian airfields.[f]

In addition to the Sixth Fleet's air arm, the United States may, in case of necessity, use air power from bases in Italy, Greece, and Turkey (possibly also from the British base on Cyprus), but only with the permission of these NATO allies. The same restrictions exist with regard to airplanes based on Spanish airfields. Should the Atlantic Alliance be involved in hostilities, Washington may also count on the support of Allied navies and air forces.

In the 1960s, Britain withdrew most of her warships from the Mediterranean, where her navy once ruled supreme. British naval units only occasionally return in strength for exer-

---

[f] These are twin-jet Tupolev (TU-16) long-range reconnaissance bombers known by the NATO code names as "Badgers" and marked with United Arab Republic insignia though manned by Soviet pilots. See William H. Honan, "Russian and American Pilots Play 'Chicken,' " *New York Times Magazine*, November 22, 1970, p. 25.

cises.[g] After the British withdrawal from East of Suez, those units of the British Navy regularly stationed in the Indian Ocean most probably would be deployed in the Mediterranean. At present this would involve one carrier or heavy cruiser and several frigates and guided-missile destroyers. [15]

The Italian Navy is larger in numbers and tonnage but weaker in fire-power than the average-strength Soviet Mediterranean fleet. [16] The strength of the Turkish Navy has been discussed earlier; the Turks expect to receive a number of additional submarines and destroyers from their allies. Greece could add her eight destroyers, four destroyer escorts, and two submarines to a combined anti-Russian action.

Both the United States and the Soviet Union maintain attack submarines and ballistic-missile submarines in the Mediterranean. The U.S. Polaris-type submarines are based at the Spanish port of Rota (near the Gibraltar entrance into the Mediterranean), where the United States continues to enjoy harbor, repair, and refueling facilities under treaty.

Submarines constitute a major danger to the two leading navies in the Mediterranean, and their early detection, in case of hostilities, could be a question of life and death for many ships and their crews. Each fleet therefore constantly shadows the other's submarines. [17] How the two major rivals and their allies would behave in the case of a threatened war would determine to a considerable extent the limits of conflagration in the area or might possibly forestall the outbreak of hostilities.

2. In case of an imminent threat of war which would involve the entire NATO Alliance and in which Turkey would

---

[g] At the meeting of the Defense Planning Committee of NATO in Brussels in May 1971 Britain proposed that the present "on call" force of destroyers or frigates from the American, British, Italian, Greek, and Turkish navies be made a permanent "standing naval force." Lord Carrington, the British defense minister, also announced that Britain would station one commando regiment, about 600 men, on Malta, as a reinforcement of the Atlantic Alliance's intervention forces, now almost entirely composed of U.S. marines. *New York Times,* May 29,1971.

consider herself directly endangered, Turkey would, according to her discretion, be legally justified in closing the Straits to warships of some powers and keeping them open for others. In the above contingency the potential peril would emanate from the Soviet Union, and therefore Soviet warships would be barred from passing through these waterways. Ankara may thus prevent Soviet vessels of war from returning to their regular Black Sea bases (Article 21 of the Montreux Convention). It is of course not to be expected that Turkey would lightheartedly resort to such a drastic measure, which could precipitate rather than postpone an outbreak of hostilities. She would use these extreme steps only when aggression would appear to be almost inevitable.

Turkey would have to report the closure of the Straits to the United Nations Security Council (in lieu of the Council of the League of Nations). How the Security Council would handle such a crisis must remain a matter of conjecture. Whether it would decide to leave or lift the closure of the Straits by a majority of two-thirds (as provided for the League Council by the Montreux Convention) or whether it would follow its own voting rules (including the so-called veto rights of its five Permanent Members) would have to be decided by the Security Council itself.

In case of a threat of war, the question of the closure of the Straits may also be brought before the signatory powers of the Convention (save Japan). Among these signatories, Britain, Australia, Greece, Italy, and of course Turkey, would in all likelihood sustain the closure, whereas the U.S.S.R., Bulgaria, and Rumania would demand its discontinuation. France would probably join the first group, Yugoslavia possibly the second group. In any case, no majority would be likely to be available which would enjoin Turkey to withdraw the closure.

But a prolonged closure of the Straits would create an intolerable situation for the Soviet Union and glaringly reveal the geographical impediments to its claim that the Mediterranean is but a continuation of the Black Sea.

A tension is more likely to be resolved by direct contact between the opposing governments, primarily between the United States (which is not one of the signatories) and the Soviet Union, rather than through the slow machinery of the Security Council or a decision by the signatory powers of Montreux. On the other hand, the tension might also escalate into a military conflagration. In the event of an acute danger of war, the need for a quick decision would exclude lengthy procedures before the United Nations or the unorganized group of signatories. This could hardly have been foreseen by the draftsmen of the Montreux Convention.

Should a danger of military conflict arise between the United States and Russia (for instance, if Israel's existence were at stake, a case which is not a NATO *casus belli*), Turkey could possibly remain a nonbelligerent. In that event she would, however, be legally obliged to close the Straits to the warships of the belligerent powers, except that she would still have to permit the withdrawal of Soviet vessels into the Black Sea (Article 19 of the Convention).

As we have seen, in any of these eventualities the attitude of Turkey and her jurisdiction over the Straits would be an element of controlling importance. In such a case, legal considerations would probably become secondary, though still employed to justify measures taken primarily for political and military reasons.

3. In the event of an outbreak of hostilities of a limited or conventional nature between the NATO powers and the Soviet Union and its allies, the primary mission of the Sixth Fleet would be to maintain supply lines to Turkey and Greece. To carry out its objective, it would have to fight and destroy the Soviet fleet in the Mediterranean, even at the potential risk of being partly or entirely destroyed. Should Turkey be immediately involved in such a war, she would probably be invaded from Bulgaria and along her Caucasian border, and she would require assistance which would have to come mostly by ship via the Mediterranean.

If Turkey were directly involved, she would naturally close and defend the Straits against attacks from the north. The Soviet fleet in the Mediterranean would be cut off from its Black Sea bases, and to run the gauntlet of the Gibraltar Strait and sail around Europe would be a hopeless undertaking. Even if the claim that Soviet warships in the Mediterranean could be destroyed within minutes is regarded as over-optimistic, those ships would almost surely suffer total destruction unless the war were to escalate quickly into a nuclear exchange (see below). The Sixth Fleet still might suffer heavy losses, in particular from submarine attacks; and the escape of Soviet submarines into the Atlantic might still be within the realm of possibility.

However, in the event that no aggression were committed against her territory, Turkey might decide to remain a nonbelligerent, as she did during World War II. In that case, the status of American bases on her territory would become highly anomalous, should such bases still exist there at that time. If she did not close the Straits to all warships, her involvement in the hostilities would be inevitable. Should she close the Straits to the warships of all belligerents, the Soviet Union's Mediterranean navy would be isolated. Thus closure of the Straits would hurt Moscow almost exclusively; we must wonder whether the Soviets could afford such a measure and whether it would not be more likely that they would try to open the Straits, first by diplomatic and later by military measures. In such an eventuality, unless Turkey submitted to Soviet pressures (in which case she would fall under Soviet control), she would inevitably be drawn into the war. Thus, while the Straits are Turkey's treasure, they could also determine her destiny.

4. It is hardly possible to predict the reactions of the superpowers in regard to the use of their nuclear arsenals. How far the conventional military contingencies outlined above are realistic depends on the moderation or obduracy of these powers and also on the calculations they may make

with regard to the intentions of their opponents. The price appears, in any case, so high that escalation into a nuclear exchange would be avoided by both sides.

In the event of a nuclear exchange—as a military expert opined in 1957—the Sixth Fleet must be considered "expendable." [18] Although one may also speculate that in the eventuality of a nuclear war the American naval vessels would be withdrawn into the vastness of the Atlantic (if time allowed), this writer is inclined to believe that they would not be ordered to desert their strategic position and would instead attempt to accomplish their mission even at the risk of total destruction. They would have to destroy the Soviet fleet very quickly and inflict crippling damage on Soviet military-industrial centers and possibly other objectives in the south of Russia.

It cannot be foreseen to what degree Turkey might become a victim in a nuclear war. There is apprehension in Turkey that she might be the target of a Soviet first strike, but this is highly unlikely. In the Mediterranean area, the first targets would be the American military installations which have nuclear retaliatory capabilities. The American bases in Turkey are hardly among this number. The Straits, in such a case, would play only a secondary role; any hit along these waterways would cause earth movements and devastation which might render their navigational use impossible for a long time. Such a result could hardly be in the interest of the Soviets. Compared to points in the Soviet Union and on the North American continent which are likely to be primary targets, the Mediterranean region would be only a "secondary war theater." Polaris or Poseidon missiles, launched from submarines in that sea, would be the really deadly danger to Soviet power; these submarines, however, would themselves be safer than surface ships in these narrow waters.

Whether Turkey could be subdued by a Soviet nuclear threat is a hypothetical question, the answer to which would largely depend on the credibility of the threat, on the credibility of the American nuclear response, and in no small degree on the determination of the Turkish leadership to refuse absolutely to submit to its historic enemy.

More likely than unprovoked Soviet nuclear blackmail is an attempt to invade Turkish territory. Under the flexible response strategy, Turks are being told that NATO will first use tactical nuclear arms and only thereafter strategic ones, should the integrity of a member country or its survival be in jeopardy. Occupation by enemy forces of any portion of Turkey's territory would be considered such a jeopardy. [19]

The danger of escalation from a minor incident into an all-out global war should constantly be in the minds of the decision-makers, provided of course that they do not think in irrational terms. A confrontation between the superpowers, short of war, is likely to remain limited to the Mediterranean area and warfare to be restricted to powers (such as the Arabs and Israelis) which can to some extent be controlled by their arms suppliers.

5. Since 1955 the Soviets have moved into the Middle East; but their most dramatic descent into that sensitive area occurred after, and as a result of, the Six-Day War of 1967. Short of a military or naval action, NATO could not have prevented that Soviet advance, carried out, as it was, in agreement with the Arab states and in accordance with international law (Montreux Convention). There was no way to force out the Soviet Union without resort to violent measures, which for psychological, political, and legal reasons had to be rejected. Thus the Soviet presence is there to stay and NATO has to accommodate its political and military posture accordingly.

The former line of containment, along the northern borders of the Northern Tier countries, has not collapsed; it has only been outflanked. NATO must seek to contain Soviet penetration by taking full account of these Soviet outflanking maneuvers. A strategic breakthrough becomes fatal only if the adversary is able to exploit such an action fully. If not, he has only increased his vulnerability. This is the case in the Mediterranean and the Middle East.

The West has, to a large extent, lost its influence over most of the Arab countries (an influence which since the collapse of the Baghdad Pact was diplomatic rather than political or military). The United States has lost its overwhelming preponderance of naval power in the Mediterranean but still maintains a superior naval potential. The American teeth were shown in October 1970 at the time of the Jordanian crisis, when joint action with Israel was planned against Syria while the Soviet Union remained inactive. [20]

Moscow may not be interested in a permanent solution to the Arab-Israeli conflict. Its influence and power base in the Arab states rests with the dependence of these countries on Soviet military and political support. On the other hand, Moscow does not want to escalate that conflict into a military confrontation with the United States. In this respect Soviet and American interests coincide. But Soviet influence is by no means as well established as British, French, or American ascendancy had been in the past in that part of the world. The greatest weakness of Soviet control lies in the lack of secure communications between the home base and its newly acquired sphere of influence. The NATO line has been pierced, but it still stands. Turkey, as well as Greece and Iran, are still in the Western camp. And the only sea-lane from the Black Sea into the Middle East, the Turkish Straits, is solidly under Turkish and, by implication, NATO control. As long as this status quo persists, Soviet penetration into the Middle East must be considered tenuous.

The suggestion that a new NATO defense line be set up is hardly supportable. [21] As long as Turkey remains committed to defend her status quo and that of the Straits, the one pocket of penetration which the Soviet Union has been able to establish "behind" the lines must be contained as effectively as possible. Moscow's plans seem to be more ambitious than gaining control over the Arab Middle East; its naval advance seems to be directed in the "general direction" of the Persian Gulf and the Indian Ocean. The closure of the Suez Canal remains a grave hindrance to Soviet shipping and to the movement of the Soviet Navy. In this respect, the U.S.S.R. appears to have stepped into the traditional role of the British, but for different reasons.[h]

Moscow has managed to enter into the "next room," the Arab Middle East, but the Kremlin has no power over the "revolving door" leading to that area—the Straits. It is dependent on Turkish consent even for direct flights from the Russian heartland to Egypt. Russia has overcome her naval weakness but she has not overcome the disadvantages which geography has placed on her path toward global penetration. Control of Turkey and of the Straits therefore must be a more highly coveted prize for Soviet leaders than that of the Arab area. If the former could be secured, the latter could be held more easily and at a lower price. It has therefore been suggested that the primary goal of Russian moves into the Middle East is to surround and force into compliance the hereditary opponent of Russian advances toward the warm seas.[22]

The developments of the past decade, and in particular the Soviet success behind the Anatolian fortress and beyond the Dardanelles, have greatly increased the dilemma facing the Turkish leadership, a dilemma which has plagued them since the foreign policy catalysis brought about by the Johnson letter of 1964.

---

[h] There are several explanations for Moscow's search for easy access to the seas east of Suez: faster transit to the Far East (Vietnam) and to the Soviet Pacific coast; shorter supply lines in case of a conflagration with China; penetration into the Persian Gulf, a potential "no man's land" following the departure of the British; or simply a desire to "show the flag" along the Asian rimlands.

TURKEY'S DILEMMA

In 1953 Moscow officially abandoned claims to Turkey's territory, claims it had advanced in 1945 and 1946. But the call for a change in the regime of the Straits has not been abandoned. Although the Kremlin was careful not to reiterate the brutal threats and overt intimidation previously practiced in pursuit of its objective, Turkey remains under constant subtle pressures in respect to these waterways, and a reopening of the question of the Turkish Straits can be expected at a moment considered suitable to Soviet planning.

The presence of the strong Soviet Navy in the Mediterranean, and the concomitant overflow of Soviet warships and supply vessels in the Bosporus and the Dardanelles, as well as the high stake Moscow has in the Middle East all suggest the near certainty of renewed pressures on Turkey. It is true that the U.S.S.R. has now turned to the sea, but she has by no means given up the traditional Russian geostrategic postulate of "contiguous land power," that is, the demand that her borders be surrounded by states which are subject to her influence. This leading policy principle has been set forth in *Pravda* as follows: "Soviet ships entered the sea on the strength of the U.S.S.R.'s sovereign right to make free use of the open sea. . . . As a Black Sea and, in this sense, a Mediterranean power, it is closely connected with all problems involving the interests of the peoples of this area of Europe, Africa, and Asia. It is directly interested in insuring the security of its southern borders." [23]

In view of these developments, it appears inconceivable that the Soviets should not feel unhappy because of their dependence on Turkey's authority over the "umbilical cord" connecting their navy in the Mediterranean with its home base in the Black Sea. On the other hand, Turkey is bound to be most apprehensive of any claim according to which she belongs to the "Soviet security sphere," and she considers the Soviet strategem to be a move to encircle her from the south. As one Turkish commentator put it: "The purpose is evident:

to make a sandwich of the Anatolian Peninsula with Soviet navies both in the Mediterranean and in the Black Sea." [24]

Under such circumstances, expressions of Soviet friendship are of little assurance to Ankara, as it anticipates being presented again with a Soviet bill which it must reject while in the matrix of a constantly deteriorating geostrategic position. Turkey has to weigh possible measures to meet the dangers threatening her security and the status quo of the Straits. These fears have been muted so far because an overt expression of them would betray distrust of Soviet intentions and would hardly improve Turkey's diplomatic posture. She certainly has no intention of interfering with Soviet passage through the Straits as established by the Convention of Montreux. Ankara wants to apply this international instrument scrupulously, and in the spirit of Montreux. There is no wish by the Turkish government to give the slightest provocation to Moscow, nor is there any willingness to jeopardize the security of the Turkish nation. Turkey would like to impress upon the Soviets that her control over the Straits should not impair Moscow's sense of security as to the passage of warships or other ships. There is, however, a latent suspicion that Soviet power hunger and expansionist ambitions can never be satisfied.

Even before the Soviet build-up in the Mediterranean, Turkey was carefully reappraising her role in the Atlantic Alliance. The relaxation of the Cold War, the realization that her monorail-like reliance on the United States was unrealistic, and the example of Gaullist France induced her to seek greater flexibility and mobility, though still within NATO. From August 24, 1969, member states were entitled to renounce their NATO membership after giving one year's notice. The great debate over whether Turkey should leave the Alliance has ended, at least for the time being, with a resolution to stay. Nevertheless, earnest soul searching (which should be clearly distinguished from propagandistic, ill-informed, and highly prejudiced criticism against the United States and the Atlantic Alliance) continues over whether a posture more aloof from close military and political ties would not be more advantageous to Turkey's national interests. [25]

Practically all participants in this debate, even official spokesmen, agree that reliance on a single power (meaning, of course, the United States) would not serve Turkey's best interests. Even those who otherwise strongly favor the maintenance of NATO ties advocate a de-emphasis of relations with the United States, arguing that American and Turkish interests are not always identical and that "rigid" relations should not be maintained with any particular country.

Only a few foreign policy experts have suggested a withdrawal from the Atlantic Alliance. Others, assessing the advantages and potential disadvantages of NATO membership, conclude that the former outweigh the latter. As one author expressed it: "The Soviet Union would be the greatest beneficiary of Turkish withdrawal from NATO." [26] The main arguments by the few commentators who wish Turkey to abandon NATO somewhat resemble those put forth in Gaullist France. Because of her NATO commitments, this line of reasoning goes, Turkey would be dragged into war should there be hostilities anywhere in Europe. In case of a nuclear war, Turkey could become the first target. On the other hand, if she had no nuclear arms or radar detection devices in her territory, she would be spared devastation. In case of a Russian attack on Turkey, the United States would, in any case, come to her defense because Washington could not afford to lose her.

While supporting a flexible foreign policy and a revision of NATO arrangements (including strategic planning), the principal opposition party, led by the octogenarian elder statesman Ismet Inönü, has opposed abandonment of the alliance. It is generally believed that with Inönü's advocacy of a continued alliance policy, the debate—at least temporarily—has ended. [27]

On behalf of the government of the Justice Party, Foreign Minister Çağlayangil in 1970 advanced the following reasons against a neutralist stance for Turkey: "Europe without NATO would be a disunited Europe—the divided Europe of 1939, and such a state of affairs would be even more to our disadvantage because the balance between the potential aggressor and the attacked is more in favor of the aggressor today." He also sought to refute the argument that Turkey has lost her independence by her membership in NATO: "Turkey has lived in alliances in every stage of her history. The balance of power notion which is the most dominant feature of Turkey's foreign policy is a requirement dictated by the *historic and geopolitical situation of our country*. It was the same in Atatürk's time too. . . . Atatürk's independence policy does not mean a principle of living alone with your own might, no matter what the political conditions and necessities of foreign security are." [28]

For the same reasons the government refused to dismantle American bases; this could be done only when "all the clouds have been dispelled" from Turkey's relations with the Soviet Union.[29] In fact, because of the Soviet concentration in the Mediterranean and Russia's new power base on the other side of Turkey, the clouds have become thicker than when the above declarations were made.

In March 1971, following an intervention by the military leadership, a new Turkish government was formed under the premiership of Professor Nihat Erim, a staunch supporter of the Western alliance. Osman Olcay, deputy secretary general of NATO, joined the new cabinet as minister of foreign affairs, an event which also demonstrated Turkey's unchanged policy orientation.

As so candidly admitted in Khrushchev's letter to General Gürsel in 1960, the primary goal of Moscow's Turkish policy is to squeeze Turkey out of NATO. Should Turkey become "neutralist" it could be—in view of existing power relations—only a Finland-type neutrality. With a Finlandized Turkey, so the masters of the Kremlin may think, it would be possible "to share in the defenses of the Straits."

Although it seems unquestionable that Moscow is supporting some of the pro-neutral and leftist tendencies of Turkish radicals, the prevailing anti-Russian phobia requires that such moves be extremely discreet. At the time of this writing, official Soviet policy emphasizes Moscow's friendship toward its southern neighbor, and the Kremlin's advocacy for Turkey's leaving the "one-track" foreign policy (namely, NATO membership) is tactful and restrained. Evidently, after the past mistakes, Soviet diplomacy wishes to practice fraternization rather than intimidation. Nevertheless, it also believes in "intimidation by implication." The dramatic deployment of Soviet strength in the Mediterranean is to serve as a reminder to Ankara that it should not rely solely on its friends in the West but should seek security in more realistic power relations.

No doubt the status of an uncommitted nation may have many attractions for the Turkish leaders. But Turkey is not strong enough to become a "balancer" rather than a weight in the balance of the power structure. And she is, primarily because of her geopolitical location, far too significant to be left alone. In fact the guardianship of the Straits, more than anything else, determines her stand on the side of the Western powers. Also, her drive to reach "the level of contemporary civilization" is tied up with her Western orientation.[30] She will soon complete her Second Five Year Plan and embark upon the Third in her drive to achieve modernization and industrialization. Her models are not the Eastern totalitarian regimes but the prosperous nations of Europe. Her desire—since Atatürk's time—to be accepted as and to develop into a European nation-state cannot but affect her foreign policy orientation. Only if the status of an uncommitted nation would definitely accrue to her national interest, or if she felt abandoned by her present allies, would she return to neutralism.

Turkey is an indispensable element in the power balance of the Eastern Mediterranean region and the Middle East. Her possession of the Straits is a geostrategic phenomenon which deserves the highest consideration. The character of this control is double-edged: it raises the value of Turkey as an ally but it attracts potential aggressors. On the other hand, mastery of the Straits is a vital requisite of Turkey's genuine independence. While she cannot survive without them, with the Straits Turkey leads a dangerous life. And, being realistic, she must clearly see in which corner the danger lies, which power has the greatest interest in depriving her of this invaluable possession.

Turkey is not expected to sacrifice herself for NATO. If she must make sacrifices, she will have to do so primarily in her own well-considered interest. It is important for Turkey to realize that her interests on the main security issue run parallel with those of her NATO allies. And the West also clearly has to recognize that Turkey's independence, her welfare, and her control over the Straits are essential to the security of the West and to international peace and stability.

- 7 -

The Turkish Straits: Issues and Options

At the end of the eighteenth century Russia succeeded in turning the Black Sea from Turkish into predominantly Russian waters. But she endeavored in vain during the next century and a half to turn the Bosporus and the Dardanelles into Russian straits. Conversely, for over two centuries with brief exceptions, Britain and France pursued a policy of containment with the objectives being to preserve the Ottoman Empire and block Russian political and military power in the Black Sea. To counterbalance the offensive and defensive strategies of Russia and the Western powers, Constantinople closed the Straits to all foreign warships. The status quo of Europe, and in particular that of the Mediterranean region, depended largely upon the regime maintained in the Straits.

Turkey, the residual legatee of the Ottoman Empire, inherited the essence of her predecessor's problems. The complete exclusion of foreign warships from the Straits has now been superseded by a balanced compromise as laid down by

136

the Convention of Montreux. With the implementation of this international instrument, as long as the interested powers refrain from using political or military means of coercion, dissension surrounding these all-important waterways is reduced to an exchange of legal arguments.

A change in the present regime of the Straits may be brought about by peaceful agreement, a revision of the existing Convention or its replacement by another convention. The issues and options of such a change, consistent with the norms of international law, must first be examined. But it is by no means certain that Moscow will not once again attempt a change in the status quo by the use of coercive moves. The issues which have to be faced by Turkey and her NATO allies in such a contingency will have to be discussed next. The interest which the United States should display toward the Straits question, and in general toward Turkey, deserves further scrutiny. Because the problem of the Straits cannot now be separated from the wider issues of the Middle East, the containment of Soviet expansion into that region should be the topic of our final comments.

REVISION OF THE MONTREUX CONVENTION

1. At the time of this writing, neither Turkey nor the NATO powers have any interest in urging a revision of the Convention regarding the regime of the Straits as accepted in Montreux in 1936. After three and a half decades there is no doubt that the present Convention has become antiquated or superseded in some respects by international developments. At the same time, it has also proved to be a sound and equitable instrument for the balancing of interests. Thus, a revision of the obsolete or outdated clauses of the Convention would be desirable, though their maintenance does not disadvantage Turkey or any of her Western allies. Constant practice has shown that despite its shortcomings or obsolescent features it has remained a workable instrument.

As long as Turkey continues to be a trusted ally and friend, her implementation of the provisions of Montreux can be relied on and it would be wise to leave things as they are. It is therefore suggested that NATO or the United States should not, unless there is a basic change in their relations with Turkey, initiate a revision of the Convention. Even if Turkey should withdraw from NATO and become a genuinely uncommitted nation, there would seem to be no urgent reason for the United States or other NATO powers to propose a revision of the present regime of the Straits. Should Turkey become compliant with Soviet desires for a change in the status quo—a contingency which cannot be expected to occur without Soviet coercion—the issue of the Straits will cease to be one governed by international law and will certainly degenerate into one of naked power politics.

2. It can be expected, however, that the Soviet Union will raise the issue of changing the present regime of the Straits at a time it deems appropriate. If the Soviet government is ready to comply with existing treaty obligations, it has two options for promoting peaceful change:

a. Since November 9, 1954, the signatory powers of the Montreux Convention may inform the French government of their intention to denounce it; the denunciation, in such a case, would take effect two years after notice had been given. The Soviet government may thus denounce the Convention at any time now and the withdrawal would become effective two years thereafter. However, the signatories are committed to be represented at a conference to be convoked upon the act of denunciation for the purpose of concluding a new convention (Article 28).[a]

---

[a] For the Montreux Convention, see Appendix 12. It should be remembered that Article 1 of the Convention, which enacted "the principle of freedom of transit and navigation by sea in the Straits," cannot be denounced. This freedom is, however, subject to regulation, that is, restriction. The present and any future convention is to provide for the manner in which navigation through the Straits is regulated.

b. Three months before the end of each five-year period following the entry into force of the Montreux Convention, the signatory powers are entitled to propose amendments of the treaty.[b] Such proposals must be supported by two other Montreux signatories, unless the proposed modification touches on questions relating to the tonnage of warships permitted to pass through the Straits, in which case the support of only one more signatory power is required. The details of revision are to be discussed through diplomatic channels. If no agreement can be reached in such a manner, the signatories are committed to attend a conference to be summoned for the purpose of revising the Convention (Article 29). It can be assumed that the Soviet Union would, if it wanted to propose amendments to the Convention, be able to obtain the support of Bulgaria and Rumania.

3. If the Convention were to be denounced by the Soviet Union, the international conference which is to convene for the purpose of drafting a new convention could be attended by any power provided the other participants do not object. Thus, the United States would certainly be a participant in such a conference. Which other states, in addition to the present signatories of the Montreux instrument, should be invited, could become a central issue. Presently, the Montreux treaty may only be acceded to by signatories of the Lausanne Treaty (Article 27). The Soviet Union is likely to propose that all Mediterranean countries be invited. Such an increase of participants would not necessarily upset the balance and should not be opposed by the NATO signatories or the United States.

In such a case, the conference would be attended by Britain, France, Italy, Turkey, Greece, Bulgaria, Rumania, the U.S.S.R., Yugoslavia, and Australia (Japan has been excluded by the San Francisco Peace Treaty of 1950) as former signa-

---

[b] Such five-year periods expire on August 9, 1971; August 9, 1976; August 9, 1981; and so on.

tories, and by the United States, Albania, Algeria, Cyprus, Israel, Lebanon, Libya, Malta, Spain, Syria, Tunisia, and the Arab Republic of Egypt as new participants (the inclusion of Morocco, which may also be considered a Mediterranean country, can also be contemplated).

4. If a conference is convoked for the amendment of the Montreux Convention, initially only the signatory powers may attend it. However, it seems legally possible that even before they decide to amend Article 27 by opening the treaty to countries other than the Lausanne signatories, they may unanimously invite such other states, including, for instance, the United States. It must, however, be remembered that the conference for amending the Montreux Convention may only take decision by unanimous vote, except as regards the revision of the clauses relating to the tonnage of warships allowed to pass through the Straits (Article 29, par. 5), for which a majority of three quarters of the signatories is sufficient.

It cannot be doubted that the majority of the present signatories would insist that the United States participate in an international conference, either for the revision of certain provisions of the Convention or for the acceptance of a new convention. Accordingly, it is more likely that such a conference would be convoked under Article 28 (the denunciation clause) than under Article 29 (the conference to deal strictly with "amendments" only).

5. Should the present Convention be denounced by the Soviet Union and the subsequently convoked international conference fail to agree on a new convention, the new situation could be given highly different interpretations by the two opposing groups. The Montreux Convention would still be considered valid and applicable by those signatory powers which did not denounce it. As things stand now, Turkey, Britain, France, Italy, Greece, Australia, and possibly Yugo-

slavia would continue to regard the Convention as being in force; Bulgaria and probably Rumania would join the U.S.S.R. in considering it no longer applicable. Following their denunciation of it, the Soviet Union and the Soviet-camp powers might even support the view that the Montreux Convention has completely lapsed, even between the other signatories. Such a view, however, should be strongly opposed by the NATO participants to Montreux and by the United States.[c] The legal status of those powers which might denounce the Convention may be considered from two drastically different angles:

a. Turkey would probably rely on the view expressed in her diplomatic note of October 18, 1946 (Appendix 26), according to which the Lausanne and Montreux regimes of the Straits only replaced, with the consent of Turkey, the ancient rule of the Ottoman Empire which allowed the territorial sovereign (now the Republic of Turkey) to close the Straits to the warships of all foreign powers. While the principle of freedom of navigation through the Straits cannot be denounced, Ankara may still claim that with denunciation of the Montreux Convention she regains the right to regulate, according to her judgment, the navigation in those waterways vis-à-vis those powers which consider the Convention no longer valid. However, it seems more probable that Ankara would continue to apply the Convention to the warships of the Soviet Union just as before. One should remember that Moscow failed to ratify the Lausanne Convention on the Straits but nevertheless cooperated with Turkey in its implementation. It would be desirable for the United States and NATO powers, in agreement with Turkey, to take a common stand in this new situation and jointly oppose the probable Soviet position on this issue.

---

[c] Non-signatory powers, like the United States, are indirectly also beneficiaries of the Convention by enjoying the rights of passage provided by it.

b. Should the U.S.S.R. denounce the Montreux Convention and agree on no other international treaty to replace it, it probably would claim, under the general rules of international law applicable to straits, complete freedom for its warships to pass through the Turkish Straits, at least in time of peace. The Russian contention would probably be based on Article 16 of the Convention on the Territorial Sea and the Contiguous Zone signed at Geneva on April 29, 1958, which became effective on September 10, 1964 (after having been ratified by thirty states including the United States, the Soviet Union, Britain, and France).[1] Paragraph 4 of Article 16 provides: "There shall be no suspension of the innocent passage of foreign ships through straits which are used for international navigation between one part of the high seas and another part of the high seas or the territorial sea of a foreign state."

Such a claim should be strongly opposed by NATO powers, as it would no doubt be opposed by Turkey. The very special geographical character of the Turkish Straits, since the beginnings of the development of international law, always assured them an exceptional status.[2] The ancient rule of the Ottoman Empire was rightly considered as part of the "public law of Europe," and this status was replaced first by the Lausanne and then by the presently valid Montreux regime. The application of general rules of maritime law to waterways which always enjoyed a special status appears wholly unjustified. Besides, it should be recalled that Russia, and now the Soviet Union, has claimed a special status for the Black Sea. Should the general rule be applied to the Turkish Straits, warships of non-Black Sea powers would also enjoy the right to enter the Black Sea without the restrictions now imposed on them by the Montreux Convention.

6. It is in the interest of NATO that an international conference on the revision of the Straits Convention be attended by the United States with equal rights, whether such a con-

ference be convoked because of a denunciation or for the purpose of discussing proposed amendments. As mentioned above under point 4, the present NATO signatories of the Convention should see that Washington is invited. In Lausanne as well as in Montreux, the representatives of the United Kingdom played a dominant role in the forging of the Convention. Britain was in those days the major Mediterranean naval power. This position is now held by the United States. However, when participating in such a conference, Washington must fully face up to the delicate questions which are to be treated. As we have noted, the American approach at Yalta and Potsdam largely ignored the intricate fabric and legal-political balance established by the draftsmen of Montreux.

The American note of November 2, 1945, practically accepted the Soviet claim for unrestricted passage of its warships through the Straits and for a denial of the right of entry into the Black Sea to warships of non-Black Sea powers (Appendix 28). During the Potsdam conference a State Department briefing paper even recommended that the United States not object to the establishment of Russian bases on the Straits, naïvely adding, "with the free consent of Turkey."[3] It is to be wondered what the political-military balance in the Eastern Mediterranean would be now had these suggestions been followed.

The revision of the Montreux Convention is not a topic that could be successfully handled at the Olympian heights of a summit conference; it is a matter that requires patient spadework and legal and naval-military expertise in addition to an understanding of power realities. A contempt for the "legal subtleties" of a Straits convention would be just as harmful in negotiations as reliance on truistic "principles" often pronounced without an adequate knowledge of the complexities involved. Should a conference be convoked for the revision of the Montreux Convention, the United States would have to be represented at it by delegates fully compe-

tent to deal with all aspects of the problem, both historical-
legal and political-military, and fully able to cooperate usefully with other NATO delegations, including the Turkish.

7. An international conference for the renegotiation of
the Straits Convention would have to face the following
issues[4] and should probably adopt the positions suggested
below:

a. The regime of the Straits should continue to be governed by an international convention; any bilateral (Soviet-
Turkish) arrangement or one concluded solely between Black
Sea riparian powers should be strongly opposed. On the other
hand, internationalization of the Straits (that is, the establishment of an international commission to administer navigation
through the Straits and their demilitarization) should also be
rejected. Turkey would never willingly agree to such a return
to the Lausanne system; her conduct in applying the Montreux Convention has been praiseworthy. The interests of
peace and the international community do not demand internationalization.[d]

b. The new convention should not be allowed to depart from the balance of interests struck at Montreux. Turkish
control of the Straits with the right to fortify the area and
limitations on the entry of non-Black Sea warships into that
sea should be maintained, as should restrictions on numbers
and tonnage of such vessels in transit through the Straits.

c. The present convention should be updated technologically; Annexes II and IV should be replaced by a modern
classification of warships; limitations with regard to the caliber of guns should be amended by provisions with regard to
missile-launchers; provisions regarding nuclear warheads

---

[d] Nor does the Soviet Union favor an international regime of the
Straits. Of course, Moscow would object to it because she wishes to
deal with Turkey only.

should be introduced and the use of helicopters regularized. While it seems desirable that the general prohibition on the passage of submarines be maintained, concessions may be made to the Russians in regard to aircraft-carriers (the limitation of 15,000 tons might be lifted). Generally, the technological restrictions might be negotiated against other concessions to be asked for. The notification clause for warships should be maintained; time limits might be eased.

d. The League of Nations should be replaced with the United Nations in the revised convention.

e. The provisions of Montreux with regard to Turkey's right to close the Straits in time of war to warships of belligerents should be maintained. Similarly, the right of Turkey to close the Straits when she considers herself threatened should be upheld. This measure should be reported to the Security Council of the United Nations; the Council, using its voting rules on nonprocedural matters (Article 27, paragraph 3 of the U.N. Charter), could decide that closure might not be justified. It appears undesirable, however, to uphold the right of signatory powers to decide on the discontinuation of measures taken by the Turkish government, whether by a majority of two-thirds or otherwise.

f. In time of war (Turkey not being a belligerent), Turkey should be obliged to allow passage of warships if so ordered by the Security Council in implementation of its enforcement measures under Chapter VII of the U. N. Charter. It would seem, however, impractical to renew the provision (Article 19, par. 2, of the Montreux Convention) under which warships of belligerents are permitted to pass the Straits to render assistance, by virtue of a mutual assistance treaty binding Turkey, to a state which is a victim of aggression.

g. Otherwise it should be left to the discretion of Turkey to rule whether there is a state of war in the meaning of the Convention, and to determine which states are to be considered belligerents.

h. It should be considered whether the revised Straits Convention should not be made an "open" treaty, to which any state (or only members of the United Nations) might accede.

DEFENSE OF THE STRAITS

The previous recommendations assume a call in which the Soviet Union attempts to bring about a change of the present status of the Straits by using methods within the frame of the rule of law as laid down by the Convention of Montreux. It must be considered, however, that Moscow might attempt to upset the status quo by other measures, which might range from diplomatic persuasion to expected or direct threats of war, resort to various coercive measures including subversion or infiltration, or to war itself. The procedures for peaceful change, in harmony with international law might also be pursued at the same time that extra-legal pressures were being applied. The persuasive or coercive steps which could be anticipated, and the measures to forestall or counteract them, are to be examined under the following four points:

1. Moscow is more likely to proceed step by step toward its desired goal than to use a sudden ultimatum-like thrust, although such a move should not be considered impossible. Soviet diplomacy will probably undertake to demonstrate: that Turkey could only gain by severing her NATO ties and establishing a relationship of "genuine confidence" with the Soviets; that Ankara cannot rely on NATO assistance; that there exists a community of interests between Russia and Turkey (especially with regard to defense of the Straits); or, finally, that because of Soviet penetration into the Mediterranean Turkey has become militarily isolated to such an extent that hope of NATO assistance is no longer realistic.

Separately or combined with the above-mentioned diplomatic steps, Moscow might encourage and assist internal subversion. Contacts with leftist opposition leaders, student or trade-union leaders, and leftist-oriented military men, whether directly by Soviet consular staff members or through intermediaries, could undermine the position of the government and result in a military takeover and the formation of a government devoted to neutralism (the first step toward a pro-Soviet orientation and possible concessions with regard to the Straits).

2. To forestall or counteract the above-listed pressures and blandishments, diplomatic suasion of the following nature should be employed by members of the Atlantic Alliance and by the Alliance collectively:

a. Turkey must be convinced that NATO is vitally interested in her defense and that her vital national interest requires her to remain an active member. She must be reminded (though present Turkish leaders are aware of this) that Russian interest in the Straits concerns not only the transit of ships but will be used as a lever to establish Soviet domination over Turkey.

b. It must be demonstrated to Ankara that NATO assistance is credible and will not fail to be effective in the event of a threat of war or the outbreak of hostilities.

c. Turkish membership in NATO is likely to deter Moscow from resorting to coercive pressures or to aggression, whereas a neutral Turkish stance will not.

d. It should be made clear that Turkey, whether a NATO member or not, will be unable to remain nonbelligerent in an armed conflict between the Warsaw Pact and NATO countries, and that her territory (primarily because of the Straits and her geopolitical location) cannot escape becoming an area of military operations, as it did during World War II.

e. Turkish leaders and public opinion must be made aware that the defense of Turkey (and of the critical Straits area) can only be immediate and therefore fully effective if joint action has been previously organized and prepared (integrated commands, joint military planning, mutual exchange of relevant information, and so forth).

f. It must further be demonstrated to Turkey that despite the Soviet power base established in the Mediterranean and in the Middle East, the balance of power is still tilted in favor of the West; that the West will be ready, in case of need, to use its power; and that NATO supplies will reach Turkey across the Mediterranean despite the Soviet presence there.

g. It should be impressed upon Turkey that only her desertion from NATO would tilt the Mediterranean balance in favor of Moscow, a state of affairs in which Turkey would become the prime victim.

h. It must be clearly stated that any attempt by Russia to change by force the existing status of the Straits will be regarded by NATO as a *casus belli*.

3. While diplomatic suasion should be constantly employed, deeds would carry greater weight with the pragmatic-minded Turks. Among such actions the following should be considered:

a. Military aid should be increased rather than decreased. Turkish armed forces should be strengthened and provided with up-to-date military equipment.

b. In case of an emergency, NATO's Mobile Forces (AMF) are at present insufficient to meet the needs of Turkey's defense. They should be raised to the strength of at least one division; their transport facilities (sea-lift facilities should be added to the present air-lift capabilities and the latter enlarged) should receive added strength and be maintained in permanent readiness. Plans and capabilities for an "air-bridge" to Turkey should be prepared. Elements for logistic support should be assigned to the combat forces of the Mobile Forces.[5]

c. Instead of technologically obsolete tactical nuclear bombs, Turkey should be provided with "clean" fission devices with small blast but predominant radiation effect. Such tactical nuclear weapons might give adequate protection against aggression in Thrace directed against the Straits area and even more so on the Caucasian border of Turkey. Release orders for the use of these weapons should reach the advanced commands in time so as to make their employment possible before an enemy could invade vital territory.

d. The question of placing atomic land mines should be reviewed again in light of the latest technological developments. Permission to place these land mines and to detonate them might possibly be given to Turkish commanders, with adequate safeguards and strict contingency instructions so as to reduce the time required to block the routes of advance in the event of an imminent attack.[e]

e. It seems imperative that NATO military exercises be conducted frequently along the vital areas of Turkey's defense, including the area of the Straits. Turkish military leaders have been rather reluctant to allow such exercises near the Soviet border in Anatolia. It is suggested that such maneuvers are necessary; Moscow might consider them provocative, but they would be evidence of Turkish determination to resist any attempt to change the status quo and any aggression.

4. There is a growing feeling in Ankara that in the assessment of NATO Turkey has lost her previous strategic importance and value.[6] While she is endeavoring to strengthen her political, economic, and cultural ties with Europe, this desire to be an equal member of the European family of nations, it

---

[e] New policy guidelines were approved by NATO's nuclear planning group in October 1970 with regard to the use of atomic land mines. Such guidelines should include special provisions affecting Turkey, taking into account her geographical position and her defense of the Straits. See the *New York Times*, October 28, 1970.

is felt, is not adequately reciprocated.[7] Whatever the merits of such a complaint, it can be correctly stated that the significance of NATO as a whole in the eyes of European leaders has suffered a considerable depreciation in the past decade. This is particularly true with regard to the role NATO is supposed to play in the Mediterranean.

The defense of Turkey and her indispensable arteries, the Straits, has certainly suffered, psychologically and materially, because of the disintegrating process which has eroded NATO's strength in many areas. France's withdrawal from military cooperation, Greek-Turkish strife over Cyprus, instability in Italy and Greece, the U.N. condemnation of Portugal because of her African policies, and a general lack of sufficient interest in the common cause may be cited as the principal signals of the weakening of the Atlantic Alliance. In this dismantling and decomposing process, the Mediterranean region of NATO has been primarily affected.

The Mediterranean is not only the "soft underbelly" of Europe; until the closure of the Suez Canal in 1967, most of Europe's oil passed through those waters. Greece and Italy as well as France are Mediterranean countries, and their security is closely allied with the control of the Midland Sea. It therefore seems essential that European NATO members be awakened to the possible consequences if the southeastern bastion of NATO were to be lost or if Russian power were to flow into the Mediterranean unrestricted by the sluices of the Straits. A complete loss of the Middle East to Russia could deprive Europe of the source of vital oil; the substitution of the supply route around Africa might become irrelevant in such an event.[8]

Turkey is striving to become or to be accepted as European. She has joined practically all the Western and European organizations, such as the European Recovery Program, the Organization for Economic Cooperation and Development, the Council of Europe, and the Atlantic Alliance. She has even embarked on the slow process of becoming a member of the European Economic Community. Her foreign and defense policy is also geared to adjust to this orientation. All this would make it more difficult for her to take a neutralist or anti-Western stance. But foreign relations are based, if they are to be healthy and enduring, on mutuality. The Soviet thrust into the area behind her southern shores has further jeopardized Turkey's security, and her security is the key to any defense of Europe's southern flank.

It is primarily in the interest of NATO's European members to strengthen their position along the Mediterranean and to oppose any further deterioration in the power equilibrium of that vital area. The defense of Turkey, and the retention of control of the Straits in the safe hands of their territorial sovereign, is an essential element of Europe's defense. This was recognized for several centuries when Britain and France were ready to rescue the Ottoman Empire from the dangers threatening it from the north. The validity of such a policy should be recognized again today: the protection of Mediterranean Europe is primarily a European affair. It cannot be expected that all the efforts and risks involved should be shouldered by a power which has to stretch out its helping hand from across the Atlantic.

AMERICAN INTEREST IN THE STRAITS

1. The agonizing developments in Indochina have created an acute need for a reassessment of American interests throughout the world. Few have denied the vital interests which the United States has in Western Europe and in the exclusion of that region from the Soviet domination which so tragically descended on Eastern Europe and part of Central Europe in the aftermath of World War II. Western Europe alone cannot be protected unless the defense of its northern and southern flanks is secured. Hitler realized this in reverse when he seized Europe's northern flank and attempted to place the Mediterranean under his control. The conquest of

the Mediterranean area by American and British forces in 1942-43 exposed the southern approaches to Western and Central Europe and presaged the defeat of the Axis.

The inclusion of the Mediterranean Sea in the area to be protected by the Atlantic Alliance occurred simultaneously with the admission of Greece and Turkey. These steps resulted from the conviction, not easily arrived at, that the defense of Western Europe is unavoidably linked with the security of the Mediterranean. The gates from Russia into that sea lead through the Turkish Straits.

In the early 1950s, when Turkey and Greece joined NATO, it must have appeared inconceivable to extend the protecting NATO shield over the Mediterranean without extending it over Turkey. The fact that Turkey's territory jutted far out into the area between Soviet Transcaucasia, Iran, and Iraq was considered an additional strain on the resources of the Atlantic Alliance; but the fact that Turkey controlled the Straits was regarded as a strategic asset to NATO. Turkey and the Turkish Straits area were deemed to be an essential pillar in the defense of the Mediterranean region and the countries bordering that sea—Greece, Italy, and also France. As long as the United States maintains its interest in the defense of Western Europe the defense of the Mediterranean, together with Turkey and the Turkish Straits, must be paramount in Washington's geostrategic approach.

The Mediterranean Sea is, of course, an open sea and under the existing international rules commercial and naval vessels of any nation may freely pass over its waters or linger outside the territorial sea of the coastal states. The United States itself took advantage of this "freedom of the seas" when it dispatched the Sixth Fleet (a task force of the Atlantic Fleet) to stay in the Mediterranean. Thus even before the establishment of NATO (and especially after the reduction of British naval forces in the Mediterranean) it was thought that American interests required the presence of the United States Navy there.

American interest in the defense of the Straits remains essential. The Sixth Fleet is the chief instrument for maintaining the balance and protecting American interests; it is also the instrument which must safeguard the line of communication with Turkey, the guardian of the Straits. In order to fulfill these tasks, the Sixth Fleet must be strengthened to meet the threat offered by the presence of considerable Soviet naval forces with the potential to oppose its assignments.

2. The role of the Sixth Fleet is not only military but also political. It represents the interest and commitment of the United States in that crucial part of the world; in fact, it is a vital element in the global balance of power. The Soviet naval presence in the Mediterranean has made this clear, if it was ever in doubt. Now that the two navies are facing each other in these narrow waters, the importance of the American units has become more tangible and their responsibility has greatly increased.[f]

The political role which the Sixth Fleet is called upon to play cannot be divorced from its military-strategic impact, and certainly not from its qualitative and quantitative strength. In addition to the great-power rivalry in the Mediterranean, the global maritime expansion of the Soviet Union emphasizes the oceanic aspects of the nuclear arms race. The deployment of nuclear weapons is now closely linked with naval construction. Whether large carrier fleets will eventually share the fate of the battleship cannot as yet be foreseen.[9] However, it appears that for the time being large attack-

---

[f] Helmut Schmidt, the West German minister of defense, has said that if the Sixth Fleet were withdrawn from the Mediterranean for even two weeks, the political effects would be immediately felt in Lebanon, the United Arab Republic, Libya, Algeria, Turkey, Greece, Italy, and France. He added: "The American presence in the Mediterranean is of the greatest psychological-political significance. This is known in the Atlantic Alliance and the countries around the Mediterranean." *The Bulletin* (Bonn), February 24, 1970, p. 40.

carriers are indispensable for the maintenance of American superiority over the Soviets in the Mediterranean Sea.

The role of the navy in securing surface communications is most essential in the case of Turkey and the Straits. Russia once complained that the Turks hold the keys to her door.[g] For Turkey to be able to close this door, in case of an emergency, she will need help. Surface transports, protected by surface warships and the aircraft launched from them, may have to carry the bulk of the material assistance. It seems imperative that the size of the Sixth Fleet should not only be maintained but gradually increased. It should be provided with modern units. To a large extent, the Soviet warships are not more than four to six years old; the majority of the American naval vessels are overage.[10]

Even if at present the Sixth Fleet could "more than take care of" the growing Soviet surface fleet in the Mediterranean,[11] the American Task Force still has to be strengthened, not only for strictly military reasons but also to demonstrate determination in the face of its rival. Turkish cooperation can only be ensured when strength is shown—strength in determination and in hardware.

A belief in United States commitments depends largely on the capability to meet these commitments. The construction of warships, including the costly carriers, is still cheaper than waging war. In the Mediterranean the carriers of the Sixth Fleet provide the credible air power deterrent needed to forestall Soviet aggressive actions against Turkey and the Straits.[12] A belief in American strength and in willingness to assist is a crucial ingredient of cooperation between Washington and Ankara.

3. Turkish-American relations must be considered on a purely realistic and pragmatic basis. The "honeymoon" that

---

[g] Tsar Alexander I spoke of the Straits as "the key to the door of my house." Puryear, *Napoleon and the Dardanelles*, pp. 325-26.

characterized these relations until the early 1960s was unrealistic and contributed to the anti-American reaction which is widespread among intellectual circles in Turkey. Indeed, the Turkish foreign policy elite is polarized in regard to its views of the alliance with the United States. But as long as there is a democratic type of government there, no sudden change in foreign policy is to be expected.

Turkish sensitivity concerning her sovereign rights, non-interference in domestic affairs, and equality within the Atlantic Alliance must be respected. But only her extremists or emotionally influenced intellectuals consider the stationing of American forces, joint defense installations, or other common defense measures as interference in Turkey's internal affairs. It should be understood that those who wish to ignore the potential Soviet threat are living in a fool's paradise. Should the present Soviet efforts at improving relations with Turkey reveal themselves as artful coaxing to gain concessions on the Straits, the inanity of their anti-American stance will become obvious.

The official Turkish leadership is well aware of the usefulness of American friendship. The Cyprus incident disabused them of the belief that American and Turkish interests are in every respect identical and that they can count on American support in every eventuality. But they must know, and should be constantly reminded, that in regard to Turkey's protection against Soviet aggression, and also in regard to the Turkish sovereign rights over the Straits, American and Turkish interests are identical. Naturally, it is also necessary that the United States leadership share this attitude.

What amount of American military presence would be required to assist Turkey in the first hours of an attack against her territory may be questioned. The American Air Force units stationed in Turkey, however, would certainly play a major role in the defense of the Straits, and from this point of view their continued maintenance seems indispensable at present. Only when the Turkish Air Force can be considered fully capable of replacing that of the United States should American forces be withdrawn. But such a development would also presuppose a further strengthening of the Turkish air arm with fighter planes which are a match for Soviet aircraft.

There are many seeming inconsistencies in Turkish attitudes toward the United States. Ankara wishes to enjoy the security and other benefits of the Atlantic Alliance; at the same time, it wishes to practice a flexibility in its foreign policy which is not always compatible with the purpose and spirit of this partnership. To allow Soviet military aircraft destined for Egypt to land and refuel on Turkish airfields seems incompatible with cooperation in defense matters with the United States.[13] The Arab-Israeli conflict is technically not a NATO matter. But Soviet-supplied and Soviet-manned aircraft—allowed to pass over Turkish territory—might, in the eventuality of an East-West conflict, be employed against the Sixth Fleet, which would attempt to provide assistance to Turkey. It is suggested that Turkey should tactfully be reminded that such conduct might be self-defeating and in the long run disastrous, besides being hostile to the concept of the Atlantic Alliance.

Turkey fears that she might be involved in any violent conflict between the superpowers, even if the immediate cause of such a conflict does not affect her interests. The United States probably would have supported Turkey in the Cyprus conflict had the other protagonist of that conflict not been another NATO member, Greece. Commitment to common defense involves the danger of being drawn into a distant conflict. The futility of such a slogan as "Why fight for Danzig? " was demonstrated by the experiences of World War II, and most Turkish leaders are aware of the necessity to stand up for their commitments.

There is, however, another apprehension beclouding American-Turkish relations which Washington should be anxious to eliminate. This is the fear of Turkey's being "left out" of decision-making in areas important or even vital to its welfare. The real Turkish nightmare would be the recurrence of situations in which great powers reach understandings directly between each other affecting the Straits or other essentials of Turkish independence. The ominous exchanges between Napoleon and Tsar Alexander I and between Hitler and Stalin, or the summit conferences of Yalta and Potsdam, when there was a danger that Turkey would be disposed of, are still vivid in the imagination of Turkish leaders. A deal between Washington and Moscow concerning Turkish interests would be considered a greater danger in Ankara than acute hostility between the superpowers.

It thus seems very important that Turkey be constantly informed and consulted by American diplomats. Such contacts should naturally be based on full reciprocity, so that Turkey could maintain much of the flexibility she desires without jeopardizing the interests of the United States and her other allies. It is understandable that Ankara should try to please Moscow in any way not to the detriment of Turkish interests; but she must be reminded to consider not only her immediate advantage but also the far-reaching consequences of her actions.

Turkey can be best impressed and sincere contacts with her maintained by frequent visits of American leaders to Ankara and Turkish leaders to Washington. If demonstrations are to be avoided, such meetings could take place in towns other than Ankara or Istanbul, perhaps even outside Turkey. President Nixon's Mediterranean trip in September 1970, even if he was not prepared to go to Turkey, certainly afforded an opportunity to meet Turkish leaders somewhere in the area. Defense Secretary Laird's visit to Ankara was not regarded there as an adequate substitute. On the other hand, the presence of Secretary of State Rogers at the CENTO Council meeting in Ankara in May 1971 was beneficial.

What would most enhance American credibility in Turkish eyes is action in critical situations. The apparent readiness of the Sixth Fleet to intervene against the Syrians in the Jordanian civil war in October 1970 was a morale-booster to Turkey and an encouragement for her to resist future encroachments on her status and that of the Straits. It is now felt in Ankara, as it is in Washington, that the dynamism and latent potentialities of the Arab-Israeli conflict, coupled with the Soviet military and naval involvement in that conflict, might ominously revive the now seemingly dormant question of the Turkish Straits. [14]

CONTAINMENT IN THE MIDDLE EAST

The Soviet breakthrough into the Mediterranean and the Middle East leapfrogged the barrier which was created by NATO's southeastern extension and its connection with CENTO. This advance was made possible partly by Arab dependence on Soviet military support against Israel, partly by the Russian naval build-up in the Mediterranean, and largely by the use of the right of passage through the Turkish Straits. As pointed out in Chapter Six, this breakthrough would become fatal only if the protecting barrier that has been pierced were to collapse altogether. Turkey is the keystone of this barrier and her hold on the Straits is an important, perhaps the most important, linchpin of the still-existing defensive axis. The strategic importance of the Turkish Straits, and of the geopolitical role of Turkish territory and air space, has been made clear by these dramatic developments.

These developments have also complicated the issues that might have to be faced by the United States, by Turkey, and, indeed, by NATO at large. But in international politics a decision-maker must always place himself in the position of the potential or real opponent. If so, it must be evident that the Soviet commitment and involvement in the Middle East has presented Moscow with a snarl of problems which it will not be easy for it to disentangle. The issues—taking into account the role of the Turkish Straits in the Middle Eastern imbroglio—confronting the main protagonists, as well as some of the options available to them, may be summarized as follows:

1. The Soviets cannot be "rolled back" from the Middle East and the Mediterranean without a third world war or a nuclear exchange. But their further advance may be slowed down and eventually contained. Moscow is likely to avail itself of every opportunity to extend its influence in the Arab World and beyond. The closure of the Suez Canal remains an obstacle in its apparent drive toward the Indian Ocean. It is therefore not in the interests of the West to speed up the opening of the Canal. Events have proved that the West can live without the Canal whereas Moscow's advance is slowed down by its closure.

2. Even if it may not be in the interests of the Soviet Union to end the Arab-Israeli conflict, Moscow may not wish to see it escalate; another Egyptian defeat might force the U.S.S.R. into direct military involvement against Israel, which could provoke a similar counteraction by the United States. It may be the Kremlin's intention to let the Arab-Israeli conflict simmer, and to exploit Arab dependence without allowing its clients to waste the expensive military hardware supplied them. In return, what the United States should do is to promote compromise and settlement between the contentious parties. Washington should practice a genuinely "even-handed" policy between the Arabs and the Israelis and prevent any imbalance in disfavor of the latter. In addition to prohibiting the destruction of Israel, Washington should have it in view to counteract a growing Soviet military preponderance in the areas in question. Not only should the Sixth Fleet be strengthened, but American naval strength, sufficient to outweigh Soviet penetration, should be established in the Indian Ocean and also in the Persian Gulf. In the event that

the Arab-Israeli conflict loses some of its intensity through yet unforeseen diplomatic developments, the Russians may find themselves less welcome in Arab countries. Moscow might then be faced with the dilemma of trying to find a way to remain there against the will of its clients or of leaving these overextended positions altogether.

3. It is hardly conceivable that the Soviet Union would risk a direct military clash with the United States in the Mediterranean. However, in order to avoid such risks Moscow must be clearly informed of the tripwire which it is not supposed to cross without the danger of being forcefully opposed. NATO's tripwire system has operated successfully in the past—the critical line has not been crossed. In the Middle East there is a wide "gray area" into which the Kremlin might believe itself free to move without provoking resistance. Washington might have other views and consider a certain intrusion to be one that affects its vital interests. To clarify such issues before a crisis occurs would be the task of prudent statesmanship.

4. Israel is not a NATO issue, but it is an issue in which the United States is, if only for domestic reasons, seriously concerned. Should the United States be forced to take naval or military steps for the protection of Israel, it will have to do so, probably, alone. But if a conventional or all-out clash should ensue between the Americans and the Russians, it would be impossible for NATO to keep out of the arena.

5. Should there be such an outbreak of hostilities, Turkey would be treaty-bound to close the Straits to the warships of the belligerents. If she would live up to these obligations, the Soviet forces in the Mediterranean (and also, as far as supply is concerned, the Soviet elements in the United Arab Republic) would be cut off from their Black Sea bases and would

face destruction. Should Turkey refuse to close the Straits to Soviet shipping, United States forces might set up a naval and air blockade at the "choke-point," the entrance to the Dardanelles, which would have the same effect as if Turkey had blocked the Straits. Should Turkey—in accordance with the Montreux Convention—choose to close the Straits, the Soviet Union might invade her and try to open up the Straits by military force. NATO would then become fully involved.

6. To what extent Moscow (or Washington, for that matter) would find a humiliating retreat from the Mediterranean or a defeat by conventional forces acceptable cannot be clearly foreseen. If such a defeat were considered unacceptable by either power it could only resort to a global conventional war along the whole of the European demarcation line and in all the waters where it deploys naval or other forces, including the Pacific; or it could trigger a nuclear cataclysm. Surely the leaders in both countries will back away from such fatal options and avoid practicing brinkmanship on these issues.

7. The above considerations clearly point out the controlling strategic function that the Turkish Straits may have to fulfill in the event of a major confrontation in the Middle East or on the Mediterranean Sea. Moscow may have already realized this. It may have concluded that before going further in those regions it will have to secure its "rear"—the transit through the Straits—regardless of the restrictions and sanctions provided by the Montreux Convention. We may therefore envisage one or several of those Soviet measures for a peaceful or coercive change of the status of the Straits described earlier in the present chapter.

8. The Turkish Straits and thus the Turkish state hold a key role in the preservation of the balance in the Mediterra-

nean and the Middle East; therefore, it is imperative that they be given primary attention.[h] As long as Turkey and her all-important Straits stand in line with the defense of the Western world, containment of Soviet advances is a likely possibility; should these strategic points be lost, the entire NATO and United States position in the Mediterranean is likely to crumble. Turkey and the Straits are the West's Stalingrad—a fortress where all available resources, diplomatic and military, must be concentrated against the possibility of an eventual assault.

In 1964 a Turkish parliamentary delegation visited Moscow and was received by Premier Khrushchev. The leader of the delegation, the later Turkish Prime Minister Suat Hayrı Ürgüplü, touched on the deterioration of Turkish-Soviet relations after the end of World War II and said the responsibility for this did not rest with Turkey. Khrushchev replied: "True, we claimed land from you and submitted further demands. You believed it and took offense, rightly so because the demands were made by the Prime Minister of the U.S.S.R." With a twinkle in his eye, he added: "It was actually not the Prime Minister but Beria who did all that but nonetheless you were right to believe those demands. But now, as the Prime Minister of the U.S.S.R., I am telling you that we are giving up all these claims, so why don't you believe me?" [15]

---

[h] Illicit drug traffic from Turkey, slowly checked by Turkish authorities, is giving rise to unrealistic views concerning the value of the alliance with Ankara. Thus Senator William Proxmire, at the meeting of the Senate's Appropriations Subcommittee, suggested that any advantage from a military alliance with Turkey was "far outweighed" by the misery and loss of life caused to the United States by Turkish opium production. Secretary of Defense Melvin Laird answered that it was more important that Turkey (and Greece) remain in the North Atlantic Treaty Organization during the 1970s than it was in the 1960s because of the presence of Soviet naval forces in the Mediterranean and the need to maintain the balance of power in the Middle East. *New York Times,* June 23, 1971.

The Turks and also their Western allies would like to believe that no such demands concerning the Straits will be made by Moscow. But developments since 1964 hardly encourage such a belief. The geography of the area has not changed; and as long as Soviet leaders, like the Tsars before them, continue to want to reach out in force into the Mediterranean and the other warm seas beyond, the lifeline for such endeavors, the Straits, will remain a prize to be captured.

APPENDIXES

APPENDIX 1

Treaty of Peace of Küçük Kaynarca between Russia and the Ottoman Empire

July 10/21, 1774

[excerpts]

ART. III. All the Tartar peoples . . . shall, without any exception, be acknowledged by the two Empires as free nations, and entirely independent of every foreign Power, governed by their own Sovereign, of the race of Ghengis Khan, elected and raised to the throne by all the Tartar peoples; which Sovereign shall govern them according to their ancient laws and usages, being responsible to no foreign Power whatsoever; for which reason, neither the Court of Russia nor the Ottoman Porte shall interfere, under any pretext whatever, with the election of the said Khan, or in the domestic, political, civil, and internal affairs of the same; but, on the contrary, they shall acknowledge and consider the said Tartar nation, in its political and civil state, upon the same footing as the other Powers who are governed by themselves, and are dependent upon God alone. As to the ceremonies of religion, as the Tartars profess the same faith as the Mahometans, they shall regulate themselves, with respect to His Highness, in his capacity of Grand Caliph of Mahometanism, according to the precepts prescribed to them by their law, without compromising, nevertheless, the stability of their political and civil liberty. Russia leaves to this Tartar nation, with the exception of the fortresses of Kertach and Jenicale (with their districts and ports, which Russia retains for herself), all the towns, fortresses, dwellings, territories, and ports which it has conquered in Crimea and in Kuban; . . . the Sublime Ottoman Porte engages, in like manner, on its part, to abandon all right whatsoever which it might have over the fortresses, towns, habitations, etc., in Crimea, in Kuban, and in the island of Taman; to maintain in those places no garrison nor other armed forces, ceding these States to the Tartars in the same manner as the Court of Russia has done, that is to say, in full power and in absolute and independent sovereignty. In like manner the Sublime Porte engages, in the most solemn manner, and promises neither to introduce nor maintain, in future, any garrison or armed forces whatsoever in the above-mentioned towns, fortresses, lands, and habitations, nor, in the interior of those States, any intendant or military agent, of whatsoever denomination, but to leave all the Tartars in the same perfect liberty and independence in which the Empire of Russia leaves them.

*   *   *

ART. XI. For the convenience and advantage of the two Empires, there shall be a free and unimpeded navigation for the merchant ships belonging to the two Contracting Powers, in all the seas which wash their shores; the Sublime Porte grants to Russian merchant-vessels, namely, such as are universally employed by the other Powers for commerce and in the ports, a free passage from the Black Sea into the White Sea [the Mediterranean], and reciprocally from the White Sea into the Black Sea, as also the power of entering all the ports and harbours situated either on the sea-coasts, or in the passages and channels which join those seas. In like manner, the Sublime Porte allows Russian subjects to trade in its States by land as well as by water and upon the Danube in their ships, in conformity with what has been specified above in this Article, with all the same privileges and advantages as are enjoyed in its States by the most friendly nations, whom the Sublime Porte favours most in trade, such as the French and the English; and the capitulations of those two nations and others shall, just as if they were here inserted word for word, serve as a rule, under all circumstances and in every place, for whatever concerns commerce as well as Russian merchants, who upon paying the same duties may import and export all kinds of goods, and disembark their merchandise at every port and harbour as well upon the Black as upon the other Seas, Constantinople being expressly included in the number.*

---

*Source: J. C. Hurewitz, *Diplomacy in the Near and Middle East. A Documentary Record, 1535-1914*, Vol. I (Princeton, N.J.: D. Van Nostrand, 1956), pp. 54-61.

APPENDIX 2

Treaty between Great Britain and the Ottoman Empire (called Treaty of the Dardanelles)

January 5, 1809

[excerpt]

Article XI.—As ships of war have at all times been prohibited from entering the Canal of Constantinople, viz., in the Straits of the Dardanelles and of the Black Sea, and as this ancient regulation of the Ottoman Empire is in future to be observed by every Power in time of peace, the Court of

Great Britain promises on its part to conform to this principle.*

---

*Source: Department of State, United States of America, *The Problem of the Turkish Straits* (Washington, D.C.: U.S. Government Printing Office, 1947), p. 15.

APPENDIX 3

Treaty of Defensive Alliance between Russia and the Ottoman Empire

September 11/23, 1805

[excerpts]

(Secret) Article 7. (Noradounghian version)

ART. 7. The two contracting parties, having agreed on the closure of the Black Sea, declare that any attempt by any power whatsoever to violate it shall be considered a hostile act against them. Consequently, they pledge to oppose with all their naval forces the entrance into that sea of every vessel of war and every ship carrying military stores.

(Secret) Article 7. (Russian version)

ART. 7. The two high contracting parties agree to consider the Black Sea as closed and not to permit the appearance therein of any flag of war or armed vessel of any power whatsoever, and if any should attempt to appear there in arms, the two high contracting parties undertake to regard such an attempt as a *casus foederis* and to oppose it with all their naval forces, as being the only means of assuring their mutual tranquillity; it is understood that the free passage through the canal of Constantinople will continue in effect for the vessels of war and military transports of His Imperial Majesty of All the Russias, to which in each instance the Sublime Porte will furnish every assistance and grant every facility that may be required.*

---

*Source: J. C. Hurewitz, *Diplomacy in the Near and Middle East. A Documentary Record, 1535-1914*, Vol. I (Princeton, N.J.: D. Van Nostrand, 1956), pp. 72-77. The two versions of the secret Article 7 were taken from G. Noradounghian (ed.), *Receuil d'actes internationaux de l'Empire Ottoman...*, Vol. 2 (Paris: F. Pichon, 1897), pp. 70-77; and Serge M. Goriainov, *Le Bosphore et les Dardanelles. Etude historique sur la question des Détroits, d'après la correspondance diplomatique deposée aux Archives centrales de Saint-Petersbourg et à celles de l'Empire* (Paris: Plan-Nourrit, 1910), p. 6.

APPENDIX 4

Treaty of Defensive Alliance (of Hünkâr Iskelesi) between the Ottoman Empire and Russia

June 26/July 8, 1833

[excerpts]

ART. 1. There shall be for ever peace, amity, and alliance between His Majesty the Emperor of all the Russias and His Majesty the Emperor of the Ottomans, their empires and their subjects, as well by land as by sea. This alliance having solely for its object the common defence of their dominions against all attack, their Majesties engage to come to an unreserved understanding with each other upon all the matters which concern their respective tranquillity and safety, and to afford to each other mutually for this purpose substantial aid, and the most efficacious assistance.

* * *

ART. 3. In consequence of the principle of conservation and mutual defence, which is the basis of the present Treaty of Alliance, and by reason of a most sincere desire of securing the permanence, maintenance, and entire independence of the Sublime Porte, his Majesty the Emperor of all the Russias, in the event of circumstances occurring which should again determine the Sublime Porte to call for the naval and military assistance of Russia, although, if it please God, that case is by no means likely to happen, engages to furnish, by land and by sea, as many troops and forces as the two high contracting parties may deem necessary. It is accordingly agreed, that in this case the land and sea forces, whose aid the Sublime Porte may call for, shall be held at its disposal.

* * *

ART. 5. Although the two high contracting parties sincerely intend to maintain this engagement to the most distant period of time, yet, as it is possible that in process of time circumstances may require that some changes should be made in this Treaty, it has been agreed to fix its duration at eight years from the day of the exchange of the Imperial Ratifications. The two parties, previously to the expiration of that term, will concert together, according to the state of affairs at that time, as to the renewal of the said Treaty. . . .

SEPARATE AND SECRET ARTICLE

In virtue of one of the clauses of the first Article of the Patent Treaty of Defensive Alliance concluded between the Imperial Court of Russia and the Sublime Porte, the two high contracting parties are bound to afford to each other mutually substantial aid, and the most efficacious assistance for the safety of their respective dominions. Nevertheless, as his

Majesty the Emperor of all the Russias, wishing to spare the Sublime Ottoman Porte the expense and inconvenience which might be occasioned to it, by affording substantial aid, will not ask for that aid if circumstances should place the Sublime Porte under the obligation of furnishing it, the Sublime Ottoman Porte, in the place of the aid which it is bound to furnish in case of need, according to the principle of reciprocity of the Patent Treaty, shall confine its action in favour of the Imperial Court of Russia to closing the strait of the Dardanelles, that is to say, to not allowing any foreign vessels of war to enter therein under any pretext whatsoever [sic].

The present Separate and Secret Article shall have the same force and value as if it was inserted word for word in the Treaty of Alliance of this day.*

---

*Source: J. C. Hurewitz, *Diplomacy in the Near and Middle East. A Documentary Record, 1535-1914*, Vol. I (Princeton, N.J.: D. Van Nostrand, 1956), pp. 105-6.

APPENDIX 5

Convention of London Regarding the Straits between Austria, France, Great Britain, Prussia, Russia, and the Ottoman Empire

July 13, 1841

[complete text]

ART. I. His Highness the Sultan, on the one part, declares that he is firmly resolved to maintain for the future the principle invariably established as the ancient rule of his Empire, and in virtue of which it has at all times been prohibited for the Ships of War of Foreign Powers to enter the Straits of the

Dardanelles and of the Bosphorus; and that, so long as the Porte is at peace, His Highness will admit no foreign Ship of War into the said Straits.

And their Majesties the Queen of the United Kingdom of Great Britain and Ireland, the Emperor of Austria, King of Hungary and Bohemia, the King of the French, the King of Prussia, and the Emperor of all the Russias, on the other part, engage to respect this determination of the Sultan, and to conform themselves to the principle above declared.

ART. II. It is understood that in recording the inviolability of the ancient rule of the Ottoman Empire mentioned in the preceding Article, the Sultan reserves to himself, as in past times, to deliver firmans of passage for light vessels under flag of war, which shall be employed as is usual in the service of the Missions of foreign Powers.

ART. III. His Highness the Sultan reserves to himself to communicate the present Convention to all the Powers with whom the Sublime Porte is in relations of friendship, inviting them to accede thereto.*

---

*Source: United States Department of State, *The Problem of the Turkish Straits* (Washington, D.C.: U.S. Government Printing Office, 1947), p. 17; J. C. Hurewitz, *Diplomacy in the Near and Middle East. A Documentary Record. 1535-1914*, Vol. I (Princeton, N.J.: D. Van Nostrand, 1956), p. 123.

APPENDIX 6

**Treaty of Peace of Paris between Great Britain, France,
Austria, Prussia, Sardinia, ~~and~~ the Ottoman Empire, *and Russia,*
with the Annexed Convention Regarding the Straits**

March 30, 1856

[excerpts]

Article X. The Convention of 13th July, 1841, which maintains the ancient rule of the Ottoman Empire relative to the closing of the Straits of the Bosphorus and of the Dardanelles, has been revised by common consent.

The Act concluded for that purpose, and in conformity with that principle, between the High Contracting Parties is and remains annexed to the present Treaty, and shall have the same force and validity as if it formed an integral part thereof.

Article XI. The Black Sea is neutralized: its waters and its ports, thrown open to the mercantile marine of every nation, are formally and in perpetuity interdicted to the flag of war, either of the Powers possessing its coasts, or of any other Power, with the exceptions mentioned in Articles XIV and XIX of the present treaty.

Article XII. Free from any impediment, the commerce in the ports and waters of the Black Sea shall be subject only to regulations of health, customs, and police, framed in a spirit favorable to the development of commercial transactions.

In order to afford to the commercial and maritime interests of every nation the security which is desired, Russia and the Sublime Porte will admit Consuls in to their ports situated upon the coast of the Black Sea, in conformity with the principles of international law.

Article XIII. The Black Sea being neutralized according to the terms of Article XI, the maintenance or establishment upon its coast of military-maritime arsenals becomes alike unnecessary and purposeless; in consequence, His Majesty the Emperor of all the Russias and His Imperial Majesty the Sultan engage not to establish or to maintain upon that coast any military-maritime arsenal.

Article XIV. Their Majesties the Emperor of all the Russias and the Sultan having concluded a Convention for the purpose of settling the force and the number of light vessels necessary for the service of their coasts, which they reserve to themselves to maintain in the Black Sea, that Convention is annexed to the present Treaty, and shall have the same force and validity as if it formed an integral part thereof. It cannot be either annulled or modified without the assent of the Powers signing the present Treaty.

Article XIX. In order to insure the execution of the regulations which shall have been established by common agreement, in conformity with the principles above declared, each of the Contracting Powers shall have the right to station, at all times, two light vessels at the mouths of the Danube.

Additional and Transitory Article.—The stipulations of the Convention respecting the Straits, signed this day, shall not be applicable to the vessels of war employed by the belligerent Powers for the evacuation, by sea, of the territories occupied by their armies; but the said stipulations shall resume their entire effect as soon as the evacuation shall be terminated.

ANNEXED CONVENTION REGARDING THE STRAITS

Article I. His Majesty the Sultan on the one part, declares that he is firmly resolved to maintain for the future the principle invariably established as the ancient rule of his Empire, and in virtue of which it has, at all times, been prohibited for the ships of war of foreign Powers to enter the Strait of the

Dardanelles and of the Bosphorus; and that, so long as the Porte is at peace, His Majesty shall admit no foreign ship of war into the said Straits.

And their Majesties the Queen of the United Kingdom of Great Britain and Ireland, the Emperor of Austria, the Emperor of the French, the King of Prussia, the Emperor of all the Russias, and the King of Sardinia, on the other part, engage to respect this determination of the Sultan, and to conform themselves to the principle above declared.

Article II. The Sultan reserves to himself, as in past times, to deliver firmans of passage for light vessels under flag of war, which shall be employed, as is usual, in the service of the Missions of foreign Powers.

Article III. The same exception applies to the light vessels under flag of war which each of the Contracting Powers is authorized to station at the mouths of the Danube in order to secure the execution of the regulations relative to the liberty of that river, and the number of which is not to exceed two for each Power.*

---

*Source: United States Department of State, *The Problem of the Turkish Straits*, (Washington, D.C.: U.S. Government Printing Office, 1947), pp. 17-18.

APPENDIX 7

Convention of London for the Revision of Certain Clauses in the Paris Peace Treaty of 1856 between Great Britain, Austria, France, Germany (Prussia), Italy (Sardinia), Russia, and the Ottoman Empire

March 13, 1871

[excerpts]

Article I. Articles XI, XIII, and XIV of the Treaty of Paris of March 30, 1856, as well as the special Convention concluded between Russia and the Sublime Porte, and annexed to the said Article XIV, are abrogated, and replaced by the following Article.

Article II. The principle of the closing of the Straits of the Dardanelles and the Bosphorus, such as it has been established by the separate Convention of March 30, 1856, is maintained, with power to His Imperial Majesty the Sultan to open the said Straits in time of peace to the vessels of war of friendly and allied Powers, in case the Sublime Porte should judge it necessary in order to secure the execution of the stipulations of the Treaty of Paris of March 30, 1856.

Article III. The Black Sea remains open, as heretofore, to the mercantile marine of all nations.*

---

*Source: United States Department of State, *The Problem of the Turkish Straits* (Washington, D.C.: U.S. Government Printing Office, 1947), p. 18.

APPENDIX 8

Secret Agreements Regarding Constantinople and the Straits between Great Britain and Russia, and between France and Russia

March 4 - April 10, 1915

Aide-Mémoire FROM RUSSIAN FOREIGN MINISTER TO BRITISH AND FRENCH AMBASSADORS AT PETROGRAD, 19 FEBRUARY/4 MARCH 1915

The course of recent events leads His Majesty Emperor Nicholas to think that the question of Constantinople and of the Straits must be definitively solved, according to the time-honored aspirations of Russia.

Every solution will be inadequate and precarious if the city of Constantinople, the western bank of the Bosphorus, of the Sea of Marmara and of the Dardanelles, as well as southern Thrace to the Enez-Midye line, should henceforth not be incorporated into the Russian Empire.

Similarly, and by strategic necessity, that part of the Asiatic shore that lies between the Bosphorus, the Sakarya River, and a point to be determined on the Gulf of Izmit, and the islands of the Sea of Marmara, the Imbros Islands, and the Tenedos Islands must be incorporated into the [Russian] Empire.

The special interests of France and of Great Britain in the above region will be scrupulously respected.

The Imperial Government entertains the hope that the above considerations will be sympathetically received by the two Allied Governments. The said Allied Governments are assured similar understanding on the part of the Imperial Government for the realization of plans which they may frame with reference to other regions of the Ottoman Empire or elsewhere.

BRITISH *Aide-Mémoire* TO THE RUSSIAN GOVERNMENT, 27 FEBRUARY/12 MARCH 1915

Subject to the war being carried on and brought to a successful conclusion, and to the desiderata of Great Britain and France in the Ottoman Empire and elsewhere being realised, as indicated in the Russian communication herein referred to, His Majesty's Government will agree to the Russian Government's *aide-mémoire* relative to Constantinople and the Straits, the text of which was communicated to His Britannic Majesty's Ambassador by his Excellency M. Sazonof on February 19th/March 4th instant.

BRITISH MEMORANDUM TO THE RUSSIAN GOVERNMENT, 27 FEBRUARY/12 MARCH 1915

His Majesty's Ambassador has been instructed to make the following observations with reference to the *aide-mémoire* which this Embassy had the honour of addressing to the Imperial Government on February 27/March 12, 1915.

The claim made by the Imperial Government in their *aide-mémoire* of February 19/March 4, 1915, considerably exceeds the desiderata which were foreshadowed by M. Sazonof as probable a few weeks ago. Before His Majesty's Government have had time to take into consideration what their own desiderata elsewhere would be in the final terms of peace, Russia is asking for a definite promise that her wishes shall be satisfied with regard to what is in fact the richest prize of the entire war. Sir Edward Grey accordingly hopes that M. Sazonof will realise that it is not in the power of His Majesty's Government to give a greater proof of friendship than that which is afforded by the terms of the above-mentioned *aide-mémoire*. That document involves a complete reversal of the traditional policy of His Majesty's Government, and is in direct opposition to the opinions and sentiments at one time universally held in England and which have still by no means died out. Sir Edward Grey therefore trusts that the Imperial Government will recognise that the recent general assurances given to M. Sazonof have been most loyally and amply fulfilled. In presenting the *aide-mémoire* now, His Majesty's Government believe and hope that a lasting friendship between Russia and Great Britain will be assured as soon as the proposed settlement is realised.

From the British *aide-mémoire* it follows that the desiderata of His Majesty's Government, however important they may be to British interests in other parts of the world, will contain no condition which could impair Russia's control over the territories described in the Russian *aide-mémoire* of February 19/March 4, 1915.

In view of the fact that Constantinople will always remain a trade *entrepôt* for South-Eastern Europe and Asia Minor, His Majesty's Government will ask that Russia shall, when she comes into possession of it, arrange for a free port for goods in transit to and from non-Russian territory. His Majesty's Government will also ask that there shall be commercial freedom for merchantships passing through the Straits, as M. Sazonof has already promised.

Except in so far as the naval and military operations on which His Majesty's Government are now engaged in the Dardanelles may contribute to the common cause of the Allies, it is now clear that these operations, however successful, cannot be of any advantage to His Majesty's Government in the final terms of peace. Russia alone will, if the war is successful, gather the direct fruits of these operations. Russia should therefore, in the opinion of His Majesty's Government, not now put difficulties in the way of any Power which may, on reasonable terms, offer to co-operate with the Allies. The only Power likely to participate in the operations in the Straits is Greece. Admiral Carden has asked the Admiralty to send him more destroyers, but they have none to spare. The assistance of a Greek flotilla, if it could have been secured, would thus have been of inestimable value to His Majesty's Government.

To induce the neutral Balkan States to join the Allies was one of the main objects which His Majesty's Government had in view when they undertook the operations in the Dardanelles. His Majesty's Government hope that Russia will spare no pains to calm the apprehensions of Bulgaria and Roumania as to Russia's possession of the Straits and Constantinople being to their disadvantage. His Majesty's Government also hope that Russia will do everything in her power to render the co-operation of these two States an attractive prospect to them.

Sir E. Grey points out that it will obviously be necessary to take into consideration the whole question of the future interests of France and Great Britain in what is now Asiatic Turkey; and, in formulating the desiderata of His Majesty's Government with regard to the Ottoman Empire, he must consult the French as well as the Russian Government. As soon, however, as it becomes known that Russia is to have Constantinople at the conclusion of the war, Sir E. Grey will wish to state that throughout the negotiations, His Majesty's Government have stipulated that the Mussulman Holy Places and Arabia shall under all circumstances remain under independent Mussulman dominion.

Sir E. Grey is as yet unable to make any definite proposal on any point of the British desiderata; but one of the points of the latter will be the revision of the Persian portion of the Anglo-Russian Agreement of 1907 so as to recognise the present neutral sphere as a British sphere.

Until the Allies are in a position to give to the Balkan States, and especially to Bulgaria and Roumania, some satisfactory assurance as to their prospects and general position with regard to the territories contiguous to their frontiers to the possession of which they are known to aspire; and until a more advanced stage of the agreement as to the French and British desiderata in the final peace terms is reached, Sir E. Grey points out that it is most desirable that the understanding now arrived at between the Russian, French, and British Governments should remain secret.

RUSSIAN FOREIGN MINISTER TO RUSSIAN AMBASSADOR IN PARIS, 5/18 MARCH 1915

On 23 February [8 March 1915] the Ambassador of France declared to me, in the name of his Government, that France was prepared to consider in the most benevolent manner the realization of our desires relative to Constantinople and the Straits, which I explained to you in my telegram No. 937 and for which I charged you to express my gratitude to M. Delcassé. In these earlier conversations with you Delcassé had assured us several times that we could count on the sympathy of France and had simply pleaded the necessity of elucidating the attitude of England, from whom he feared objections, before he could himself give more formal assurances in the sense already indicated.

Now, today, the British Government has expressed to us in writing its full accord in the matter of the annexation by Russia of the Straits and Constantinople within the boundaries fixed by us; it has simply formulated one reservation concerning the safeguard of its economic interests and an equally benevolent attitude on our part toward the political aspirations of England in other areas.

Insofar as it concerns me personally, the assurance received from Delcassé is amply sufficient, because of the complete confidence that he inspires in me; but the Imperial Government would desire the French Government to issue more precise declarations like [those of the] British Government regarding its assent to the complete realization of our desires.

RUSSIAN FOREIGN MINISTER TO RUSSIAN AMBASSADOR IN LONDON, 7/20 MARCH 1915 [excerpt]

Referring to the memorandum of the British Embassy here of 12 March, will you please express to Grey the profound gratitude of the Imperial Government for the complete and definitive approval of Great Britain to a solution of the question of the Straits and Constantinople that satisfies Russia's desires. The Imperial Government appreciates fully the sentiments of the British Government and is convinced that the sincere recognition of their respective interests will guarantee in perpetuity firm friendship between Russia and Great Britian. Having already given assurances respecting the commercial regime in the Straits and Constantinople, the Imperial Government sees no objection to confirming its assent to the establishment (1) of free transit through Constantinople for all goods not deriving from or destined for Russia and (2) free passage through the Straits for merchant vessels.

With a view to facilitating the capture of the Dardanelles undertaken by the Allies, the Imperial Government will endeavor to obtain the intervention on reasonable terms of those states whose help is considered useful by Great Britain and France. . . .

Note *Verable,* FROM FRENCH AMBASSADOR AT PETROGRAD TO RUSSIAN FOREIGN MINISTER, 28 MARCH/10 APRIL 1915

The Government of the [French] Republic will give its agreement to the Russain *aide-mémoire* addressed by M. Isvolsky to M. Delcassé on 6 March last [Doc. 1, above], relating to Constantinople and the Straits, on condition that war shall be prosecuted until victory and that France and Great Britain realise their plans in the Orient as elsewhere, as it is stated in the Russian *aide-mémoire.* *

---

*Source: J. C. Hurewitz, *Diplomacy in the Near and Middle East. A Documentary Record, 1914-1956*, Vol. II (Princeton, N.J.: D. Van Nostrand, 1956), pp. 7-11.

APPENDIX 9

Treaty of Friendship between Turkey and the Russian Socialist Federated Soviet Republic

March 16, 1921

[excerpt]

Article V.—In order to assure the opening of the Straits to the commerce of all nations, the contracting parties agree to entrust the final elaboration of an international agreement concerning the Black Sea to a conference composed of delegates of the littoral States, on condition that the decisions of the above-mentioned conference shall not be of such a nature as to diminish the full sovereignty of Turkey or the security of Constantinople, her capital.*

---

*Source: Department of State, United States of America, *The Problem of the Turkish Straits* (Washington, D.C.: U.S. Government Printing Office, 1947), p. 21.

APPENDIX 10

Convention Relating to the Regime of the Straits (Lausanne Convention) Concluded between the British Empire, France, Italy, Japan, Bulgaria, Greece, Rumania, Soviet Russia, Yugoslavia, and Turkey

July 24, 1923

[partial text]

Article 1.—The High Contracting Parties agree to recognize and declare the principle of freedom of transit and of navigation by sea and by air in the Strait of the Dardanelles, the Sea of Marmora and the Bosphorus, hereinafter comprised under the general term of the "Straits."

Article 2.—The transit and navigation of commercial vessels and aircraft, and of war vessels and aircraft in the Straits in time of peace and in time of war shall henceforth be regulated by the provisions of the attached Annex.

ANNEX. RULES FOR THE PASSAGE OF COMMERCIAL VESSELS AND AIRCRAFT, AND OF WAR VESSELS AND AIRCRAFT THROUGH THE STRAITS

1. *Merchant Vessels, Including Hospital Ships, Yachts and Fishing Vessels, and Non-Military Aircraft.*

(*a*) *In Time of Peace.*

Complete freedom of navigation and passage by day and by night under any flag and with any kind of cargo, without any formalities, or tax, or charge whatever (subject, however, to international sanitary provisions) unless for services directly rendered, such as pilotage, light, towage or other similar charges, and without prejudice to the rights exercised in this respect by the services and undertakings now operating under concessions granted by the Turkish Government.

To facilitate the collection of these dues, merchant vessels passing the Straits will communicate to stations appointed by the Turkish Government their name, nationality, tonnage, and destination.

(b) *In Time of War, Turkey Being Neutral.*

Complete freedom of navigation and passage by day and by night under the same conditions as above. The duties and rights of Turkey as a neutral Power cannot authorise her to take any measures liable to interfere with navigation through the Straits, the waters of which, and the air above which, must remain entirely free in time of war, Turkey being neutral just as in time of peace.

Pilotage remains optional.

(c) In Time of War, Turkey Being a Belligerent

Freedom of navigation for neutral vessels and neutral non-military aircraft, if the vessel or aircraft in question does not assist the enemy, particularly by carrying contraband, troops or enemy nationals. Turkey will have the right to visit and search such vessels and aircraft, and for this purpose aircraft are to alight on the ground or on the sea in such areas as are specified and prepared for this purpose by Turkey. The rights of Turkey to apply to enemy vessels the measures allowed by international law are not affected.

Turkey will have full power to take such measures as she may consider necessary to prevent enemy vessels from using the Straits. These measures, however, are not to be of such a nature as to prevent the free passage of neutral vessels, and Turkey agrees to provide such vessels with either the necessary instructions or pilots for the above purpose.

2. *Warships, Including Fleet Auxiliaries, Troopships, Aircraft Carriers, and Military Aircraft.*

(a) *In Time of Peace.*

Complete freedom of passage by day and by night under any flag, without any formalities, or tax, or charge whatever, but subject to the following restrictions as to the total force:

The maximum force which any one Power may send through the Straits into the Black Sea is not to be greater than that of the most powerful fleet of the littoral Powers of the Black Sea existing in that sea at the time of passage; but with the proviso that the Powers reserve to themselves the right to send into the Black Sea at all times and under all circumstances, a force of not more than three ships, of which no individual ship shall exceed 10,000 tons.

Turkey has no responsibility in regard to the number of war vessels which pass through the Straits.

In order to enable the above rule to be observed the Straits Commission provided for in Article 10 will, on the 1st January and the 1st July of each year, enquire of each Black Sea littoral Power the number of each of the following classes of vessel which such Power possess in the Black Sea: Battleships, battlecruisers, aircraft carriers, cruisers, destroyers, submarines, or other types of vessels as well as naval aircraft; distinguishing between the ships which are in active commission and the ships with reduced complements, the ships in reserve and the ships undergoing repairs or alterations.

The Straits Commission will then inform the Powers concerned that the strongest naval force in the Black Sea comprises: Battleships, battle cruisers, aircraft carriers, cruisers, destroyers, submarines, aircraft, and units of other types which may exist. The Straits Commission will also immediately inform the Powers concerned when, owing to the passage into or out of the Black Sea of any ship of the strongest Black Sea force, any alteration in that force has taken place.

The naval force that may be sent through the Straits into

the Black Sea will be calculated on the number and type of the ships of war in active commission only.

(*b*) *In Time of War, Turkey Being Neutral.*

Complete freedom of passage by day and by night under any flag, without any formalities, or tax, or charge whatever, under the same limitations as in paragraph 2 (*a*).

However, these limitations will not be applicable to any belligerent Power to the prejudice of its belligerent rights in the Black Sea.

The rights and duties of Turkey as a neutral Power cannot authorise her to take any measures liable to interfere with navigation through the Straits, the waters of which, and the air above which, must remain entirely free in time of war, Turkey being neutral, just as in time of peace.

Warships and military aircraft of belligerents will be forbidden to make any capture, to exercise the right of visit and search, or to carry out any other hostile act in the Straits.

As regards revictualling and carrying out repairs, war vessels will be subject to the terms of the Thirteenth Hague Convention of 1907, dealing with maritime neutrality.

Military aircraft will receive in the Straits similar treatment to that accorded under the Thirteenth Hague Convention of 1907 to warships, pending the conclusion of an international Convention establishing the rules of neutrality for aircraft.

(*c*) *In Time of War, Turkey Being Belligerent.*

Complete freedom of passage for neutral warships, without any formalities, or tax, or charge whatever, but under the same limitations as in paragraph 2(*a*).

The measures taken by Turkey to prevent enemy ships and aircraft from using the Straits are not to be of such a nature as to prevent the free passage of neutral ships and aircraft, and Turkey agrees to provide the said ships and aircraft with either the necessary instructions or pilots for the above purpose.

Neutral military aircraft will make the passage of the Straits at their own risk and peril, and will submit to investigation as to their character. For this purpose aircraft are to alight on the ground or on the sea in such areas as are specified and prepared for this purpose by Turkey.

3. (*a*) The passage of the Straits by submarines of Powers at peace with Turkey must be made on the surface.

(*b*) The officer in command of a foreign naval force, whether coming from the Mediterranean or the Black Sea, will communicate, without being compelled to stop, to a signal station at the entrance to the Dardanelles or the Bosphorus, the number and the names of vessels under his orders which are entering the Straits.

These signal stations shall be notified from time to time by Turkey; until such signal stations are notified, the freedom of passage for foreign war vessels in the Straits shall not thereby be prejudiced, nor shall their entry into the Straits be for this reason delayed.

(*c*) The right of military and non-military aircraft to fly over the Straits, under the conditions laid down in the present rules, necessitates for aircraft—

(i) Freedom to fly over a strip of territory of five kilometres wide on each side of the narrow parts of the Straits;

(ii) Liberty, in the event of a forced landing, to alight on the coast or on the sea in the territorial waters of Turkey.

4. *Limitation of Time of Transit for Warships.*

In no event shall warships in transit through the Straits, except in the event of damage or peril of the sea, remain therein beyond the time which is necessary for them to effect their passage, including the time of anchorage during the night if necessary for safety of navigation.

5. *Stay in the Ports of the Straits and of the Black Sea.*

(*a*) Paragraphs 1, 2, and 3 of this Annex apply to the passage of vessels, warships and aircraft through and over the Straits and do not affect the right of Turkey to make such regulations as she may consider necessary regarding the number of men-of-war and military aircraft of any one Power which may visit Turkish ports or aerodromes at one time, and the duration of their stay.

(*b*) Littoral Powers of the Black Sea will also have a similar right as regards their ports and aerodromes.

(*c*) The light-vessels which the Powers at present represented on the European Commission of the Danube maintain as *stationnaires* at the mouths of that river as far up as Galatz will be regarded as additional to the men-of-war referred to in paragraph 2, and may be replaced in case of need.

6. *Special Provisions Relating to Sanitary Protection.*

Warships which have on board cases of plague, cholera, or typhus, or which have had such cases on board during the last seven days, and warships which have left an infected port within less than five times 24 hours must pass through the Straits in quarantine and apply by the means on board such prophylactic measures as are necessary to prevent any possibility of the Straits being infected.

The same rule shall apply to merchant ships having a doctor on board and passing straight through the Straits without calling at a port or breaking bulk.

Merchant ships not having a doctor on board shall be obliged to comply with the international sanitary regulations before entering the Straits, even if they are not to call at a port therein.

Warships and merchant vessels calling at one of the ports in the Straits shall be subject in that port to the international sanitary regulations applicable in the port in question.

Article 3.—With a view to maintaining the Straits free from any obstacle to free passage and navigation, the provisions contained in Articles 4 to 9 will be applied to the waters and shores thereof as well as to the islands situated therein, or in the vicinity.

Article 4.—The zones and islands indicated below shall be demilitarised:

1. Both shores of the Straits of the Dardanelles and the Bosphorus over the extent of the zones delimited below. . . :

Dardanelles:

On the north-west, the Gallipoli Peninsula and the area southeast of a line traced from a point on the Gulf of Xeros 4 kilometres northeast of Bakla-Burnu, reaching the Sea of Marmora at Kunbaghi and passing south of Kavak (this village excluded);

On the south-east, the area included between the coast and a line 20 kilometres from the coast, starting from Cape Eski-Stamboul opposite Tenedos and reaching the Sea of Marmora at a point on the coast immediately north of Karabigha.

Bosphorus (without prejudice to the special provisions relating to Constantinople contained in Article 8):

On the east, the area extending up to a line 15 kilometres from the eastern shore of the Bosphorus;

On the west, the area up to a line 15 kilometres from the western shore of the Bosphorus.

2. All the islands in the Sea of Marmora, with the exception of the island of Emir Ali Adasi.

3. In the Aegean Sea, the islands of Samothrace, Lemnos, Imbros, Tenedos, and Rabbit Islands.

Article 5.—A Commission composed of four representatives appointed respectively by the Governments of France,

Great Britain, Italy and Turkey shall meet within 15 days of the coming into force of the present Convention to determine on the spot the boundaries of the zone laid down in Article 4(1).

The Governments represented on that Commission will pay the salaries of their respective representatives.

Any general expenses incurred by the Commission shall be borne in equal shares by the Powers represented thereon.

Article 6. —Subject to the provisions of Article 8 concerning Constantinople, there shall exist, in the demilitarised zones and islands, no fortifications, no permanent artillery organisation, no submarine engines of war other than submarine vessels, no military aerial organisation, and no naval base.

No armed forces shall be stationed in the demilitarised zones and islands except the police and gendarmerie forces necessary for the maintenance of order; the armament of such forces will be composed only of revolvers, swords, rifles and four Lewis guns per hundred men, and will exclude any artillery.

In the territorial waters of the demilitarised zones and islands, there shall exist no submarine engines of war other than submarine vessels.

Notwithstanding the preceding paragraphs Turkey will retain the right to transport her armed forces through the demilitarised zones and islands of Turkish territory, as well as through their territorial waters, where the Turkish fleet will have the right to anchor.

Moreover, in so far as the Straits are concerned, the Turkish Government shall have the right to observe by means of aeroplanes or balloons both the surface and the bottom of the sea. Turkish aeroplanes will always be able to fly over the waters of the Straits and the demilitarised zones of Turkish territory, and will have full freedom to alight therein, either on land or on sea.

In the demilitarised zones and islands and in their territorial waters, Turkey and Greece shall similarly be entitled to effect such movements of personnel as are rendered necessary for the instruction outside these zones and islands of the men recruited therein.

Turkey and Greece shall have the right to organize in the said zones and islands in their respective territories any system of observation and communication, both telegraphic, telephonic, and visual. Greece shall be entitled to send her fleet into the territorial waters of the demilitarised Greek islands, but may not use these waters as a base of operations against Turkey nor for any military or naval concentration for this purpose.

Article 7.—No submarine engines of war other than submarine vessels shall be installed in the waters of the Sea of Marmora.

The Turkish Government shall not install any permanent battery or torpedo tubes, capable of interfering with the passage of the Straits, in the coastal zone of the European shore of the Sea of Marmora or in the coastal zone of the Anatolian shore situated to the east of the demilitarised zone of the Bosphorus as far as Darije.

Article 8.—At Constantinople, including for this purpose Stamboul, Pera, Galata, Scutari, as well as the Princes Islands, and in the immediate neighbourhood of Constantinople, there may be maintained for the requirements of the capital, a garrison with a maximum strength of 12,000 men. An arsenal and naval base may also be maintained at Constantinople.

Article 9.—If, in case of war, Turkey, or Greece, in pursuance of their belligerent rights, should modify in any way the provisions of demilitarisation prescribed above, they will be bound to re-establish as soon as peace is concluded the regime laid down in the present Convention.

Article 10.—There shall be constituted at Constantinople an International Commission composed in accordance with Article 12 and called the "Straits Commission."

Article 11.—The Commission will exercise its functions over the waters of the Straits.

Article 12.—The Commission shall be composed of a representative of Turkey, who shall be President, and representatives of France, Great Britain, Italy, Japan, Bulgaria, Greece, Roumania, Russia, and the Serb-Croat-Slovene State, in so far as these Powers are signatories of the present Convention, each of these Powers being entitled to representation as from its ratification of the said Convention.

The United States of America, in the event of their acceding to the present Convention, will also be entitled to have one representative on the Commission.

Under the same conditions any independent littoral States of the Black Sea which are not mentioned in the first paragraph of the present Article will possess the same right.

Article 13.—The Governments represented on the Commission will pay the salaries of their representatives. Any incidental expenditure incurred by the Commission will be borne by the said Governments in the proportion laid down for the division of the expenses of the League of Nations.

Article 14.—It will be the duty of the Commission to see that the provisions relating to the passage of warships and military aircraft are carried out; these provisions are laid down in paragraphs 2, 3, and 4 of the Annex to Article 2.

Article 15.—The Straits Commission will carry out its functions under the auspices of the League of Nations, and will address to the League an annual report giving an account of its activities, and furnishing all information which may be useful in the interests of commerce and navigation; with this object in view the Commission will place itself in touch with the departments of the Turkish Government dealing with navigation through the Straits.

Article 16. – It will be the duty of the Commission to prescribe such regulations as may be necessary for the accomplishment of its task.

Article 17. – The terms of the present Convention will not infringe the right of Turkey to move her fleet freely in Turkish waters.

Article 18. – The High Contracting Parties, desiring to secure that the demilitarisation of the Straits and of the contiguous zones shall not constitute an unjustifiable danger to the military security of Turkey, and that no act of war should imperil the freedom of the Straits or the safety of the demilitarised zones, agree as follows:

Should the freedom of navigation of the Straits or the security of the demilitarised zones be imperilled by a violation of the provisions relating to freedom of passage, or by a surprise attack or some act of war or threat of war, the High Contracting Parties, and in any case France, Great Britain, Italy, and Japan, acting in conjunction, will meet such violation, attack, or other act of war or threat of war, by all the means that the Council of the League of Nations may decide for this purpose.

So soon as the circumstances which may have necessitated the action provided for in the preceding paragraph shall have ended, the regime of the Straits as laid down by the terms of the present Convention shall again be strictly applied.

The present provision, which forms an integral part of those relating to the demilitarisation and to the freedom of the Straits, does not prejudice the rights and obligations of the High Contracting Parties under the Covenant of the League of Nations.

Article 19.–The High Contracting Parties will use every possible endeavour to induce non-signatory Powers to accede to the present Convention.

This adherence will be notified through the diplomatic channel to the Government of the French Republic, and by that Government to all signatory or adhering States. The adherence will take effect as from the date of notification to the French Government.

Article 20.–The present Convention shall be ratified. The ratifications shall be deposited at Paris as soon as possible. . . .*

---

*Source: *League of Nations Treaty Series*, Vol. XXVIII (1924), pp. 115-37.

APPENDIX 11

Note of the Turkish Government Addressed to the Signatories of the Lausanne Convention

April 10, 1936

[complete text]

In 1923, when Turkey agreed at Lausanne to sign the Straits Convention prescribing freedom of transit and demilitarization, the general situation of Europe, from the political and military point of view, presented an aspect totally different from that of to-day.

Europe was progressing towards disarmament, and the political organization of Europe was to be based solely on the unchanging principles of law embodied in international engagements. The land, naval, and air forces were much less formidable and were showing a tendency towards decrease. At that time, Turkey signed the restrictive clauses of the Straits Convention. She had the assurance given her by Article 18, which added to the guarantee afforded by Article 10 of the Covenant of the League of Nations an undertaking that the signatories, and in any case four great Powers, conjointly undertook, by all the means decided upon for that purpose by the Council of the League, the defence of the Straits if threatened.

Since then, the situation in the Black Sea has come to present an aspect of concord which has been reassuring in every respect. Uncertainty has gradually arisen, however, in the Mediterranean; naval conferences have shown a tendency towards rearmament, and the naval shipyards will soon launch upon the seas vessels of a power never previously attained. In the air, the curve of increase has shown a swift upward turn, and continental and insular fortifications are constantly being multiplied.

During this complete change of conditions the only guarantee intended to guard against the total insecurity of the Straits has just disappeared in its turn, and while the Powers most closely concerned are proclaiming the existence of a threat of general conflagration, Turkey finds herself exposed at her most vulnerable point to the worst dangers without any counterpart for this disquieting insecurity.

In response to the urgent demands addressed to her, Turkey accepted the demilitarization of the Straits, then wholly occupied by foreign forces, after having very fully considered, in the existing conditions, the value of the minimum guarantees granted to her in order that the demilitarization of the Straits and of the contiguous zones should not constitute an unjustifiable danger to the military security of Turkey.

To Article 18 of the Convention, which provided a guarantee of security indissolubly bound up with the body of clauses regulating the regime of the Straits, the signatories attached such importance that they solemnly affirmed that the guarantee in question formed an integral part of the clauses regarding demilitarization and freedom of transit.

This means that without an effective, practical, and efficacious assurance, Turkey's sovereignty could not have been diminished over a portion of her territory the security of which is indispensable to that of the country as a whole.

It is also evident that if this guarantee becomes inoperative or uncertain, the equilibrium of the whole Convention is overthrown, to the prejudice of Turkey and to that of European peace.

Political crises have made it clear that the present machinery for collective guarantees is too slow in coming into operation and that a delayed decision is likely in most cases to cause the advantage of international action to be lost. It was for this reason that Turkey in 1923, like many other Powers at the present time, could not be content with the collective guarantee which would be ensured to her by the Covenant on her becoming a Member of the League of Nations; that she considered the collective guarantee of all the signatories of the Straits Convention insufficient; and that only the conjoint guarantee of the four great Powers seemed to her calculated to ensure in the conditions then existing the minimum of security indispensable for her territorial integrity.

But, if this minimum itself is weakened or rendered problematical by political and military circumstances entirely different from those which existed when the security was given, the Government of the Republic cannot, without being guilty of serious negligence, expose the whole country to an irreparable *coup de main*.

The position of the guarantors of the security of the Straits *vis-à-vis* the League of Nations, the particular circumstances which render doubtful, to say the least, the effective military collaboration of these guarantors to secure the object assigned to them—these factors have upset the general economy of the Convention of 1923.

It cannot be said to-day that the security of the Straits is still ensured by a real guarantee, and Turkey cannot be asked to remain indifferent to the possibility of a dangerous failure to act.

Besides these considerations it should be added that the Straits Convention mentions only a state of peace and a state of war, Turkey being a neutral or a belligerent in the latter case, but does not provide for the contingency of a special or general threat of war or enable Turkey in such a case to provide for her legitimate defence.

It is amply proved to-day, however, that the most delicate stage of danger from without is this very stage of a threat of war in which a state of war may arise unexpectedly and without any formality.

This omission may in itself render the guarantees contemplated ineffective, whatever their value.

From the beginning of its existence the Turkish Republic has followed a policy of peace and understanding, the carrying-out of which in every field has necessarily imposed upon her sacrifices, often heavy sacrifices.

The Turkish Government has shown, in the many circumstances which have arisen in the last decade, a spirit of conciliation, of loyalty to her engagements, and of sincere attachment to the cause of peace, which has been appreciated by all the Powers. Turkey is entitled to claim for herself the security which she has always ensured to others.

Circumstances independent of the will of the Lausanne signatories, have rendered inoperative clauses which were drawn up in all good faith, and as the issue at stake is the existence of Turkey herself and the security of her whole territory, the Government of the Republic may be led to take before the nation the responsibility incumbent upon it by adopting the measures dictated by the imperious necessity of circumstances.

In view of the above considerations, and rightly holding that the provisions of Article 18 of the Straits Convention relating to a joint guarantee of the four great Powers have become uncertain and inoperative and that they can no longer in practice shield Turkey from an external danger to her territory, the Government of the Republic has the honour to inform the Powers which took part in the negotiations for the conclusion of the Straits Convention that it is prepared to enter into negotiations with a view to arriving in the near future at the conclusion of agreements for regulation of the régime of the Straits under the conditions of security which are indispensable for the inviolability of Turkey's territory, in the most liberal spirit, for the constant development of commercial navigation between the Mediterranean and the Black Sea.

TEVFIK RÜŞTÜ ARAS,
Turkish Minister for Foreign Affairs*

---

*Source: *Documents on International Affairs, 1936* (London: Oxford University Press [for the Royal Institute of International Affairs], 1937), pp. 645-48.

APPENDIX 12

Convention Regarding the Regime of the Straits (Montreux Convention) between Bulgaria, France, Great Britain (also on Behalf of Parts of the British Empire Not Represented at the Montreux Conference), Australia, Greece, Japan, Rumania, Turkey, Union of Soviet Socialist Republics, and Yugoslavia

July 20, 1936

[complete text]

HIS MAJESTY THE KING OF THE BULGARIANS, THE PRESIDENT OF THE FRENCH REPUBLIC, HIS MAJESTY THE KING OF GREAT BRITAIN, IRELAND AND THE BRITISH DOMINIONS BEYOND THE SEAS, EMPEROR OF INDIA, HIS MAJESTY THE KING OF THE HELLENES, HIS MAJESTY THE EMPEROR OF JAPAN, HIS MAJESTY THE KING OF ROUMANIA, THE PRESIDENT OF THE TURKISH REPUBLIC, THE CENTRAL EXECUTIVE COMMITTEE OF THE UNION OF SOVIET SOCIALIST REPUBLICS, AND HIS MAJESTY THE KING OF YUGOSLAVIA:

Desiring to regulate transit and navigation in the Straits of the Dardanelles, the Sea of Marmora and the Bosphorus comprised under the general term "Straits" in such manner as to safeguard, within the framework of Turkish security and of the security, in the Black Sea, of the riparian States, the principle enshrined in Article 23 of the Treaty of Peace signed at Lausanne on the 24th July 1923;

Have resolved to replace by the present Convention the Convention signed at Lausanne on the 24th July, 1923, and have appointed as their Plenipotentiaries:

HIS MAJESTY THE KING OF THE BULGARIANS:
  Dr. Nicolas P. NICOLAEV, Minister Plenipotentiary, Secretary-General of the Ministry of Foreign Affairs and of Cults;
  M. Pierre NEÏCOV, Minister Plenipotentiary, Director of Political Affairs at the Ministry of Foreign Affairs and of Cults;

THE PRESIDENT OF THE FRENCH REPUBLIC:
  M. PAUL-BONCOUR, Senator, Permanent Delegate of France to the League of Nations, former President of the Council, former Minister for Foreign Affairs, Chevalier of the Legion of Honour, Croix de Guerre;
  M. Henri PONSOT, Ambassador Extraordinary and Plenipotentiary of the French Republic at Angora, Grand Officer of the Legion of Honour;

HIS MAJESTY THE KING OF GREAT BRITAIN, IRELAND AND THE BRITISH DOMINIONS BEYOND THE SEAS, EMPEROR OF INDIA:

FOR GREAT BRITAIN AND NORTHERN IRELAND AND ALL PARTS OF THE BRITISH EMPIRE WHICH ARE NOT SEPARATE MEMBERS OF THE LEAGUE OF NATIONS:
  The Right Honourable Lord STANLEY, P.C., M.C., M.P., Parliamentary Secretary to the Admiralty;

FOR THE COMMONWEALTH OF AUSTRALIA:
  The Right Honourable Stanley Melbourne BRUCE, C.H., M.C., High Commissioner for the Commonwealth of Australia in London;

HIS MAJESTY THE KING OF THE HELLENES:
  M. Nicolas POLITIS, Envoy Extraordinary and Minister Plenipotentiary of Greece in Paris, former Minister for Foreign Affairs;

M. Raoul BIBICA ROSETTI, Permanent Delegate of Greece to the League of Nations;

HIS MAJESTY THE EMPEROR OF JAPAN:
M. Naotake SATO, Jusammi, Grand-Cordon of the Order of the Rising Sun, Ambassador Extraordinary and Plenipotentiary in Paris;
M. Massa-aki HOTTA, Jushii, Second Class of the Order of the Rising Sun, Envoy Extraordinary and Minister Plenipotentiary at Berne;

HIS MAJESTY THE KING OF ROUMANIA:
M. Nicolas TITULESCO, Minister Secretary of State for the Department of Foreign Affairs;
M. Constantin CONTZESCO, Minister Plenipotentiary, Delegate of Roumania to the European and International Commissions of the Danube;
M. Vespasien PELLA, Envoy Extraordinary and Minister Plenipotentiary at The Hague;

THE PRESIDENT OF THE TURKISH REPUBLIC:
Dr. Rüştü ARAS, Minister for Foreign Affairs, Deputy for Smyrna;
M. Suad DAVAZ, Ambassador Extraordinary and Plenipotentiary of the Turkish Republic in Paris;
M. Numan MENEMENÇIOĞLU, Ambassador of Turkey, Secretary-General of the Ministry for Foreign Affairs;
M. Asim GÜNDÜZ, General Commanding an Army Corps, Deputy Chief of the General Staff;
M. Necmeddin SADAK, Permanent Delegate of Turkey to the League of Nations, Deputy for Sivas, *Rapporteur* for the Committee of Foreign Affairs;

THE CENTRAL EXECUTIVE COMMITTEE OF THE UNION OF SOVIET SOCIALIST REPUBLICS:
M. Maxime LITVINOFF, Member of the Central Executive

Committee of the Union of Soviet Socialist Republics, People's Commissar for Foreign Affairs;

HIS MAJESTY THE KING OF YUGOSLAVIA:
M. Ivan SOUBBOTITCH, Permanent Delegate of the Kingdom of Yugoslavia to the League of Nations;

Who, after having exhibited their full powers, found in good and due form, have agreed on the following provisions;

Article 1.

The High Contracting Parties recognise and affirm the principles of freedom of transit and navigation by sea in the Straits.

The exercise of this freedom shall henceforth be regulated by the provisions of the present Convention.

SECTION I.
MERCHANT VESSELS.

Article 2.

In time of peace, merchant vessels shall enjoy complete freedom of transit and navigation in the Straits, by day and by night, under any flag and with any kind of cargo, without any formalities, except as provided in Article 3 below. No taxes or charges other than those authorised by Annex I to the present Convention shall be levied by the Turkish authorities on these vessels when passing in transit without calling at a port in the Straits.

In order to facilitate the collection of these taxes or charges merchant vessels passing through the Straits shall communicate to the officials at the stations referred to in Article 3 their name, nationality, tonnage, destination, and last port of call (provenance).

Pilotage and towage remain optional.

Article 3.

All ships entering the Straits by the AEgean Sea or by the Black Sea shall stop at a sanitary station near the entrance to the Straits for the purposes of the sanitary control prescribed by Turkish law within the framework of international sanitary regulations. This control, in the case of ships possessing a clean bill of health or presenting a declaration of health testifying that they do not fall within the scope of the provisions of the second paragraph of the present Article, shall be carried out by day and by night with all possible speed, and the vessels in question shall not be required to make any other stop during their passage through the Straits.

Vessels which have on board cases of plague, cholera, yellow fever, exanthematic typhus, or smallpox, or which have had such cases on board during the previous seven days, and vessels which have left an infected port within less than five times twenty-four hours shall stop at the sanitary stations indicated in the preceding paragraph in order to embark such sanitary guards as the Turkish authorities may direct. No tax or charge shall be levied in respect of these sanitary guards and they shall be disembarked at a sanitary station on departure from the Straits.

Article 4.

In time of war, Turkey not being belligerent, merchant vessels, under any flag or with any kind of cargo, shall enjoy freedom of transit and navigation in the Straits subject to the provisions of Articles 2 and 3.

Pilotage and towage remain optional.

Article 5.

In time of war, Turkey being belligerent, merchant vessels not belonging to a country at war with Turkey shall enjoy freedom of transit and navigation in the Straits on condition that they do not in any way assist the enemy.

Such vessels shall enter the Straits by day and their transit shall be effected by the route which shall in each case be indicated by the Turkish authorities.

Article 6.

Should Turkey consider herself to be threatened with imminent danger of war, the provisions of Article 2 shall nevertheless continue to be applied except that vessels must enter the Straits by day and that their transit must be effected by the route which shall, in each case, be indicated by the Turkish authorities.

Pilotage may, in this case, be made obligatory, but no charge shall be levied.

Article 7.

The term "merchant vessels" applies to all vessels which are not covered by Section II of the present Convention.

SECTION II.
VESSELS OF WAR.

Article 8.

For the purposes of the present Convention, the definitions of vessels of war and of their specification together with those relating to the calculation of tonnage shall be as set forth in Annex II to the present Convention.

Article 9.

Naval auxiliary vessels specifically designed for the carriage of fuel, liquid or non-liquid, shall not be subject to the provisions of Article 13 regarding notification, nor shall they be counted for the purpose of calculating the tonnage which is subject to limitation under Articles 14 and 18, on condition that they shall pass through the Straits singly. They shall, however, continue to be on the same footing as vessels of war for the purpose of the remaining provisions governing transit.

The auxiliary vessels specified in the preceding paragraph shall only be entitled to benefit by the exceptional status therein contemplated if their armament does not include: for use against floating targets, more than two guns of a maximum calibre of 105 millimetres; for use against aerial targets, more than two guns of a maximum calibre of 75 millimetres.

Article 10.

In time of peace, light surface vessels, minor war vessels and auxiliary vessels, whether belonging to Black Sea or non-Black Sea Powers, and whatever their flag, shall enjoy freedom of transit through the Straits without any taxes or charges whatever, provided that such transit is begun during daylight and subject to the conditions laid down in Article 13 and the Articles following thereafter.

Vessels of war other than those which fall within the categories specified in the preceding paragraph shall only enjoy a right of transit under the special conditions provided by Articles 11 and 12.

Article 11.

Black Sea Powers may send through the Straits capital ships of a tonnage greater than that laid down in the first paragraph of Article 14, on condition that these vessels pass through the Straits singly, escorted by not more than two destroyers.

Article 12.

Black Sea Powers shall have the right to send through the Straits, for the purpose of rejoining their base, submarines constructed or purchased outside the Black Sea, provided that adequate notice of the laying down or purchase of such submarines shall have been given to Turkey.

Submarines belonging to the said Powers shall also be entitled to pass through the Straits to be repaired in dockyards outside the Black Sea on condition that detailed information on the matter is given to Turkey.

In either case, the said submarines must travel by day and on the surface, and must pass through the Straits singly.

Article 13.

The transit of vessels of war through the Straits shall be preceded by a notification given to the Turkish Government through the diplomatic channel. The normal period of notice shall be eight days; but it is desirable that in the case of non-Black Sea Powers this period should be increased to fifteen days. The notification shall specify the destination, name, type and number of the vessels, as also the date of entry for the outward passage and, if necessary, for the return journey. Any change of date shall be subject to three days' notice.

Entry into the Straits for the outward passage shall take place within a period of five days from the date given in the original notification. After the expiry of this period, a new notification shall be given under the same conditions as for the original notification.

When effecting transit, the commander of the naval force shall, without being under any obligation to stop, communicate to a signal station at the entrance to the Dardanelles or the Bosphorus the exact composition of the force under his orders.

Article 14.

The maximum aggregate tonnage of all foreign naval forces which may be in course of transit through the Straits shall not exceed 15,000 tons, except in the cases provided for in Article 11 and in Annex III to the present Convention.

The forces specified in the preceding paragraph shall not, however, comprise more than nine vessels.

Vessels, whether belonging to Black Sea or non-Black Sea Powers, paying visits to a port in the Straits, in accordance with the provisions of Article 17, shall not be included in this tonnage.

Neither shall vessels of war which have suffered damage during their passage through the Straits be included in this tonnage; such vessels, while undergoing repair, shall be subject to any special provisions relating to security laid down by Turkey.

Article 15.

Vessels of war in transit through the Straits shall in no circumstances make use of any aircraft which they may be carrying.

Article 16.

Vessels of war in transit through the Straits shall not, except in the event of damage or peril of the sea, remain therein longer than is necessary for them to effect the passage.

Article 17.

Nothing in the provisions of the preceding Articles shall prevent a naval force of any tonnage or composition from paying a courtesy visit of limited duration to a port in the Straits, at the invitation of the Turkish Government. Any such force must leave the Straits by the same route as that by which it entered, unless it fulfils the conditions required for passage in transit through the Straits as laid down by Articles 10, 14 and 18.

Article 18.

(1) The aggregate tonnage which non-Black Sea Powers may have in that sea in time of peace shall be limited as follows:

(*a*) Except as provided in paragraph (*b*) below, the aggregate tonnage of the said Powers shall not exceed 30,000 tons;

(*b*) If at any time the tonnage of the strongest fleet in the Black Sea shall exceed by at least 10,000 tons the

tonnage of the strongest fleet in that sea at the date of the
signature of the present Convention, the aggregate tonnage
of 30,000 tons mentioned in paragraph (*a*) shall be increased by the same amount, up to a maximum of 45,000
tons. For this purpose, each Black Sea Power shall, in conformity with Annex IV to the present Convention, inform
the Turkish Government, on the 1st January and the 1st
July of each year, of the total tonnage of its fleet in the
Black Sea; and the Turkish Government shall transmit this
information to the other High Contracting Parties and to
the Secretary-General of the League of Nations;

(*c*) The tonnage which any one non-Black Sea Power
may have in the Black Sea shall be limited to two-thirds of
the aggregate tonnage provided for in paragraphs (*a*) and
(*b*) above;

(*d*) In the event, however, of one or more non-Black
Sea Powers desiring to send naval forces into the Black Sea,
for a humanitarian purpose, the said forces, which shall in
no case exceed 8,000 tons altogether, shall be allowed to
enter the Black Sea without having to give the notification
provided for in Article 13 of the present Convention, provided an authorisation is obtained from the Turkish Government in the following circumstances: if the figure of the
aggregate tonnage specified in paragraphs (*a*) and (*b*) above
has not been reached and will not be exceeded by the
despatch of the forces which it is desired to send, the Turkish Government shall grant the said authorisation within
the shortest possible time after receiving the request which
has been addressed to it; if the said figure has already been
reached or if the despatch of the forces which it is desired
to send will cause it to be exceeded, the Turkish Government will immediately inform the other Black Sea Powers
of the request for authorisation, and if the said Powers
make no objection within twenty-four hours of having
received this information, the Turkish Government shall,

within forty-eight hours at the latest, inform the interested Powers of the reply which it has decided to make to their request.

Any further entry into the Black Sea of naval forces of non-Black Sea Powers shall only be effected within the available limits of the aggregate tonnage provided for in paragraphs (*a*) and (*b*) above.

(2) Vessels of war belonging to non-Black Sea Powers shall not remain in the Black Sea more than twenty-one days, whatever be the object of their presence there.

Article 19.

In time of war, Turkey not being belligerent, warships shall enjoy complete freedom of transit and navigation through the Straits under the same conditions as those laid down in Articles 10 to 18.

Vessels of war belonging to belligerent Powers shall not, however, pass through the Straits except in cases arising out of the application of Article 25 of the present Convention, and in cases of assistance rendered to a State victim of aggression in virtue of a treaty of mutual assistance binding Turkey, concluded within the framework of the Covenant of the League of Nations, and registered and published in accordance with the provisions of Article 18 of the Covenant.

In the exceptional cases provided for in the preceding paragraph, the limitations laid down in Articles 10 to 18 of the present Convention shall not be applicable.

Notwithstanding the prohibition of passage laid down in paragraph 2 above, vessels of war belonging to belligerent Powers, whether they are Black Sea Powers or not, which have become separated from their bases, may return thereto.

Vessels of war belonging to belligerent Powers shall not make any capture, exercise the right of visit and search, or carry out any hostile act in the Straits.

Article 20.

In time of war, Turkey being belligerent, the provisions of Articles 10 to 18 shall not be applicable; the passage of war-ships shall be left entirely to the discretion of the Turkish Government.

Article 21.

Should Turkey consider herself to be threatened with imminent danger of war she shall have the right to apply the provisions of Article 20 of the present Convention.

Vessels which have passed through the Straits before Turkey has made use of the powers conferred upon her by the preceding paragraph, and which thus find themselves separated from their bases, may return thereto. It is, however, understood that Turkey may deny this right to vessels of war belonging to the State whose attitude has given rise to the application of the present Article.

Should the Turkish Government make use of the powers conferred by the first paragraph of the present Article, a notification to that effect shall be addressed to the High Contracting Parties and to the Secretary-General of the League of Nations.

If the Council of the League of Nations decide by a majority of two-thirds that the measures thus taken by Turkey are not justified, and if such should also be the opinion of the majority of the High Contracting Parties signatories to the present Convention, the Turkish Government undertake to discontinue the measures in question as also any measures which may have been taken under Article 6 of the present Convention.

Article 22.

Vessels of war which have on board cases of plague, cholera, yellow fever, exathematic typhus or smallpox or which have had such cases on board within the last seven days, and vessels of war which have left an infected port within less than five times twenty-four hours must pass through the Straits in quarantine and apply by the means on board such prophylactic measures as are necessary in order to prevent any possibility of the Straits being infected.

SECTION III.
AIRCRAFT.

Article 23.

In order to assure the passage of civil aircraft between the Mediterranean and the Black Sea, the Turkish Government will indicate the air routes available for this purpose, outside the forbidden zones which may be established in the Straits. Civil aircraft may use these routes provided that they give the Turkish Government, as regards occasional flights, a notification of three days, and as regards flights on regular services, a general notification of the dates of passage.

The Turkish Government moreover undertake, notwithstanding any remilitarisation of the Straits, to furnish the necessary facilities for the safe passage of civil aircraft authorised under the air regulations in force in Turkey to fly across Turkish territory between Europe and Asia. The route which is to be followed in the Straits zone by aircraft which have obtained an authorisation shall be indicated from time to time.

SECTION IV.
GENERAL PROVISIONS.

Article 24.

The functions of the International Commission set up under the Convention relating to the régime of the Straits of the 24th July, 1923, are hereby transferred to the Turkish Government.

The Turkish Government undertake to collect statistics

and to furnish information concerning the application of Articles 11, 12, 14 and 18 of the present Convention.

They will supervise the execution of all the provisions of the present Convention relating to the passage of vessels of war through the Straits.

As soon as they have been notified of the intended passage through the Straits of a foreign naval force the Turkish Government shall inform the representatives at Angora of the High Contracting Parties of the composition of that force, its tonnage, the date fixed for its entry into the Straits, and, if necessary, the probable date of its return.

The Turkish Government shall address to the Secretary-General of the League of Nations and to the High Contracting Parties an annual report giving details regarding the movements of foreign vessels of war through the Straits and furnishing all information which may be of service to commerce and navigation, both by sea and by air, for which provision is made in the present Convention.

Article 25.

Nothing in the present Convention shall prejudice the rights and obligations of Turkey, or of any of the other High Contracting Parties members of the League of Nations, arising out of the Covenant of the League of Nations.

SECTION V.
FINAL PROVISIONS.

Article 26.

The present Convention shall be ratified as soon as possible.

The ratifications shall be deposited in the archives of the Government of the French Republic in Paris.

The Japanese Government shall be entitled to inform the Government of the French Republic through their diplomatic representative in Paris that the ratification has been given, and in that case they shall transmit the instrument of ratification as soon as possible.

A *procès-verbal* of the deposit of ratifications shall be drawn up as soon as six instruments of ratification, including that of Turkey, shall have been deposited. For this purpose the notification provided for in the preceding paragraph shall be taken as the equivalent of the deposit of an instrument of ratification.

The present Convention shall come into force on the date of the said *procès-verbal*.

The French Government will transmit to all the High Contracting Parties an authentic copy of the *procès-verbal* provided for in the preceding paragraph and of the *procès-verbaux* of the deposit of any subsequent ratifications.

Article 27.

The present Convention shall, as from the date of its entry into force, be open to accession by any Power signatory to the Treaty of Peace at Lausanne signed on the 24th July, 1923.

Each accession shall be notified, through the diplomatic channel, to the Government of the French Republic, and by the latter to all the High Contracting Parties.

Accessions shall come into force as from the date of notification to the French Government.

Article 28.

The present Convention shall remain in force for twenty years from the date of its entry into force.

The principle of freedom of transit and navigation affirmed in Article 1 of the present Convention shall however continue without limit of time.

If, two years prior to the expiry of the said period of twenty years, no High Contracting Party shall have given notice of denunciation to the French Government the present Convention shall continue in force until two years after such notice shall have been given. Any such notice shall be communicated by the French Government to the High Contracting Parties.

In the event of the present Convention being denounced in accordance with the provisions of the present Article, the High Contracting Parties agree to be represented at a conference for the purpose of concluding a new Convention.

Article 29.

At the expiry of each period of five years from the date of the entry into force of the present Convention each of the High Contracting Parties shall be entitled to initiate a proposal for amending one or more of the provisions of the present Convention.

To be valid, any request for revision formulated by one of the High Contracting Parties must be supported, in the case of modifications to Articles 14 or 18, by one other High Contracting Party, and, in the case of modifications to any other Article, by two other High Contracting Parties.

Any request for revision thus supported must be notified to all the High Contracting Parties three months prior to the expiry of the current period of five years. This notification shall contain details of the proposed amendments and the reasons which have given rise to them.

Should it be found impossible to reach an agreement on these proposals through the diplomatic channel, the High Contracting Parties agree to be represented at a conference to be summoned for this purpose.

Such a conference may only take decisions by a unanimous vote, except as regards cases of revision involving Articles 14 and 18, for which a majority of three-quarters of the High Contracting Parties shall be sufficient.

The said majority shall include three-quarters of the High Contracting Parties which are Black Sea Powers, including Turkey.

In witness whereof, the above-mentioned Plenipotentiaries have signed the present Convention.

Done at Montreux the 20th July, 1936, in eleven copies, of which the first copy, to which the seals of the Plenipotentiaries have been affixed, will be deposited in the archives of the Government of the French Republic and of which the remaining copies have been transmitted to the signatory Powers.

(L.S.) N. P. NICOLAEV.
(L.S.) Pierre NEICOV.
(L.S.) J. PAUL-BONCOUR.
(L.S.) H. PONSOT.
(L.S.) STANLEY.
(L.S.) S. M. BRUCE.
(L.S.) N. POLITIS.
(L.S.) Raoul BIBLICA ROSETTI.

The undersigned, Plenipotentiaries of Japan, declare, in the name of their Government, that the provisions of the present Convention do not in any sense modify the position of Japan as a State not a member of the League of Nations, whether in relation to the Covenant of the League of Nations or in regard to treaties of mutual assistance concluded within the framework of the said Covenant, and that in particular Japan reserves full liberty of interpretation as regards the provisions of Articles 19 and 25 so far as they concern that Covenant and those treaties.

(L.S.) N. SATO.
(L.S.) Massa-aki HOTTA.
(L.S.) N. TITULESCO.
(L.S.) Cons. CONTZESCO.
(L.S.) V. V. PELLA.
(L.S.) Dr. R. ARAS.
(L.S.) Suad DAVAZ.
(L.S.) N. MENEMENCIOĞLU.
(L.S.) Asim GÜNDÜZ.
(L.S.) N. SADAK.
(L.S.) Maxime LITVINOFF.
(L.S.) Dr. I. V. SOUBBOTITCH.

ANNEX I.

The taxes and charges which may be levied in accordance with Article 2 of the present Convention shall be those set forth in the following table. Any reductions in these taxes or charges which the Turkish Government may grant shall be applied without any distinction based on the flag of the vessel:

Nature of service rendered	Amount of tax or charge to be levied on each ton of net register tonnage
	Francs gold
(*a*) Sanitary Control Stations	0.075
(*b*) Lighthouses, Light and Channel Buoys:	
Up to 800 tons	0.42
Above 800 tons	0.21
(*c*) Life Saving Services, including Lifeboats, Rocket Stations, Fog Sirens, Direction-finding Stations, and any Light Buoys not comprised in (*b*) above, or other similar installations . .	0.10

2. The taxes and charges set forth in the table attached to paragraph 1 of the present Annex shall apply in respect of a return voyage through the Straits (that is to say, a voyage from the AEgean Sea to the Black Sea and return back to the AEgean Sea or else a voyage through the Straits from the Black Sea to the AEgean Sea followed by a return voyage into the Black Sea); if, however, a merchant vessel re-enters the Straits with the object of returning into the AEgean Sea or to the Black Sea, as the case may be, more than six months after the date of entry into the Straits for the outward voyage, such vessel may be called upon to pay these taxes and charges a second time, provided no distinction is made based on the flag of the vessel.

3. If, on the outward voyage, a merchant vessel declares an intention of not returning, it shall only be obliged as regards the taxes and charges provided for in paragraphs (*b*) and (*c*) of the first paragraph of the present Annex, to pay half the tariff indicated.

4. The taxes and charges set forth in the table attached to the first paragraph of the present Annex, which are not to be greater than is necessary to cover the cost of maintaining the services concerned and of allowing for the creation of a reasonable reserve fund or working balance, shall not be increased or added to except in accordance with the provisions of Article 29 of the present Convention. They shall be payable in gold francs or in Turkish currency at the rate of exchange prevailing on the date of payment.

5. Merchant vessels may be required to pay taxes and charges for optional services, such as pilotage and towage, when any such service shall have been duly rendered by the Turkish authorities at the request of the agent or master of any such vessel. The Turkish Government will publish from time to time the tariff of the taxes and charges to be levied for such optional services.

6. These tariffs shall not be increased in cases in the event of the said services being made obligatory by reason of the application of Article 5.

ANNEX II.

A. STANDARD DISPLACEMENT.

(1) The standard displacement of a surface vessel is the displacement of the vessel, complete, fully manned, engined, and equipped ready for sea, including all armament and ammunition, equipment, outfit, provisions and fresh water for crew, miscellaneous stores and implements of every description that are intended to be carried in war, but without fuel or reserve feed water on board.

(2) The standard displacement of a submarine is the surface displacement of the vessel complete (exclusive of the water in non-watertight structure), fully manned, engined and equipped ready for sea, including all armament and ammunition, equipment, outfit, provisions for crew, miscellaneous stores and implements of every description that are intended to be carried in war, but without fuel, lubricating oil, fresh water or ballast water of any kind on board.

(3) The word "ton" except in the expression "metric tons" denotes the ton of 2,240 lb (1,016 kilos).

B. CATEGORIES.

(1) *Capital Ships* are surface vessels of war belonging to one of the two following sub-categories:

(*a*) Surface vessels of war, other than aircraft-carriers, auxiliary vessels, or capital ships of sub-category (*b*), the standard displacement of which exceeds 10,000 tons (10,160 metric tons) or which carry a gun with a calibre exceeding 8 in. (203 mm.);

(*b*) Surface vessels of war, other than aircraft-carriers, the standard displacement of which does not exceed 8,000 tons (8,128 metric tons) and which carry a gun with a calibre exceeding 8 in. (203 mm.).

(2) *Aircraft-Carriers* are surface vessels of war, whatever their displacement, designed or adapted primarily for the purpose of carrying and operating aircraft at sea. The fitting of a landing-on or flying-off deck on any vessel of war, provided such vessel has not been designed or adapted primarily for the purpose of carrying and operating aircraft at sea, shall not cause any vessel so fitted to be classified in the category of aircraft-carriers.

The category of aircraft-carriers is divided into two sub-categories as follows:

(*a*) Vessels fitted with a flight deck, from which aircraft can take off, or on which aircraft can land from the air;

(*b*) Vessels not fitted with a flight deck as described in (*a*) above.

(3) *Light Surface Vessels* are surface vessels of war other than aircraft-carriers, minor war vessels or auxiliary vessels, the standard displacement of which exceeds 100 tons (102 metric tons) and does not exceed 10,000 tons (10,160 metric tons), and which do not carry a gun with a calibre exceeding 8 in. (203 mm.).

The category of light surface vessels is divided into three sub-categories as follows:

(*a*) Vessels which carry a gun with a calibre exceeding 6.1 in. (155 mm.);

(*b*) Vessels which do not carry a gun with a calibre exceeding 6.1 in. (155 mm.) and the standard displacement of which exceeds 3,000 tons (3,048 metric tons);

(*c*) Vessels which do not carry a gun with a calibre exceeding 6.1 in. (155 mm.) and the standard displacement of which does not exceed 3,000 tons (3,048 metric tons).

(4) *Submarines* are all vessels designed to operate below the surface of the sea.

(5) *Minor War Vessels* are surface vessels of war, other than auxiliary vessels, the standard displacement of which exceeds 100 tons (102 metric tons) and does not exceed 2,000 tons (2,032 metric tons), provided they have none of the following characteristics:

(*a*) Mount a gun with a calibre exceeding 6.1 in. (155 mm.);

(*b*) Are designed or fitted to launch torpedoes;

(*c*) Are designed for a speed greater than twenty knots.

(6) *Auxiliary Vessels* are naval surface vessels the standard displacement of which exceeds 100 tons (102 metric tons), which are normally employed on fleet duties or as troop transports, or in some other way than as fighting ships,

and which are not specifically built as fighting ships, provided they have none of the following characteristics:

(*a*) Mount a gun with calibre exceeding 6.1 in. (155 mm.);

(*b*) Mount more than eight guns with a calibre exceeding 3 in. (76 mm.);

(*c*) Are designed or fitted to launch torpedoes;

(*d*) Are designed for protection by armour plate;

(*e*) Are designed for a speed greater than twenty-eight knots;

(*f*) Are designed or adapted primarily for operating aircraft at sea;

(*g*) Mount more than two aircraft-launching apparatus.

C. OVER-AGE.

Vessels of the following categories and sub-categories shall be deemed to be "over-age" when the undermentioned number of years have elapsed since completion:

(*a*) Capital ships . . . . 26 years;
(*b*) Aircraft-carriers . . . . 20 years;
(*c*) Light surface vessels, sub-categories (*a*) and (*b*):
    (i) If laid down before 1st January, 1920 . 16 years;
    (ii) If laid down after 31st December, 1919 20 years;
(*d*) Light surface vessels, sub-category (*c*) . . . . 16 years;
(*e*) Submarines . . . . 13 years;

ANNEX III.

It is agreed that, of the three over-age training ships, as indicated below, belonging to the Japanese Fleet, two units may be allowed to visit ports in the Straits at the same time.

The aggregate tonnage of these two vessels shall in this case be considered as being equivalent to 15,000 tons.

	Date when laid down	Date of entry into Service	Standard displace- ment (tons)	Armaments
Asama	20-X-1896	18-III-1899	9,240	IVx200 mm. XIIx150 mm.
Yakumo ..	1-IX-1898	20-VI-1900	9,010	IVx200 mm. XIIx150 mm.
Iwate	11-XI-1898	18-III-1901	9,180	IVx200 mm. XIVx150 mm.

ANNEX IV.

1. The categories and sub-categories of vessels to be included in the calculation of the total tonnage of the Black Sea Powers provided for in Article 18 of the present Convention are the following:
    Capital Ships:
        Sub-category (*a*);
        Sub-category (*b*).
    Aircraft-Carriers:
        Sub-category (*a*);
        Sub-category (*b*).
    Light Surface Vessels:
        Sub-category (*a*);
        Sub-category (*b*);
        Sub-category (*c*).
    Submarines:
        As defined in Annex II to the present Convention.
The displacement which is to be taken into consideration in the calculation of the total tonnage is the standard displacement as defined in Annex II. Only those vessels shall be taken into consideration which are not over-age according to the definition contained in the said Annex.

2. The notification provided for in Article 18, paragraph (*b*), shall also include the total tonnage of vessels belonging to the categories and sub-categories mentioned in paragraph 1 of the present Annex.

PROTOCOL.

At the moment of signing the Convention bearing this day's date, the undersigned Plenipotentiaries declare for their respective Governments that they accept the following provisions:

(1) Turkey may immediately remilitarise the zone of the Straits as defined in the Preamble to the said Convention.

(2) As from the 15th August, 1936, the Turkish Government shall provisionally apply the régime specified in the said Convention.

(3) The present Protocol shall enter into force as from this day's date.

Done at Montreux, the 20th July, 1936.

N. P. NICOLAEV.
Piere NEÏCOV.
J. PAUL-BONCOUR.
H. PONSOT.
STANLEY.
S. M. BRUCE.
N. POLITIS.
Raoul BIBLICA ROSETTI.
N. SATO. (ad referendum)
Massa-aki HOTTA (ad referendum)
N. TITULESCO.
Cons. CONTZESCO.
V. V. PELLA.
Dr. R. ARAS.
Dr. R. ARAS.
Suad DAVAZ.
N. MENEMENCIOĞLU.
Asim GÜNDÜZ.
N. SADAK.
Maxime LITVINOFF.
Dr. I. V. SOUBBOTITCH.*

---

*Source: *League of Nations Treaty Series,* Vol. CLXXIII (1936), pp. 215-41.

APPENDIX 13

Draft Agreement between the Axis Powers (Germany,
Italy, and Japan) and the Soviet Union

Submitted to the Soviet People's Commissar for Foreign
Affairs, Vyacheslav M. Molotov, by the German Foreign
Minister, Joachim von Ribbentrop, during the former's
visit to Berlin on November 12-13, 1940

[complete text]

The Governments of the states of the Three Power Pact,
Germany, Italy and Japan, on the one side, and the Government of the U.S.S.R. on the other side, motivated by the
desire to establish in their natural spheres of influence in
Europe, Asia, and Africa a new order serving the welfare of
all peoples concerned and to create a firm and enduring foundation for their common labors toward this goal, have agreed
upon the following:

ART. I. In the Three Power Pact of Berlin, of September
27, 1940, Germany, Italy, and Japan agreed to oppose the
extension of the war into a world conflict with all possible
means and to collaborate toward an early restoration of
world peace. They expressed their willingness to extend their
collaboration to nations in other parts of the world which are
inclined to direct their efforts along the same course as theirs.
The Soviet Union declares that it concurs in these aims of the
Three Power Pact and is on its part determined to cooperate
politically in this course with the Three Powers.

ART. II. Germany, Italy, Japan, and the Soviet Union undertake to respect each other's natural spheres of influence.
In so far as these spheres of interest come into contact with
each other, they will constantly consult each other in an
amicable way with regard to the problems arising therefrom.

Germany, Italy, and Japan declare on their part that they recognize the present extent of the possessions of the Soviet Union and will respect it.

ART. III. Germany, Italy, Japan, and the Soviet Union undertake to join no combination of powers and to support no combination of powers which is directed against one of the Four Powers.

The Four Powers will assist each other in economic matters in every way and will supplement and extend the agreements existing among themselves.

ART. IV. This agreement shall take effect upon signature and shall continue for a period of ten years. The Governments of the Four Powers shall consult each other in due time, before the expiration of that period, regarding the extension of the agreement.

Draft. Secret Protocol No. 1

Upon the signing today of the Agreement concluded among them, the Representatives of Germany, Italy, Japan and the Soviet Union declare as follows:

1) Germany declares that, apart from the territorial revisions in Europe to be carried out at the conclusion of peace, her territorial aspirations center in the territories of Central Africa.

2) Italy declares that, apart from the territorial revisions in Europe to be carried out at the conclusion of peace, her territorial aspirations center in the territories of Northern and Northeastern Africa.

3) Japan declares that her territorial aspirations center in the area of Eastern Asia to the south of the Island Empire of Japan.

4) The Soviet Union declares that its territorial aspirations center south of the national territory of the Soviet Union in the direction of the Indian Ocean.

The Four Powers declare that, reserving the settlement of specific questions, they will mutually respect these territorial aspirations and will not oppose their achievement.

Draft. Secret Protocol No. 2 To be Concluded
Among Germany, Italy, and the Soviet Union

On the occasion of the signing today of the Agreement among Germany, Italy, Japan, and the Soviet Union, the Representatives of Germany, Italy and the Soviet Union declare as follows:

1) Germany, Italy, and the Soviet Union agree in the view that it is in their common interest to detach Turkey from her existing international commitments and progressively to win her over to political collaboration with themselves. They declare that they will pursue this aim in close consultation, with a common line of action which is still to be determined.

2) Germany, Italy, and the Soviet Union declare their agreement to conclude, at a given time, a joint agreement with Turkey, wherein the Three Powers would recognize the extent of Turkey's possessions.

3) Germany, Italy, and the Soviet Union will work in common toward the replacement of the Montreux Straits Convention now in force by another convention. By this convention the Soviet Union would be granted the right of unrestricted passage of its navy through the Straits at any time, whereas all other Powers except the other Black Sea countries, but including Germany and Italy, would in principle renounce the right of passage through the Straits for their naval vessels. The passage of commercial vessels through the Straits would, of course, have to remain free in principle.*

---

*Source: J. C. Hurewitz, *Diplomacy in the Near and Middle East: A Documentary Record, 1914-1956*, Vol. II (Princeton, N.J.: D. Van Nostrand, 1956), pp. 228-29.

APPENDIX 14

Soviet Counter-Draft Containing the Conditions of the USSR's Acceptance of the Four-Power Agreement

Submitted by German Ambassador Schulenburg to the German Foreign Office on November 26, 1940

[complete text]

For the Reich Minister in person.

Molotov asked me to call on him this evening [25 November 1940] and in the presence of Dekanosov stated the following:

The Soviet Government has studied the contents of the statements of the Reich Foreign Minister in the concluding conversation on November 13 and takes the following stand:

"The Soviet Government is prepared to accept the draft of the Four Power Pact which the Reich Foreign Minister outlined in the conversation of November 13, regarding political collaboration and reciprocal economic [support] subject to the following conditions:

"1) Provided that the German troops are immediately withdrawn from Finland, which, under the compact of 1939, belongs to the Soviet Union's sphere of influence. At the same time the Soviet Union undertakes to ensure peaceful relations with Finland and to protect German economic interests in Finland (export of lumber and nickel).

"2) Provided that within the next few months the security of the Soviet Union in the Straits is assured by the conclusion of a mutual assistance pact between the Soviet Union and Bulgaria, which geographically is situated inside the security zone of the Black Sea boundaries of the Soviet Union, and by the establishment of a base for land and naval forces of the

U.S.S.R. within range of the Bosphorus and the Dardanelles by means of a long-term lease.

"3) Provided that the area south of Batum and Baku in the general direction of the Persian Gulf is recognized as the center of the aspirations of the Soviet Union.

"4) Provided that Japan [renounces] her rights to concessions for coal and oil in Northern Sakhalin.

"In accordance with the foregoing, the draft of the protocol concerning the delimitation of the spheres of influence as outlined by the Reich Foreign Minister would have to be amended so as to stipulate the focal point of the aspirations of the Soviet Union south of Batum and Baku in the general direction of the Persian Gulf.

"Likewise, the draft of the protocol or agreement between Germany, Italy, and the Soviet Union with respect to Turkey should be amended so as to guarantee a base for light naval and land forces of the U.S.S.R. on [am] the Bosporus and the Dardanelles by means of a long-term lease, including—in case Turkey declares herself willing to join the Four Power Pact—a guarantee of the independence and of the territory of Turkey by the three countries named.

"This protocol should provide that in case Turkey refuses to join the Four Powers, Germany, Italy, and the Soviet Union agree to work out and to carry through the required military and diplomatic measures, and a separate agreement to this effect should be concluded.

"Furthermore there should be agreement upon:

"*a*) a third secret protocol between Germany and the Soviet Union concerning Finland (see Point 1 above).

"*b*) a fourth secret protocol between Japan and the Soviet Union concerning the renunciation by Japan of the oil and coal concession in Northern Sakhalin (in return for an adequate compensation).

"*c*) a fifth secret protocol between Germany, the Soviet Union, and Italy, recognizing that Bulgaria is geographically located inside the security zone of the Black Sea boundaries of the Soviet Union and that it is therefore a political necessity that a mutual assistance pact be concluded between the Soviet Union and Bulgaria, which in no way shall affect the internal regime of Bulgaria, her sovereignty or independence."

In conclusion Molotov stated that the Soviet proposal provided for five protocols instead of the two envisaged by the Reich Foreign Minister.*

---

*Source: J. C. Hurewitz, *Diplomacy in the Near and Middle East: A Documentary Record, 1914-1956*, Vol. II (Princeton, N.J.: D. Van Nostrand, 1956), p. 230.

APPENDIX 15

Briefing Paper Submitted by the Department of State to President Roosevelt Prior to the Conference at Yalta, 1945

No date

[complete text]

This Government hopes that *no* question regarding the Turkish Straits will be raised because:

(*a*) The Montreux Convention (signed July 20, 1936; signatories Belgium, France, Great Britain, Greece, Japan, Rumania, Turkey, U.S.S.R., Yugoslavia) has worked well, and the Soviet Government so declared to the Turks jointly with Great Britain on August 10, 1941. Non-use of the Straits as an avenue of supply to Russia during this war was due to Axis command of Rumania, Bulgaria, Greece, and the Aegean, not to the Montreux Convention.

(*b*) Any major changes in the regime of the Straits probably would violate Turkish sovereignty and affect adversely the strategic and political balance in the Balkans and the Near East. By and large Turkey has been a good custodian of the Straits.

(*c*) The Convention was drafted to fit into the League of Nations' collective security system and consequently can be adapted to the Dumbarton Oaks pattern.

This Government might not object if minor changes in the Convention are suggested by the U.S.S.R. (the Great Power primarily at interest), or Great Britain. Such proposals should, of course, be carefully considered by the Navy and War Departments.

No valid claim can be made for altering the Convention so far as merchant vessels are concerned, because, under its provisions, defensively armed merchant vessels of any flag, with any cargo, are free to transit the Straits subject to certain Turkish security provisions.

Under its terms the Montreux Convention can be reconsidered in 1946—it would be preferable to leave all changes until then and to have them made within the framework of the Convention itself.

"Internationalization" of the Straits is not a practical solution at this time because, if that is done, the Suez Canal and the Panama Canal logically should receive the same treatment. Turkey would strongly resist such a proposal.

If asked whether the United States would be willing to participate in a revised Montreux Convention in 1946 or some other future regime of the Straits, the reply might be that we, having in mind Dumbarton Oaks, would be prepared to give sympathetic consideration to the idea.

Note: Navy and War Departments concur with the above.*

---

*Source: United States, Department of State, *The Conferences at Malta and Yalta, 1945*, Foreign Relations of the United States, Diplomatic Papers, (Washington, D.C.: U.S. Government Printing Office, 1955), pp. 328-29. Footnotes omitted.

APPENDIX 16

Excerpt from the Minutes of the Yalta Conference Relating to the Discussion on the Turkish Straits Between President Roosevelt, British Prime Minister Churchill, and Marshal Stalin of the Soviet Union

February 10, 1945

*   *   *

MARSHAL STALIN then said that he would like to say a few words about the Montreux Convention regarding the Dardanelles. He said the treaty was now outmoded. As he recalled, the Japanese Emperor played a big part in the treaty, even greater than that of the Soviet Union. The treaty was linked with the League which does not exist just as the Japanese Emperor was not present at this Conference. Under the Montreux Convention the Turks have the right to close the Straits not only in time of war but if they feel that there is a threat of war. He said that the treaty was made at a time when the relations between Great Britain and the Soviet Union were not perfect, but he did not think now that Great Britain would wish to strangle Russia with the help of the Japanese. The treaty needed revision. He thought that there would be no objection to a consideration of the revision of that treaty. He said in what manner the treaty should be revised he did not know and he did not wish to prejudge any decisions, but he felt that the interests of Russia should be considered. He said that it was impossible to accept a situation in which Turkey had a hand on Russia's throat. He added, however, that it should be done in such a manner as not to harm the legitimate interests of Turkey. This was a question which an appropriate organization could consider and he thought that the three Foreign Ministers who were to meet periodically—every two or three months—might well consider this matter at their first meeting and report to their respective cabinets.

THE PRESIDENT said he had one general observation to make and that was that in the United States we had a frontier of over 3,000 miles with Canada and there was no fort and no armed forces. This situation had existed over a hundred years and it was his hope that other frontiers in the World would eventually be without forts or armed forces on any part of their national boundaries.

THE PRIME MINISTER said that Marshal Stalin had reminded them of the question of the Straits when they were in Moscow last autumn. They had said then that they were in sympathy with the revision of the treaty and had suggested to the Soviet Government that a note be sent on the subject but none has as yet been received. He said that he thought that the method proposed by Marshal Stalin was a wise one. The British certainly felt that the present position of Russia with their great interests in the Black Sea should not be dependent on the narrow exit. He said if the matter is brought up at the meeting with the Foreign Ministers he hoped the Russians would make their proposals known. In the meantime, it might be well to inform the Turks that the matter of revision of the Montreux Convention would be under consideration. This was particularly true if the Allies desired them to come into the war on their side. Mr. Eden reminded him that he had mentioned the matter several times to the Turkish Ambassador in London. He said it might be advisable to give the Turks at the same time some assurance that their independence and integrity will be guaranteed.

MARSHAL STALIN replied it was impossible to keep anything secret from the Turks and that such assurance should be expressed.

THE PRESIDENT agreed to this.

MARSHAL STALIN said the Foreign Ministers could meet at the United Nations Conference and discuss the question of the Straits.

THE PRIME MINISTER said that he thought that this matter affected the position of Great Britain in the Mediterranean more than it did that of the United States and that he felt that if the Foreign Ministers had a meeting in London that that would be the proper place to discuss this question. He went on to say that some years ago he had tried very hard to get through the Dardanelles and then the Russian Government had made available an armed force to help but it did not succeed.

MARSHAL STALIN said that the Prime Minister had been in too much of a hurry in withdrawing his troops since the Germans and Turks were on the verge of surrender.

THE PRIME MINISTER replied that by that time he was out of the government because of the Dardanelles campaign and had had nothing to do with that decision. . . .*

---

*Source: United States, Department of State, *The Conferences at Malta and Yalta, 1945*, Foreign Relations of the United States, Diplomatic Papers, (Washington, D.C.: U.S. Government Printing Office, 1955), pp. 903-5. Footnotes omitted.

APPENDIX 17

Excerpts from the Minutes of the Potsdam (Berlin) Conference Relating to the Discussion on the Turkish Straits between President Truman, Prime Minister Churchill, and Marshal Stalin (and People's Commissar for Foreign Affairs Molotov)

July 22, 23, 24, and 25, 1945

[July 22, 1945]

CHURCHILL said this was not the first time he had discussed this matter with Marshal Stalin. It became important because of the admitted need to modify the Montreux Convention. He had agreed with the Marshal in these discussions that insofar as the British Government was concerned they favored revision. Revision could only be made by agreement with the signatories with the exception, of course, of Japan. He had also frequently expressed his readiness to welcome an arrangement for the free movement of Russian ships, naval or merchant, through the Black Sea and back. He, therefore, opened the discussion on the basis of a friendly agreement. At the same time he wished to impress on Marshal Stalin the importance of not alarming Turkey. Undoubtedly Turkey was very much alarmed by a strong concentration of Bulgarian and Soviet troops in Bulgaria; by continuous attacks in the Soviet press and radio; and, of course, by the turn which the conversations between the Turkish Ambassador and Mr. Molotov had taken in which modifications of Turkey's eastern frontier were mentioned, as well as a Soviet base in the Straits. This led Turkey to fear for the integrity of her empire and her power to defend Constantinople. He understood, however, that these were not demands on Turkey by the Soviet Government but that the Turks had asked for an alliance and then Molotov had stated the conditions for such an alliance. He quite saw that if Turkey asked for an offensive and defensive alliance, this would be the occasion when the Soviets would say what improvement they wanted in the Turkish situation. However, the Turks were alarmed by the mention of these conditions. He did not know what had happened beyond these conversations. What he should like to know was the present Russian position on the subject.

MOLOTOV said that he would circulate a letter to the President and Churchill giving the point of view of the Soviet Government on this question. He would like to explain the origin of the matter. The Turkish Government had taken the initiative through the Turkish Ambassador in Moscow and had proposed an alliance. This question had been brought up before their Ambassador in Ankara and again in Moscow at the end of May by the Turkish Ambassador. Early in June he had had two conversations with the Turkish Ambassador. In reply to the Turkish proposals he had stated that the Soviet Government had no objection to a treaty of alliance subject to certain conditions. He pointed out the fact that in doing so they should settle their mutual claims. On the Soviet side there were two. The conclusion of a treaty of alliance meant that they undertook each to defend the frontiers of both states. He had pointed out that there were several sections of their frontiers which they considered unjust. In 1921 a portion of their territory had been torn from Soviet Armenia and Soviet Georgia. He pointed out that he was bound to settle this question before the conclusion of a treaty of alliance.

The second question was that of the Black Sea Straits. The Soviet Union had repeatedly let their allies know that they could not regard the Montreux Convention as a correct arrangement and that they were not satisfied with it. The rights of the Soviet Union under this Convention were equal to those of the Japanese Emperor. It seemed to them that this did not correspond to the present situation. On behalf of the Soviet Government he had presented certain proposals which had been set forth in the Soviet paper which he was now circulating. At the same time, he had pointed out to the Turks that if both of these issues were settled the Russians were ready to conclude an alliance. He had also informed the Turks that the Soviet Union was prepared to settle any questions which the Turks raised on their side. He had added that if the Turkish Government were not prepared to settle these two questions the Soviet Government was prepared to make an agreement on the Straits alone between the Black Sea Powers.

CHURCHILL said that this was an important document which went far beyond the conversations between Eden and himself and Stalin and Molotov.

MOLOTOV said that the treaty of alliance with Turkey had not been under consideration at that time.

CHURCHILL inquired whether the words "proper regular

procedure" in paragraph one of the Soviet paper meant that all signatories except Japan would be consulted. He repeated [that] different questions were raised in this paper, when a Russian base in the Straits was asked for; also by the proposal that no one had anything to do with the Bosporus and the Dardanelles except Russia and Turkey. He was certain that Turkey would never agree to this proposal that was being made.

MOLOTOV said that similar treaties had existed in the past between Russia and Turkey.

CHURCHILL asked if he meant the question of a Russian base in the Black Sea Straits.

MOLOTOV replied that he meant treaties which provided for the settlement of the Straits question only by Turkey and Russia. He referred to the treaties of 1805 and 1833.

CHURCHILL said he would have to ask his staff to look up these ancient treaties and added that he had only pointed out the difference between these proposals and those which had earlier been discussed. He said that the British were not prepared to push Turkey to accept these proposals.

STALIN said that they had not discussed the proposals before but had only had conversations.

MOLOTOV said that they had proposed to submit the matter to the June meeting of the Foreign Ministers which had not taken place.

CHURCHILL said that he stood by his conversations with Stalin in which he, Churchill, expressed the willingness to press for the revision of the Montreux Convention side by side with Stalin. That agreement still stood, but he felt quite free with regard to these new proposals.

STALIN said, "Yes," he was free.

THE PRESIDENT said he was not ready to express an opinion and suggested that they defer consideration of the question.

This was agreed to.

[July 23, 1945]

Returning to the subject of Turkey, THE PRESIDENT remarked that he did not think that the Prime Minister had finished his remarks when they had adjourned at the last meeting.

CHURCHILL replied that he had finished his remarks at the last meeting when he had stated that he could not consent to the establishment of a Russian base in the Straits and that he did not think that Turkey would agree to that proposal.

STALIN remarked that yesterday Churchill had said that the Russians had frightened the Turks and that one of the chief points was that the Russians had concentrated too many troops in Bulgaria. He considered it necessary to give information on this point. Churchill's information was out of date. He did not know what information Churchill had been given by the Turks, but Russia had less troops in Bulgaria than the British had in Greece.

CHURCHILL inquired how many Stalin thought the British had in Greece.

STALIN replied: "Five divisions."

CHURCHILL said there were only two.

STALIN inquired with respect to armored units, and asked how strong the British divisions were.

CHURCHILL said they had about 40,000 troops altogether.

STALIN replied that they [the Soviet Union] had about 30,000 [in Bulgaria].

CHURCHILL said he hoped that the meeting would hear Field Marshal Alexander as he preferred that he give the figures.

STALIN replied that he was not seeking for accuracy but that he believed Churchill 100 per cent. He said that should it prove necessary General Antonov could make a detailed report, but one thing was clear—the Turks had nothing of

which to be afraid. The Turks had about twenty-three divisions and there was nothing to be afraid of. That was the
Russian information.

As to the rectification of the frontiers, which might have
frightened the Turks, he said that perhaps it was the possible
restoration of the pre-war frontiers that had existed under
the Czar that had frightened the Turks. He said that he had in
mind the area of Kars, formerly in Armenia, as well as Ardahan, formerly in Georgia. He pointed out that this question
of the restoration of frontiers would not have been brought
up if the Turks had not brought up the question of an alliance. An alliance meant that they would defend the frontiers
of Turkey, just as Turkey would defend the frontiers of the
Soviet Union, but in the Soviet opinion the frontiers in the
area mentioned was [*were*] incorrect and they had told the
Turks that if there was to be an alliance the frontiers had to
be rectified. If this were not done the question of an alliance
would be dropped. What was there to be afraid of?

The third question was that of the Straits. He drew their
attention to the fact that the position of such a great state as
the Soviet Union was the following. The Montreux Convention had been decided against Russia. Russia considered it
inimical. Turkey had the right under this treaty to block the
Straits to any shipping not only if Turkey were at war but
also if it seemed to Turkey that there was a threat of war.
The Convention also left it to Turkey to decide when this
threat appeared. Thus, an impossible situation was created in
which Turkey was free to block the Straits when she thought
they were threatened. The situation at the moment was that
the Russians had the same rights in the Straits as the Japanese
Emperor. This was ridiculous, but it was a fact. The result
was that a small state supported by Great Britain held a great
state by the throat and gave it no outlet. He said that they
could imagine what commotion there would be in England if
a similar regime existed in Gibraltar or in the Suez Canal, or
what a commotion there would be in the United States if

such a regime existed with regard to the Panama Canal. Hence, the point at issue was to give Soviet shipping the possibility to pass to and from the Black Sea freely. As Turkey was too weak to guarantee the possibility of free passage in case complications arose, the Soviet Union would like to see them defended by force.

CHURCHILL, who appeared to misunderstand, said: "Not law? "

STALIN replied that force was necessary just as in the case of the Panama Canal, which was defended by the American navy, and for shipping through the Suez Canal, which was guaranteed by the British navy. He said that if they thought that naval bases in the Straits were unacceptable to the Turks, then let them give the Soviet Union some other base where the Russian fleet could repair and refuel and where in cooperation with its allies the Russian fleet could protect the Straits. For the situation to continue as it was would be ridiculous.

THE PRESIDENT said that the attitude of the American Government was that the Montreux Convention should be revised. We thought, however, that the Straits should be a free waterway open to the whole world and that they should be guaranteed by all of us. He had come to the conclusion after a long study of history that all the wars of the last two hundred years had originated in the area from the Black Sea to the Baltic and from the eastern frontier of France to the western frontier of Russia. In the last two instances the peace of the whole world had been overturned; by Austria in the case of the previous war, and by Germany in the case of this war. He thought it should be the business of this Conference and of the coming peace conference to see that this did not happen again. He thought that to a great extent this could be accomplished by arranging for the passage of goods and vessels through the Straits on the basis of free intercourse, just as was the case in American waters. He said that he was presenting a paper and that he wanted to see Russia and

England and all other countries have free access to all the seas of the world. The President then read his paper on the free and unrestricted navigation of inland waterways.

THE PRESIDENT then continued that he did not want to engage in another war twenty-five years from now over the Straits or the Danube. He said that our ambition was to have a Europe that was sound economically and which could support itself. He wanted a Europe that would make Russia, England, France and all other countries in it happy and with which the United States can trade and be happy as well as prosperous. He thought that his proposal was a step in that direction.

He said that the question of territorial concessions was a Turkish and Russian dispute which they would have to settle themselves and which the Marshal had said he was willing to do, but he pointed out that the question of the Black Sea Straits concerned the United States and the whole world.

CHURCHILL said that he strongly supported Stalin's wish for a revision of the Montreux Convention with the object of securing for Soviet Russia free and unrestricted navigation of the Straits by merchant and war ships alike in peace or war. He entirely agreed with the President when he said that this should be guaranteed by all of us. A guarantee by the Great Powers and the powers interested would certainly be effective. He earnestly hoped that the Marshal would consider this alternative in contrast to that of a base in close proximity to Constantinople. With regard to the other waterways, they were in full accord with the general line that the President had taken in his statement. He thought that the Kiel Canal should certainly be free and open and guaranteed by all the Great Powers. He also attached great importance to the free navigation of the Danube and the Rhine. He felt that there was a great measure of agreement between the Three Powers represented at the Conference.

THE PRESIDENT said there was no doubt regarding their agreement on the question of the revision of the Montreux Convention.

CHURCHILL added "and on the purpose of that revision."

STALIN said that he would have to read attentively the proposal made by the President, which was now being translated, before he could discuss it.

[July 24, 1945]

THE PRESIDENT pointed out that he had circulated a paper on inland waterways and inquired if it had been considered.

STALIN pointed out that this paper did not deal with the question of Turkey and the Straits but dealt with the Danube and the Rhine. The Soviet Delegation would like to receive a reply to their proposal in regard to the Black Sea Straits.

THE PRESIDENT replied that he wished the two questions to be considered together.

STALIN said he was afraid they would not be able to reach an agreement in regard to the Straits, since their views differed so widely. He said that perhaps they should postpone the question and take up the next question.

CHURCHILL said he understood that it was agreed that freedom in the Black Sea Straits should be approved and guaranteed by the Big Three and other powers and that the United States would come into that kind of an organization and said that to his mind this was a remarkable and important fact.

THE PRESIDENT said that the Prime Minister had clearly stated the position of the United States.

CHURCHILL pointed out that this was a big step.

STALIN said that this was correct with respect to freedom of passage, for the British were in favor of freedom for all traffic.

CHURCHILL said that they hoped that the guarantee proposed would be more than a substitute for the fortification of the Straits.

MOLOTOV inquired if the Suez Canal were under the same principle.

CHURCHILL rejoined that it was open in war and peace to all.

MOLOTOV inquired if it were under the same international control as was proposed for the Black Sea Straits.

CHURCHILL said that this question had not been raised.

MOLOTOV said that he was asking. If it was such a good rule why not apply it to the Suez.

CHURCHILL said that they had an arrangement with which they were satisfied and that this arrangement had operated for some seventy years with no complaints.

MOLOTOV said there had been a lot of complaints. They should ask Egypt.

EDEN said that Egypt had signed the treaty with them.

MOLOTOV said that the British asserted that international control was better.

CHURCHILL said that their suggestion had been made to meet the Russian position that Russia should be able to move freely in and out of the Black Sea and that they were prepared to join in a guarantee with other nations and were prepared to press it upon Turkey. Was it to be supposed that Turkey would resist when the three Great Powers agreed and took an interest in the matter? Freedom could be attained in this way and without trouble for Turkey. He quite agreed that the question must be put off, but he hoped that the tremendous fact that they had heard at this meeting should not be underestimated by their Russian friends.

THE PRESIDENT said he wished to make clear his understanding of an international guarantee of the freedom of the Straits; it meant that any nation had free ingress for any purpose whatever. He did not contemplate any fortifications of any kind.

CHURCHILL said he fully sympathized and agreed with Stalin that a great power, such as the Soviet Union, must not have to go to a smaller power, like Turkey, hat in hand, any time it wanted to send ships through the Straits, only because

Turkey said she had fears of war. He did not oppose Stalin's complaint in this respect.

STALIN pointed out that this question had been raised at the Conference by Great Britain. It was evident that they differed in their views. They had many more urgent questions before them and this one could be put off.

CHURCHILL said the question had been brought up following all their conversations with the Russians regarding the Soviet wish to change the Montreux Convention, which position they were prepared to support.

STALIN said the question was not yet ripe. Some talks with the Turks should take place.

CHURCHILL inquired "With Turkey by whom? "

STALIN replied that the Russians had interrupted their conversations with the Turks, but only temporarily. The United States could talk with Turkey as well as Great Britain. He was not certain whether Turkey would be prepared to agree to international control.

CHURCHILL said it was more likely that they would agree to this than to the construction of big fortifications in the Straits.

STALIN replied that this might be, he did not know.

THE PRESIDENT drew attention to the word "control." If the Straits were free there would be no control. He said that we would endeavor to make Turkey see our point of view.

STALIN then proposed that each of them work on the matter.

*U.S. Delegation's Memorandum on the Results
of the Conference*

[July 25, 1945]

Turkey and the Straits. No tripartite agreement was reached on this subject but it was dropped with the understanding that each of the three Powers would consult the Turks, the British and Americans with a view to establishing an international guarantee of free passage of the Straits for all nations at all times; the Russians presumably with a view to obtaining either exclusive Soviet-Turkish control of the Straits or Soviet-fortified bases on the Straits.*

---

*Source: United States, Department of State, *The Conference of Berlin (The Potsdam Conference, 1945*, Vol. II, Foreign Relations of the United States, Diplomatic Papers, (Washington, D.C.: U.S. Government Printing Office, 1960), pp. 256-59, 302-5, 365-67, 393. Footnotes omitted.

APPENDIX 18

Note from the American Ambassador in Turkey to the Turkish Minister of Foreign Affairs

November 2, 1945

[complete text]

ANKARA, *November 2, 1945.*

EXCELLENCY:

I have the honor, under instructions of my Government, to inform Your Excellency as follows:

The American Government has given careful consideration to the Turkish Government's note of August 20, 1945, together with the *aide-memoire* attached thereto, concerning the question of the Straits.

The Turkish Government is no doubt aware that at the

recent conference in Berlin, the President of the United States concurred with Premier Stalin and Prime Minister Attlee (1) that the convention of 1936 signed at Montreux regarding the régime of the Straits should be revised to meet present day conditions and (2) that the matter would be the subject of direct conversations between each of the three governments and the Turkish Government. It is the earnest hope of the Government of the United States that the problem of the control and use of the Straits can be solved in a manner which will promote international security, will show due consideration for the interests of Turkey and all Black Sea riparian powers, and will assure the free use of this important waterway to the commerce of all nations.

It is the understanding of the Government of the United States that the Montreux Convention is subject to revision in 1946. This government suggests that an international conference be held for the purpose of revising the convention in order that the régime of the Straits may be more in harmony with changed world conditions. The United States, if invited, would be pleased to participate in such a conference.

The Government of the United States is of the opinion that a revision of the Montreux Convention undertaken to meet changed world conditions should be based on the following principles:

(1) The Straits to be open to the merchant vessels of all nations at all times;

(2) The Straits to be open to the transit of the warships of Black Sea powers at all times;

(3) Save for an agreed limited tonnage in time of peace, passage through the Straits to be denied to the warships of non-Black Sea powers at all times, except with the specific consent of the Black Sea powers or except when acting under the authority of the United Nations; and

(4) Certain changes to modernize the Montreux Convention; such as the substitution of the United Nations system

for that of the League of Nations and the elimination of Japan as a signatory.

The British and Soviet Governments are also being informed of the American Government's views set forth above.

Please accept [etc.] EDWIN C. WILSON

His Excellency
HASAN SAKA,
   *Minister of Foreign Affairs, Ankara.**

---

*Source: United States, Department of State, *The Problem of the Turkish Straits* (Washington, D.C.: U.S. Government Printing Office, 1947), p. 47.

APPENDIX 19

Note from the Soviet Chargé d'Affaires at Washington to the Acting Secretary of State

August 7, 1946

[complete text]

EMBASSY OF THE UNION OF SOVIET SOCIALIST REPUBLICS

Washington, D.C., August 7, 1946.

SIR:

By direction of the Soviet Government I have the honor to communicate to you the following:

As is known, the Berlin Conference of the Three Powers

on the question of the Montreux Convention adopted a resolution, whereby the three governments declared that the said convention should be revised, since it does not correspond to present conditions. At the same time the three governments agreed that this question was to be the subject of direct negotiations between each of the three powers and the Turkish Government. In accordance with this, the Soviet Government on August 7 of this year addressed to the Turkish Government a note which is transcribed below:

"The Ministry of Foreign Affairs of the U.S.S.R. has the honor to inform the Turkish Government of the following:

"Events which occurred during the past war clearly indicated that the regime of the Black Sea Straits, established by the Straits Convention, signed in 1936 at Montreux, does not meet the interests of the safety of the Black Sea Powers and does not insure conditions under which the use of these Straits for purposes inimical to the Black Sea Powers would be prevented.

"It will suffice to mention a series of incidents during this war, when the Axis Powers directed their warships and auxiliary craft through the Straits into the Black Sea and out of the Black Sea, which in its turn gave rise to the corresponding steps and protests registered by the Soviet Government with the Turkish Government.

"On July 9, 1941, the German command sent the German patrol boat *Seefalke* through the Straits into the Black Sea, which was a gross violation of the Straits Convention and called forth a protest to the Turkish Government on the part of the Soviet Government.

"In August, 1941, Turkish authorities gave the Italian auxiliary war vessel *Tarvisio* permission to pass through the Straits into the Black Sea, which likewise called forth a representation on the part of the Soviet Government, calling to the attention of the Turkish Government the fact that the passage of the Italian auxiliary vessel into the Black Sea would appear to be a violation of the Straits Convention.

"On November 4, 1942, the Soviet Government again called to the attention of the Turkish Government the fact that Germany planned to send to the Black Sea through the Straits auxiliary warships under the guise of merchant vessels with a total displacement of 140,000 tons. These vessels were intended for the transfer of military forces and war materials of the Axis countries into the Black Sea. In its representation, the Soviet Government emphasized the fact that 'the admission of the aforementioned vessels through the Straits into the Black Sea would be an obvious violation of the Convention regarding the regime of the Straits concluded in Montreux, inasmuch as these vessels are left at the disposal of the German Government and are in reality auxiliary warships.'

"In June, 1944, the Soviet Government registered a protest against the fact that toward the end of May and early in June of 1944 there took place a series of passages through the straits from the Black Sea into the Aegean Sea of German warships and auxiliary warships of varying tonnage of the *Ems* (8 vessels) and *Kriegstransport* (5 vessels) types, which had taken part in the naval operations in the Black Sea.

"It is obvious from the aforementioned facts that at the time of the past war with Germany and her allies, the Straits Convention did not prevent the enemy powers from using the straits for military purposes against the U.S.S.R. and other allied powers, with the Turkish Government not being able to escape the responsibility for this situation.

"In view of this, the Soviet Government suggested to the Berlin Conference of the Three Powers—Great Britain, the United States of America and the Soviet Union—which took place in July and August 1945, to discuss the question that the regime of the Straits, established by the Montreux Convention, does not conform to present conditions and that it is necessary to establish a new regime of the Straits. As is known, the Berlin Conference of the Three Powers adopted a resolution consisting of the following:

"*a*) The three governments declared that the Convention regarding the Straits, concluded in Montreux, should be revised, as it does not meet the conditions of the present time;

"*b*) The three governments agreed that as the proper course the said question would be the subject of direct negotiations between each of the three powers and the Turkish Government.

"The Soviet Government is also acquainted with the contents of the note of November 2, 1945, of the Government of the United States of America and with the note of the British Government of November 21, 1945, addressed to the Government of Turkey on this question.

"For its own part, the Soviet Government proposes to establish for the Straits a new regime, proceeding from the following principles:

"1) The Straits should be always open to the passage of merchant ships of all countries.

"2) The Straits should be always open to the passage of warships of the Black Sea powers.

"3) Passage through the Straits for warships not belonging to the Black Sea powers shall not be permitted except in cases specially provided for.

"4) The establishment of a regime of the Straits, as the sole sea passage leading from the Black Sea and to the Black Sea, should come under the competence of Turkey and other Black Sea powers.

"5) Turkey and the Soviet Union, as the powers most interested and capable of guaranteeing freedom to commercial navigation and security in the Straits, shall organize joint means of defense of the Straits for the prevention of the utilization of the Straits by other countries for aims hostile to the Black Sea powers.

"The Soviet Government is informing the governments of the United States of America and Great Britain regarding the present declaration."

The Soviet Union has directed me to bring this to the

knowledge of the Government of the United States of America.

Accept [etc.]   FEDOR OREKHOV

Acting Secretary of State DEAN ACHESON,
        Department of State, Washington. *

---

*Source: United States, Department of State, *The Problem of the Turkish Straits* (Washington, D.C.: U.S. Government Printing Office, 1947), pp. 47-49.

APPENDIX 20

Note from the Acting Secretary of State to the Soviet Chargé d'Affaires at Washington

August 19, 1946

[complete text]

SIR:

I acknowledge receipt of your note of August 7, 1946 which sets forth the text of the note addressed on the same day by the Government of the Union of Soviet Socialist Republics to the Government of the Republic of Turkey and express the appreciation of this Government for the courtesy of the Soviet Government in making this information available.

It will be recalled that the American Embassy in Moscow made available to the Soviet Government in November 1945 a copy of the note which the American Embassy in Ankara delivered to the Turkish Government on November 2, 1945.

This Government has given careful study to the views expressed by the Soviet Government in its note to the Turkish

Government. It would appear from a comparison of this Government's note of November 2, 1945 with the Soviet note to the Turkish Government of August 7, 1946 that the views of the Governments of the United States and of the Soviet Union, while not in entire accord, are in general agreement with regard to the three following proposals set forth in the Soviet note:

"1. The Straits should be always open to the passage of merchant ships of all countries.

"2. The Straits should be always open to the passage of warships of the Black Sea powers.

"3. Passage through the Straits for warships not belonging to the Black Sea powers shall not be permitted except in cases specially provided for."

The fourth proposal set forth in the Soviet note does not appear to envisage a revision of the Montreux Convention as suggested in our note to the Turkish Government of November 2, 1945, but rather the establishment of a new regime which would be confined to Turkey and the other Black Sea powers. It is the view of this Government that the regime of the Straits is a matter of concern not only to the Black Sea powers but also to other powers, including the United States. This Government cannot, therefore, agree with the Soviet view that the establishment of the regime of the Straits should come under the competence of the Black Sea powers to the exclusion of other powers.

The fifth proposal set forth in the note of the Soviet Government was that Turkey and the Soviet Union should organize joint means of defense of the Straits. It is the firm opinion of this Government that Turkey should continue to be primarily responsible for the defense of the Straits. Should the Straits become the object of attack or threat of attack by an aggressor the resulting situation would constitute a threat to international security and would clearly be a matter for action on the part of the Security Council of the United Nations.

It is observed that the note of the Soviet Government contains no reference to the United Nations. The position of the Government of the United States is that the regime of the Straits should be brought into appropriate relationship with the United Nations and should function in a manner entirely consistent with the principles and aims of the United Nations.

The Government of the United States reaffirms its willingness to participate in a conference called to revise the Montreux Convention.

Accept [etc.[

DEAN ACHESON
Acting Secretary of State

MR. FEDOR T. OREKHOV,
*Chargé d'Affaires ad interim of the Union of Soviet Socialist Republic.**

---

*Source: United States Department of State, *The Problem of the Turkish Straits* (Washington, D.C.: U.S. Government Printing Office, 1947), pp. 49-50.

APPENDIX 21

Note from the British Secretary of State for Foreign Affairs to the Soviet Chargé d'Affaires at London

August 21, 1946

[complete text]

I have the honour to acknowledge receipt of your note of 8th August in which you communicated to me the text of a note which the Soviet Government had delivered to the Turkish Government on the 7th August concerning the future of the Montreux Convention. The Soviet Government will already be aware from the communication addressed to the Soviet Government by His Majesty's Ambassador in Moscow on the 23rd November, 1945 that His Majesty's Government are of the opinion that a revision of the Montreux Convention is desirable and that they would, if the Soviet Government or the Turkish Government desired to call a conference for the revision of the Convention, be ready to take part in its work. His Majesty's Government have consequently given careful consideration to the proposals which the Soviet Government have now put forward for the new regime which they consider should be established in the Straits.

Before, however, they comment on the proposals put forward by the Soviet Government, His Majesty's Government wish to point out that the agreements reached regarding this question at the Potsdam Conference, as recorded in Section XVI of the Protocol of the Conference, were that as a next step the matter should be the subject of direct conversations between each of the three Governments and the Turkish Government. It was not, as is suggested in the second paragraph of the note under reply, agreed at Potsdam that the matter should be the subject of direct negotiations between each of the three Powers and the Turkish Government.

As regards the proposals now put forward by the Soviet Government, His Majesty's Government note that there is no mention in these proposals of the United Nations. His Majesty's Government desire to place it on record that in any modification of the Montreux Convention the regime should be consistent with the purpose and principles of the United Nations. Subject to this His Majesty's Government wish to offer no comments at the present stage upon the first three proposals made by the Soviet Government. As regards the fourth proposal, however, His Majesty's Government would point out that it has for long been internationally recognised that the regime of the Straits is the concern of other States besides the Black Sea Powers. His Majesty's Government cannot therefore agree with the Soviet view that the future regime should be the concern of the Black Sea Powers and Turkey alone. As regards the fifth proposal, that Turkey and the Soviet Union should organise the defence of the Straits by joint means, His Majesty's Government consider that Turkey, as the territorial power concerned, should continue to be responsible for the defense and control of the Straits.

In conclusion, His Majesty's Government wish to make it clear once again that they would be ready to attend an international conference to discuss a revision of the 1936 Convention if all the interested parties agree.*

---

*Source: United States, Department of State, *The Problem of the Turkish Straits* (Washington, D.C.: U.S. Government Printing Office, 1947), p. 50.

APPENDIX 22

Note from the Turkish Ministry of Foreign Affairs to the Soviet Embassy in Turkey

August 22, 1946

[complete text]

ANKARA, *August 22, 1946.*

The Government of the Republic has examined with the greatest interest the note dated August 7, 1946 which the Embassy of the Union of Soviet Socialist Republics delivered to the Ministry of Foreign Affairs concerning the question of the Straits. The Government of the Republic has examined this note with all the more attention in that it expressed the Soviet point of view on a question of which the international importance is only surpassed by the vital interest which it represents from the Turkish national point of view.

From the reading of this note it appears that, in the opinion of the Soviet Government, the events which took place during the Second World War clearly showed that the regime established by the Montreux Convention did not correspond to the interests of the Black Sea Powers, and does not insure the conditions under which the use of the Straits for purposes hostile to the Black Sea Powers would be prevented. In support of this thesis the note recalls the passage in both directions through the Straits of war vessels and auxiliary war vessels of the Axis, such as the *Seefalke* and the *Tarvisio*, and of ships designed for the transport of troops, a combination of facts, which, in the opinion of the Soviet Government, established proof of the possibility of the use of the Straits by Powers enemy to the Soviet Union and the other allied states, a use for which the Turkish Government, adds the note, could not declare itself unresponsible.

Then, after a concise account of the Anglo-American-Soviet deliberations at Potsdam in July and August, 1945 on the subject of the Straits, deliberations as a result of which the three powers under reference decided:

a. that the Montreux Convention, as not corresponding to present conditions, should be revised,

b. that this question would be the object of direct conversations between each of the powers and the Turkish Government,

the note reveals the Soviet proposals for the establishment of a new Straits regime. These proposals are formulated as follows:

1) The Straits should be always open to the passage of merchant vessels of all countries.

2) The Straits should be always open to the passage of warships of the Black Sea Powers.

3) The passage of warships of non-Black Sea Powers through the Straits is not permitted, except in cases especially provided for.

4) The establishment of the regime of the Straits as a natural maritime route leading to and from the Black Sea should be within the competence of Turkey and the other Black Sea Powers.

5) Turkey and the Soviet Union, as the powers most interested and able to insure the freedom of merchant navigation and security in the Straits, would insure by their common means the defense of the Straits to prevent their use by other states for purposes hostile to the Black Sea Powers.

Before beginning any examination as to the form and basis of the Soviet *démarche*, the Ministry of Foreign Affairs considers it necessary to pause on the cases of passage through the Straits by certain Axis vessels, cases cited in the above-mentioned note in contention of the inefficacy of the Montreux Convention in order to deduce therefrom a supposed responsibility on the part of the Turkish Government.

The motor-vessel *Seefalke* of 37 tons, flying the German

commercial flag and not listed in the record of war fleets arrived at the entrance of the Dardanelles on July 6, 1941. It requested passage through the Straits to go to Constanza.

The vessel was not armed and it only carried on board a large life raft and a life boat. There was discovered no indication leading to the supposition of its use for purposes of war.

Given that the vessel in question presented none of the characteristics mentioned in Annex II of the Montreux Convention, treating of the definition, tonnage, and specifications of warships, the *Seefalke* was authorized to pass through the Straits.

In the case of the Italian oil tanker *Tarvisio* the facts are as follows:

The *Tarvisio* passed through the Straits in June 1941 as a commercial vessel. Its passage was brought to the attention of the Ministry of Foreign Affairs as a case of fraud, in view of the fact that the ship in question also appeared on the list of auxiliary ships of the Italian war fleet. When explanations were requested of the Italian Embassy, the latter declared that the *Tarvisio* had been removed from the list of auxiliary war vessels and was sailing exclusively for commercial purposes. The Government of the Republic none the less gave the appropriate authorities the order to stop the *Tarvisio* upon its next attempt at passage.

The *Tarvisio* appeared a second time on August 9, 1941 at the entrance of the Dardanelles. Passage was refused it. Despite the insistence of the Italian Embassy, the Government of the Republic did not change its point of view, which consisted of not recognizing the right to change, in time of war, auxiliary war vessels into commercial vessels. The *Tarvisio* after having been at anchor for 25 days off Çanakkale, with its radio apparatus sealed, turned back into the Mediterranean on September 2.

The Ambassador of the Union of Soviet Socialist Republics, at the time of his visit to the Minister of Foreign Affairs on August 25, 1941, expressed the gratitude of the Government of the Union of Soviet Socialist Republics for the decision of the Government of the Republic in this case and confirmed that his Government fully shared the Turkish point of view as regards the admissibility of the right to change auxiliary war vessels into commercial vessels.

The Honorable Embassy mentions as well in its note a *démarche* dated November 4, 1942, having for purpose the drawing of the attention of the Turkish Government to the intention of Germany to pass through the Straits into the Black Sea auxiliary war vessels displacing a total of 140,000 tons, in the form of merchant vessels.

During the months of November and December 1942, no German merchant vessels passed the Straits in the direction indicated. From the first of January 1943 to the first of January 1944 only 10 German merchant vessels, displacing in all 19,476 tons and of which the commercial character was verified beyond doubt by the appropriate authorities, passed through the Straits into the Black Sea.

As regards the passage through the Straits in May and June 1944 of ships of the types *Ems* and *Kriegstransport*, the facts can be stated as follows:

Ships of the type *Ems* displaced less than 100 tons, were not armed, had freight holds, and, at the time of their passage, carried cargos of wood, coal, or fodder. The German Embassy had declared that they belonged to private shipping companies and were sailing for purely commercial purposes.

The ships of the type of *Kriegstransport* also had the characteristics of merchant vessels, were not represented in the list of auxiliary German war vessels and could not be included in any of the categories of Annex II of the Convention.

The British Embassy having informed the Ministry of Foreign Affairs that, according to entirely reliable information from its Government, said ships, of which several had already passed through the Straits, were in the service of the (German) fleet or used as troop transports, the Turkish naval authorities stopped at the entrance of the Straits one of the

German ships belonging to this group, which was requesting passage. Passage was henceforth refused to ships of this type.

It results from the preceding explanations that the objection to the Montreux Convention concerns less the intrinsic dispositions which govern the purely juridical aspects of the regime, and which have kept pace here with circumstances, than the definitions of warships and their specifications as well as the calculation of tonnage, which form the purely technical annex of the Convention. The exigencies of war of all kinds, the tactical and strategic needs, made certain belligerents decide to adopt during the war new types of war ships which, from the point of view of specifications and tonnage, departed completely from the type of war ships defined by the Convention of Montreux, and presented all the characteristics of innocent commercial vessels, which, because of this fact, were controlled by Article 7 of the Convention.

The Government of the Republic, responsible for applying rigorously the provisions of the Montreux Convention, has always referred, for the separation of ships requesting passage into war ships or commercial vessels, to the criterions fixed by the Convention, and it is in consequence of the application of these criterions that it, in each case, refused or authorized passage to the ships in question. Therefore, there can be no complaints addressed to it on this point. Moreover, the surveillance exercised by the Turkish authorities over ships in transit through the Straits was complicated by the fact that the only kind of control to which the ships in question could be submitted according to the Convention was limited to a sanitary control to be carried out "by day and night with the greatest possible speed." If, in the extremely difficult conditions of surveillance and control, some very few ships were able, by taking on the characteristics required for commercial ships, to pass fraudulently through the Straits, the Government of the Republic hastened, as soon as it was informed of complaints, to take the necessary measures looking towards preventing the repetition of the fraud.

The Soviet Government bases all its arguments leading to obtaining a Straits regime entirely in conformity with its own interests upon the allegation that the regime established by the Montreux Convention does not assure the conditions in which the use of the Straits for purposes hostile to the Black Sea Powers would be prevented. In fact, with the exception of several cases of fraudulent passage which were the objects of *démarches* of the Soviet Embassy, not once during the course of the Second World War did the Soviet Government inform the Government of the Turkish Republic of a situation which would endanger its security in the Black Sea. This attitude, which indicated an appreciable feeling of internal tranquillity as regards the loyalty of Turkey, is perfectly understandable, because the Soviet Union, a power deeply interested in following the always uniform political line of its neighbor, was the first to declare that, despite the immeasurable advantages which the free use of the Straits could present for strategic and tactical purposes, the Axis countries never dared force the Strait in order to pass their war fleets through. The Government of the Republic must emphasize this highly significant abstention, which certainly did not result from the lack of interest which this perspective presented to the Axis countries, as the clearest proof of the unanimous conviction inspired by the capacity and absolute correctness —correctness carried at times as far as a fanaticism disregarding even purely Turkish interests—with which it fulfilled the role of guardian of the Straits which was given it by history. It is certainly not the fraudulent passage, under conditions independent of the good faith and good will of the Turkish authorities, of a very few Axis auxiliary war vessels hidden under the mask of commercial vessels which can change the approach of History as regards the loyal attitude of the Turkish Government in this connection.

In consequence, the complaint addressed to the Montreux

Convention of not responding to present conditions cannot be accepted by the Government of the Republic except in the measure that this complaint concerns the technical part of the Convention which deals with the definition applicable to war ships, with their specifications and tonnage, and the provisions treating of the control of ships in transit. The Turkish Government acknowledges that the above-mentioned definitions and provisions, by-passed by events and weakened by experience, need to be adapted to technical progress and present conditions. But it cannot admit that these facts, destined to remain specific cases, serve as motives for the rejection in its entirety of the Convention, which reveals itself as a balanced instrument, and still less for the deduction of a supposed responsibility in its regard. The Turkish Government cannot accept that an extremely limited number of cases of fraudulent passage through the Straits, moreover rapidly corrected, were able, in the totality of war operations, to acquire such an extent that they put the security of the Union of Soviet Socialist Republics in danger. The Turkish Government believes itself in a position to affirm before world public opinion, and, if such should be necessary, to prove before an arbitral authority, the good faith and the high realization of international responsibilities with which it has not ceased, in the application of the regime of Montreux, to be the guardian of the Straits.

To return to the practical ends which the Government of the Soviet Union would appear to wish to attain through its note of August 7, the Government of the Republic takes it that it is a question of putting into application the procedure for quinquennial revision provided for in Article 29 of the Montreux Convention. The choice of the date for giving notice, as well as the indication of the motives of the proposed amendments, would seem to militate in favor of such an interpretation. If such is indeed the intention of the Government of the Soviet Union, the request for revision formulated ought, in order to be admissible, to fulfill certain conditions provided for in the above-mentioned Article 29 of the Convention. It is principally necessary that the request be supported by one or two contracting parties, depending upon what articles of the Convention it is a question of modifying. Then the request thus supported must be notified to all contracting parties three months before the expiration of the current period of five years. The Government of the Republic, which has noted the desire for revision expressed by the Soviet Government, and which moreover desires to satisfy the wish expressed by American public opinion concerning the use of maritime passages, does not intend, insofar as it is concerned, to create any difficulty as regards the placing in application with the agreement of the signatories of the Montreux Convention and the United States of America, and through an international conference including the above-mentioned powers, of every demand for revision provided for by the Convention and the examination of proposed amendments, in concert with said powers.

As regards the basic part of the question raised, the Government of the Republic is cognizant of the five principles constituting the Soviet amendments. It observes that the first three points take up in more or less identical terms the suggestions presented on November 2, 1945 by the government of the United States for the readaptation of the Montreux Convention to present conditions. In the report then made to the American suggestions, the Turkish Government stated *inter alia* that it pertained to the international conference of signatories provided by the terms of the Montreux Convention to determine the best way to conciliate the principle of freedom of passage through the Straits for merchant and war vessels with the rights of sovereignty and security of Turkey.

"That once it had been informed of the full viewpoints of the three Powers represented at Potsdam regarding the Straits question it would not fail to proceed to a thorough study of the problem, a study after which it would hasten to convey its point of view to the three above-mentioned Powers; that it was none the less at the moment permitted to say that the Turkish Government received favorably the American suggestions which, under certain conditions and reservations, were worthy of being taken as a basis for discussion; that as regards the participation of the Government of the United States of America in the proposed conference, the Turkish Government regarded it not only as a realization of a warm desire but also as an imperative international necessity."

The same answer applies at present to the three first propositions contained in the Soviet note.

It is not the same case with the propositions contained in points 4 and 5 of said note, which require more thorough consideration. As regards point 4 in particular, the Soviet note seems to foresee a new Straits regime set up on a new basis and in the development of which only Turkey and the powers bordering the Black Sea would participate to the exclusion of all others. Such a concept seems in the first place to set aside the remainder of the duration of the Montreux Convention, which is scheduled to exist at least until 1956, and the procedure for revision, which excludes by definition the setting up of a new regime, the general economy of which would depart from the Montreux regime. It seems moreover to desire to ignore the interests of the other powers signatory to the Convention, which have equal right to participate in the negotiations and signature of the revised text and which are making evident in the most definite manner their desire to take part in these negotiations.

As for the fifth principle set forth in the Soviet note, the Government of the Republic states that this proposition aims at nothing less than organizing the security of the Straits against all aggression coming from the Mediterranean, by means of the establishment of a combined Turco-Soviet defense.

From the national point of view the Soviet proposition is not compatible with the inalienable rights of sovereignty of Turkey nor with its security, which brooks no restriction.

Moreover, from the international point of view, the same proposition raises as well the gravest objections.

The acceptance of the Soviet thesis would result in the suppression of the role of factor of equilibrium and liaison played by Turkey in the Straits and in building the so-called security of the Black Sea Powers upon the annihilation of the security of Turkey. The Turkish Government experiences many difficulties in understanding the Soviet apprehensions which the new security system set forth in the August 7 note would remove. The Government of the Republic considers that Turkey is herself interested in defending by all her means the country against all aggression, no matter whence it comes. History gives no example of a war in which Turkey has been involved without the Turkish nation's having accomplished its duty to the country. It is up to Turkey to take all the measures necessary to insure the security of the Country against every danger which may come from abroad. If Turkey had not been in a position to defend by its own means the sovereign rights which it exercises over the Straits, it would not have escaped during the greatest war history has known the fate of its neighbors, which were all attacked or occupied. Moreover, to desire further to strengthen a form of defense having already been proven, at the very moment when all the nations of the world are competing in order to bring their contribution to create an era of peace and security, would be to deny the existence and aims of the United Nations Charter and would show toward these same nations, of which the ideal is to preserve future generations from the scourge of war, a mistrust of which the Turkish Government is unable to understand the cause.

The surest guarantee for the security of the Union of Soviet Socialist Republics in the Black Sea resides, not in the search for a privileged strategic position in the Straits, a position incompatible with the dignity and sovereign rights of an independent country, but in the restoration of friendly and trusting relations with a strong Turkey, which, as far as it is concerned, is determined to dedicate itself with all its strength to the inauguration of this happy era, but whose efforts in this direction must be seconded by an equal good will coming from its northern neighbor. Moreover, beyond this important guarantee furnished by Turkey herself, the Turkish Government, as co-signatory with the Union of Soviet Socialist Republics of the San Francisco Charter, believes that it has the right to think that, in the new concept of war, the security of each country is under the guarantee of international forces placed in the service of the United Nations Organization by the United Nations, of which the Union of Soviet Socialist Republics as well as Turkey are members.

Consequently, even in the wholly improbable case where the Union of Soviet Socialist Republics feared an attack on its Black Sea positions as the result of aggression coming from the Mediterranean through the Straits, the Turkish Government considers that there would be reason for it to rely on the efficacy of the United Nations Organization to which Turkey, as far as it is concerned, remains firmly attached.

A copy of this note has been sent to the signatories of the Montreux Convention, as well as to the Government of the United States of America, which Turkey would be happy to see participate in an international conference for the revision of the Montreux Convention.*

---

*Source: United States, Department of State, *The Problem of the Turkish Straits* (Washington, D.C.: U.S. Government Printing Office, 1947), pp. 50-55.

APPENDIX 23

Note from the Soviet Embassy in Turkey to the Turkish Ministry of Foreign Affairs

September 24/25, 1946

[complete text]

The Soviet Government has carefully studied the note of the Turkish Government dated August 22, which was the response to the note of the U.S.S.R. Government of August 7 of this year on the subject of the regime of the Straits of the Black Sea (*Détroits de la Mer Noire*).

In its note of August 7 the Soviet Government took up a number of cases of the use of the Straits, in the course of the last war, by the states at war with the U.S.S.R. and its allies. It was at that time a question only of cases which have been the object of representations and specific protests to the Turkish Government by the Soviet Government during the years 1941-2 and 1944, which does not at all include all the cases of the use of the Straits by Germany and Italy for the passage of their warships and their auxiliary warships into the Black Sea and in the opposite direction. It is sufficient to mention the repeated passage through the Straits of German fast pinnaces (*péniches*) in 1942 and 1943, as well as other similar acts.

The Turkish Government has given its explanations on this subject. However, these explanations have not denied the statements set forth in the Soviet note of August 7 as far as the concrete facts are concerned. The reference contained in the note of the Turkish Government and according to which Turkey undertook, upon the demand of the Government of Great Britain, measures against the passage through the Straits of German vessels destined for servicing the German fleet and for the transportation of German troops while recognizing that the passage of certain of these ships through the Straits had been authorized prior to the said protest on the part of Great Britain, only confirms the justice of the statement of the Soviet Government that during the last war the Straits Convention did not prevent the enemy powers from using the Straits for purposes of the war against the Allied states.

Consequently, the Soviet Government considers it necessary to record also the fact that during the war the Turkish Government ceased to furnish the belligerent states with reports on the movement of vessels in the Straits, although Turkey was required to do this in accordance with Article 24 of the Convention.

In its note of August 22, the Turkish Government indicates certain circumstances which in its opinion rendered control in the Straits difficult. Thus, it is pointed out that in the naval annual there are no names of warships and auxiliary war vessels which illegally passed the Straits during the war. However, the Turkish Government certainly is not unaware that official annuals containing the complete list of warships and especially of auxiliary ships, do not exist, especially during wartime. The Note of the Turkish Government also states that, in accordance with the Convention, the only form of control of vessels passing through the Straits is the sanitary control. But it is known on the other hand that the Turkish authorities, by their notices to mariners dated February 25 and May 6, 1941 and June 27, 1942, established for transit vessels compulsory stops and the use of Turkish pilots in the Straits. The Customs authorities also carried out control of vessels in transit. If these control measures were however insufficient, one is nevertheless obliged to record that during the course of the war the Turkish Government did not once raise the question of whether it was necessary to strengthen the measures for the control of the passage of vessels through the Straits.

In the note of the Turkish Government it is stated that during the Second World War the Soviet Government made no declaration to the Government of the Turkish Republic concerning the existence of the threat to the security of the U.S.S.R. in the Black Sea region. From this, the said note draws the conclusion that Turkey discharged during the war the task of guardian of the Straits and that the Axis countries, in view of the attitude taken by Turkey did not decide to infringe the regime established in the Straits.

The Soviet Government does not consider this point of view justified and draws the attention of the Turkish Government to the fact that the repeated representations which the U.S.S.R. made to Turkey on the subject of the passage of enemy vessels through the Straits during the war prove the contrary. As to the extent of the above-mentioned threat, it is sufficient to recall the fact that the Soviet High Command, having in mind the repeated cases of free passage of enemy warships and auxiliary war vessels through the Straits during the war, found itself obliged to withdraw an important number of military effectives from the principal sectors of the war theater for the defense of the Black Sea region.

All the foregoing confirms that the Straits regime established by the Montreux Convention does not respond to the security interests of the Black Sea powers and does not assure conditions in which it will be possible to forestall the use of the Straits for purposes hostile to the Black Sea powers. The explanations given by the Turkish Government have not overcome, according to the Soviet Government, the above-stated conclusion. These explanations moreover do not furnish the reason why the Government of Turkey should be relieved of the responsibility which rests upon it for the violation of the Straits regime during the war.

In the note of August 7, the Soviet Government expressed an opinion on the subject of the five principles which it proposes to advance as a basis of the establishment of the new regime in the Straits. To judge from the Turkish note of

August 22, the Government of Turkey has nothing against the taking as a basis of discussion the first three points of the Soviet proposals, namely:

1. The Straits shall always be open to the passage of merchant vessels of all countries.

2. The Straits shall always be open to the passage of warships of the Black Sea Powers.

3. The passage of warships of powers nonriverain of the Black Sea through the Straits is not allowed, except in cases especially provided for. (There is no paragraph here in the French text—the text continues.)

The Soviet Government expresses its satisfaction with the fact that the Turkish Government is ready to accept as a basis the three above-mentioned principles although it pointed out that it had in view the making later on of certain reservations.

The Government of Turkey made known its own opinion with regard to the proposals of the U.S.S.R. embodied in points 4 and 5 of the Soviet note of August 7.

In point 4, the Soviet Government proposed to recognize that the establishment of the regime of the Straits should be a matter within the competence of Turkey and the other Black Sea Powers. Since the Turkish Government has indicated a certain distrust regarding this proposal, the Soviet Government considers it necessary to dwell longer on this question.

In accord with this, the Soviet Government desires before all to invite the attention of the Turkish Government to the special situation of the Black Sea as a closed sea. Such a situation means that the Straits of the Black Sea represent a seaway leading only to the shores of a limited number of powers, namely: to the shores of several Black Sea Powers. Therefore, it is entirely natural that the Soviet Union and the other Black Sea Powers are the most interested in the regulation of the regime of the Straits of the Black Sea and accordingly their situation in this matter cannot be compared with that of the other powers. The destination of these Straits, leading to the Black Sea which is a closed sea, differs from that of world seaways such as, for example, Gibraltar or the Suez Canal, giving access not to a limited number of States, and which, as is known, are seaways of world importance. With regard to such international seaways it is indeed necessary to establish an international control with the participation of the Powers most interested, which moreover has not yet been realized. With regard to the Straits of the Black Sea leading into the Black Sea, which is a closed sea, it seems proper in this case to establish such a regime of the Straits which above all would meet the special situation and the security of Turkey, the U.S.S.R., and the other Black Sea Powers.

It is the Montreux Conference of which the insufficiency in this matter is evident, which established a preferential position for the Black Sea Powers with regard to the Straits regime. On the other hand the Turkish Government has agreed to recognize as a basis the first three points of the Soviet proposals of last August 7, in which the special situation of the Black Sea Powers in the Straits was recognized in a much more definitive way than in the Montreux Convention. In these proposals it is stated that on the one hand the Straits shall be open to the passage of merchant vessels of all countries and on the other hand only warships of the Black Sea Powers shall have access to the Straits, whereas the passage through the Straits of warships of countries not on the shores of the Black Sea is not allowed, with the exception of special cases. As is known, these principles, bringing into relief the position of the Black Sea Powers in the Straits in relation with that of the other countries, have been fully recognized by the whole world, although they are not duly reflected in the Convention in force, adopted at Montreux.

With reference to the matter under consideration, the Soviet Government deems it necessary to recall that the special position of the Black Sea Powers in the Straits was further recognized in the Soviet-Turkish treaty which was signed March 16, 1921.

In Article 5 of this treaty the following is stated:

"In order to assure the opening of the Straits and free passage through these Straits for commercial relations between all peoples, the two contracting parties are agreed to entrust a special conference of delegates of the littoral countries with the definitive drafting of the international statute of the Black Sea and Straits, provided that the decisions which it shall take shall not impair the absolute sovereignty of Turkey, and her capital Constantinople."

Thus, the Turkish-Soviet treaty of 1921 is based on the recognition of the necessity of confiding the drafting of the international statute of the Black Sea and Straits, to a conference composed only of the representatives of riverain countries. There is an analogous article in the treaty concluded between Turkey and the Transcaucasian Soviet Republics on October 13, 1921, as well as in the treaty concluded between Turkey and the Ukrainian Soviet Socialist Republic on January 21, 1922. The insertion in the above-mentioned treaties of the article containing the principle of the establishment of the Straits regime by the riverain countries of the Black Sea, indicates the great importance attributed to this principle by the said countries, including Turkey.

All this demonstrates that the proposal of the Soviet Government set forth in point 4 of its note of August 7 is in full accord with the above-mentioned treaties, signed by Turkey. The subsequent postponement of the putting into force of the procedure regarding the establishment of the statute of the Black Sea and of the Straits, contemplated by these treaties, cannot be justified.

On the other hand, the experience of the last war provided that the principle of the establishment of the regime of the Straits which was recognized in these treaties by Turkey as well as by the Soviet Union, really meets the legitimate interests of the Black Sea Powers and is not at all in conflict with the interests of other countries interested in the stability of general peace and the security of nations.

The Turkish Government also opposes point five of the Soviet note of August 7 in which it is contemplated that Turkey and the Soviet Union, as the Powers most interested and best able to assure freedom of commercial navigation and security in the Straits, assure the defense of the Straits by joint defense means in order to prevent the usage of the Straits by other States for purposes hostile to the Black Sea Powers.

The Turkish Government states that the said Soviet proposal is incompatible with the sovereign rights of Turkey and would destroy her security. The Turkish Government reached this conclusion long before hearing several concrete considerations of the Soviet Government on this subject, and without even having made an attempt to put under joint study the pertinent proposals of the U.S.S.R.

In declining, *en bloc*, all possibility of joint study with the Soviet Union of this important problem, indissolubly linked with the security interests of the U.S.S.R. and the other Black Sea Powers, the Turkish Government is in complete contradiction with its declarations regarding its desire to re-establish friendly relations with the U.S.S.R., based on confidence, by considering it possible to give voice to such suspicions which had no basis at all and which moreover are incompatible with the dignity of the Soviet Union.

Despite the point of view expressed in the Turkish note, the Soviet Government is of the opinion that only the means of Turkey and the Soviet Union combined can assure the freedom of commercial navigation as well as the security of the Straits. Accordingly, the Soviet Government believes that the application of the above-mentioned Soviet proposal should not prejudice the sovereignty of Turkey and should, at the same time, meet still better the interests of its security, since the joint measures of Turkey and the Soviet Union can assure the safeguarding of these Straits in much fuller measure than those of Turkey alone.

The refusal of Turkey to assure the defense of the Straits jointly with the Soviet Union deprives the Black Sea Powers of the possibility of guaranteeing the necessary security in this region.

During the last war the Axis countries used the Black Sea for their military operations against the U.S.S.R., to which contributed the fact that they were able to send into the Black Sea certain warships and auxiliary war vessels. There is also well remembered such a fact as the sudden passage through the Straits to the Black Sea in 1914 of the German cruisers *Goeben* and *Breslau* which upon entering the Black Sea attacked the Russian fleet and the Black Sea ports. All this is taken into consideration in the proposal for the common Soviet Turkish defense of the Straits having for purpose the assuring of a strong defense of the Straits in the interest of Turkey as well as in that of those of the other Black Sea Powers, which can not be fully assured by Turkey alone. On the other hand, if Turkey, after having declined the proposal of the U.S.S.R., were to set about taking (*s'était mise à effectuer*) military measures in the Straits by common accord with several Powers nonriverain of the Black Sea, this obviously would be in contradiction with the security interests of the Black Sea Powers. It would be unjust to forget that the Soviet Black Sea shores, extending 2100 kilometers, give access to the most important regions of the country, wherefore the necessity for assuring their security with direct participation of the Soviet Union in the defense of the Straits, has its origin in the vital interests of the U.S.S.R. All this explains the reason why the Soviet Government considers it necessary that the defense of the Straits should be carried out by the joint efforts of Turkey and the Soviet Union and have for its objective the assuring of the security of all the Black Sea States.

Regarding the reference of the Turkish Government to the UNO, the Soviet Government believes it necessary to state that its proposal set forth in the note of August 7 is entirely in conformity with the principles and objectives of that organization. This proposal assures not only the general interests of international commerce, but creates also the conditions for the maintenance of the security of the Black Sea Powers and thereby even contributes to the consolidation of general peace.

The Soviet Government believes it necessary to note that the remarks of the Turkish Government, relating to the procedure for the revision of the Montreux Convention, do not take into account the decisions of the Three Power Conference at Berlin that the Straits Convention, concluded at Montreux, should be revised as not meeting present conditions. With regard to the conference on the subject of the Straits regime, the Soviet Government is of the opinion that the calling of this conference should be preceded by as full as possible a discussion of this question through direct *pourparlers* between the Governments, as was envisaged by that same decision.*

*Source: United States, Department of State, *The Problem of the Turkish Straits* (Washington, D.C.: U.S. Government Printing Office, 1947), pp. 55-58.

APPENDIX 24

Note from the American Ambassador in the Soviet Union to the Soviet People's Commissar of Foreign Affairs

October 9, 1946

[complete text]

I have the honor to inform Your Excellency that my Government has studied carefully the contents of the note of the Soviet Union to Turkey of September 24 relating to the regime of the Straits.

In pursuance of its policy of making clear to all interested parties its views on matters relating to the Straits, my Government has instructed me to inform you that after examining the note referred to above it continued to adhere to the position outlined in its note of August 19, 1946 to the Soviet Government.

It will be recalled that in the Protocol of the proceedings of the Potsdam Conference, signed by the U.S.S.R., Great Britain, and the United States, the three Governments recognized that the Convention on the Straits concluded at Montreux should be revised as failing to meet present-day conditions. It was further agreed in the Protocol that as the next step the matter should be the subject of direct conversations between each of the three Governments and the Turkish Government.

It has been the understanding of my Government that the three Governments, in agreeing with one another that the regime of the Straits should be brought into accord with present-day conditions by means of a revision of the Montreux Convention, mutually recognized that all three signatories of the Protocol have an interest in the regime of the

Straits and in any changes which might be made in that regime. My Government furthermore informed the Soviet Government in its note of August 19, that in its view the regime of the Straits is a matter of concern not only to the Black Sea powers but also to other powers, including the United States. The Soviet Government, nevertheless, in its note of September 24, apparently continues to take the position set forth in its note of August 7 to Turkey that "the establishment of a regime of the Straits . . . should come under the competence of Turkey and the other Black Sea powers." My Government does not consider that it was contemplated at the Potsdam Conference that the direct conversations which might take place between any one of the three signatory governments and the Turkish Government with regard to the regime of the Convention of the Straits concluded at Montreux should have the effect of prejudicing the participation of the other two signatory powers in the revision of the regime of the Straits. On the contrary, my Government considers that the Potsdam Agreement definitely contemplated only an exchange of views with the Turkish Government as a useful preliminary to a conference of all of the interested powers, including the United States, to consider the revision of the Montreux Convention. As stated in its note of August 19, my Government stands ready to participate in such a conference.

My Government also feels that it would be lacking in frankness if it should fail to point out again at this time, in the most friendly spirit, that in its opinion the Government of Turkey should continue to be primarily responsible for the defense of the Straits and that should the Straits become the object of attack or threat of attack by an aggressor, the resulting situation would be a matter for action on the part of the Security Council of the United Nations.*

---

*Source: United States, Department of State, *The Problem of the Turkish Straits* (Washington, D.C.: U.S. Government Printing Office, 1947), p. 59.

APPENDIX 25

Note from the British Ambassador in the Soviet Union to the Soviet People's Commissar of Foreign Affairs

October 9, 1946

[complete text]

I have been instructed by my Government to inform the Soviet Government that the following are their views on the note dated September 24th from the Soviet Government to the Turkish Government on the subject of the Straits.

The Potsdam Agreement laid it down that as the next step this matter should be the subject of direct conversations between each of the three Governments and the Turkish Government. But it is the view of my Government that this "next step" has been completed by the exchange of views which have now taken place between these Governments. My Government therefore see no need for, or purpose in, continuing direct correspondence on the subject.

While my Government's attitude towards proposals 4 and 5 of the Soviet note of August 8th remain as stated in the British note of August 21st, my Government remain ready to attend a conference of the four Powers (namely the Soviet Union, the United States, the United Kingdom and France) and all other signatories of the Montreux Convention, excepting Japan, to consider the revision of that Convention.*

---

*Source: United States, Department of State, *The Problem of the Turkish Straits* (Washington, D.C.: U.S. Government Printing Office, 1947), pp. 59-60.

APPENDIX 26

Note from the Turkish Ministry of Foreign Affairs to the Soviet Embassy in Turkey

October 18, 1946

[complete text]

ANKARA, *October 18, 1946.*

The Government of the Turkish Republic has taken cognizance of the note of the Soviet Government dated September 24, 1946, in reply to the Turkish note of August 22, regarding the eventual revision of the Montreux Convention. It hastens to set forth, hereunder, the views and reflections which the meticulous examination of the above-mentioned document has permitted it to reach.

In its first part, the Soviet note takes up again the theme of the alleged use of the Straits by ships belonging to the countries of the Axis and, replying to the refutation applied against this subject in the Turkish note of August 22, it cites the cases of passage in 1942 and 1943 of German rapid pinnaces, in order to deduce from them, once again, the justice of the Soviet allegation.

In its August 22 note in reply, the Government of the Republic furnished to the Soviet Government the most complete explanations on the subject of the perfect correctness with which Turkey was able, during the extremely difficult period of the Second World War, to acquit itself of the task which it assumes because of the Montreux Convention. It clearly set forth that the few cases of fraudulent passage which had caused the Soviet objections arose essentially from the *lacunae* of Annex II of the Convention treating of definitions [and] specifications, as well as of calculation of tonnages; that the Annex in question for this reason admitted of the necessity of an adaptation to present conditions and concepts; and that, moreover, if the Soviet Government nonetheless considered that it could raise complaints concerning the execution of the Montreux Convention, the Government of the Republic would undertake to show, if necessary, before an arbitral court, the good faith and the loyalty with which it had conducted itself in order to assure with perfection the execution of the Convention confided to its care. Therefore, the Government of the Republic is of the opinion that, given the definite position taken by the two parties as regards the appreciation of the substances and the reality of the facts, it would be desirable to consider discussion on diplomatic grounds to be exhausted, the Turkish Government holding itself at the disposition of the Soviet Government to have recourse to arbitration. As regards particularly the case of the German pinnaces of which the passage through the Straits seems to be emphasized as a violation of the terms of the Convention, let it be sufficient to observe that the pinnaces in question were constructed in shipyards on the Danube under German control, and their presence in the Black Sea was consequently completely independent of the will of the Government of the Republic. Moreover, if the ships in question were able to pass through the Straits, it is also because they did not present any of the characteristics belonging to auxiliary war vessels or war vessels.

Along these lines, the Soviet note points out that, during the war, the Turkish Government ceased to present to the belligerent states reports on the movement of ships in the Straits, as it should have done according to the terms of Article 24 of the Montreux Convention.

It is appropriate to set forth, first of all, as regards this subject, that the reports in question ought, according to the terms of Article 24, to be presented not to the belligerent states, but to the powers signatory of the Montreux Convention, as well as to the Secretariat General of the League of

Nations. As regards their non-presentation, it suffices to observe that the Turkish Government, taking on the one hand,
into consideration the principles of refusal of passage for
warships of the belligerents, and foreseeing that, on the other
hand, no neutral power would consider, during the hostilities,
sending warships through the Straits, considered that the content of the Annual Report to be furnished to the signatory
powers and to the Secretariat General of the League of Nations would, because of this, be deprived of their most important information. As regards the statistics concerning commercial movements to be included in the report, the Turkish
Government considered that this movement, reduced to ridiculous proportions because of the hostilities, could not, if it
were made public, but influence unfavorably the war efforts
of the Allied countries, without, moreover, any counterpart
of usefulness. It therefore decided to stop sending the report
while continuing to compile it regularly. Moreover, it brought
this fact to the attention of the Secretariat General of the
League of Nations and of the powers signatory of the Montreux Convention, in February, 1942 for the report of the
year 1941, and in February, 1943 for that of the year 1942.
The hostilities having ended in 1945, the Annual Reports
referring to the years 1941-44 were sent to the interested
states on January 29, 1946. It is useful to emphasize here
that no power signatory of the Montreux Convention over
raised objections concerning this attitude of the Turkish Government. Let it be equally permitted to add that another
consideration of special nature, which decided the Government of the Republic to enter upon this course, was present
in the discovery that, during the years under reference, the
powers bordering the Black Sea, including the U.S.S.R. did
not think it necessary to conform to the obligation, set forth
in Article 18, Paragraph B, of the Montreux Convention, to
advise the Turkish Government on January 1st and July 1st of
each year, of the total tonnage of their fleets in the Black
Sea. Now the figures to be furnished because of this obliga-

tion were to be the basis of the information in the Annual Report to be presented by the Turkish Government. This abstention of Moscow during the war period was perfectly understandable and it never occurred to Turkey to address a complaint to the Soviet Government because of it. The Government of the Republic hopes likewise that the cessation of the sending of the Annual Reports during the same period, for the reasons set forth above, will no longer be considered by the U.S.S.R. as having prejudiced its security in the Black Sea.

The Soviet note then passes to the discussion of the grounds of certain other arguments included in the Turkish note of August 22nd as proofs of the circumstances which made difficult the control of the Straits. Notably it denies the probative character of the official annuals of war fleets, forcedly incomplete in the war period. Moreover, as reply to the Turkish argument drawn from the fact that the only kind of control to which ships in transit could be submitted, according to the Convention, was limited to a sanitary control, the Soviet note recalls the establishment by the Turkish Government of obligatory stops and of recourse to pilots in the Straits, as well as the surveillance by the Turkish customs authorities of ships in transit. The note adds finally that if the totality of these control measures was considered insufficient, on the other hand, not once during the war did the Turkish Government inform the contracting powers of the need to strengthen them.

The Turkish Government has already strongly set forth and emphasizes once again that the essential difficulty in differentiating between warships or commercial vessels, as regards ships in transit, rested in the imperfection of Annex II of the Convention. All the other arguments advanced by the Turkish note of August 22nd have no other end than to corroborate this elementary and patent truth, and to illustrate by facts and examples the conscious and considered correctness with which the Turkish authorities applied themselves, having recourse to all the sources which could, more or less, carry authority in the matter, to discovering the true character of the ships requesting passage through the Straits. It is in this light that the recourse to the official annual should be considered. As regards the establishment of obligatory stops and the recourse to pilots, it is clear that these measures had no other end than to protect ships in transit against the risk of running into the nets installed at the entrance of the Straits. They could not, in the presence of the contractual conditions, involve any purpose of control; they do not therefore have any connection with the subject under reference. Likewise, the allegation according to which the customs authorities exercised surveillance on ships in transit is completely lacking in foundation, for the good reason that because of the stipulations of the Montreux Convention, the surveillance in question could never take on the character of a customs visit and was limited to a simple precautionary measure destined to prevent attempts at smuggling. Finally the reproach addressed to Turkey of not having asked of the contracting powers the strengthening of the measures for control of ships in transit also cannot be admitted, for it does not take into consideration either the procedure established for the revision of the Montreux Convention, above all during a war in which the signatory powers were divided between the two opposing camps, nor the fact that the question of the control today described as being imperfect, was not the object, during the war, of any request of the contracting powers who could feel the need to see bettered the conditions relative to this formality.

All the facts developed above, adding themselves to the explanations already furnished, confirm the correctness and the vigilance of which the Government of the Republic gave proof in the accomplishment of its historic task in the Straits, correction and vigilance thanks to which the U.S.S.R. was able, during the entire length of the war, to remain in the Black Sea, sheltered from every Axis attack coming from the

Mediterranean. This truth, which everybody possessing objectivity is pleased to recognize, cannot be covered up by isolated facts and specious arguments. It also suffices to refute the allegation regarding the movements of troops which, according to the Soviet note, were alleged to have as their basis the supposed free passage through the Straits of war ships belonging to the Axis countries. In effect, the note affirms that this free use of the Straits by the Axis obliged the Soviet Government to withdraw an important number of military effectives from the principal sectors of the theater of war to assign them to the defense of the Black Sea region. Such would not seem to be, in the opinion of the Turkish Government, the real motive of the troop movements thus brought about. Judged in retrospect in the light of developments of the war and on the purely military plane, the despatch of troops to the Black Sea region presents no connection with the attitude of Turkey in the Straits, and this for the following reasons:

1. The real threat to the security of the Soviet Black Sea shores came from the occupation of a large part of the shore of that Sea by the German Armies, from the German possession of the Rumanian and Bulgarian fleets, and from the presence of German and Italian ships sent to Black Sea ports by rail or through the Danube.

2. The despatch of troops to the Black Sea region is explained by the obligation to face the German offensive unleashed from the beginning of hostilities, and above all commencing in the spring of the year 1942, along the shore of that Sea. This same offensive was also the origin of the uneasiness felt in Turkey from the point of its eventual development and of the measures of defense which this country had to take on the Turkish shores of the Black Sea.

The reading of the present note, as well as the reading of that dated August 22nd, which it complements, is sufficient to determine what really should be amended in the Montreux Convention in order to give the Black Sea powers all judicious and adequate satisfaction. In the first place, Annex II should be revised, account having been taken of present conditions and technical concepts. In the second place, the provisions of the Montreux Convention relative to the role and to the intervention of the League of Nations should give way to the system established by the United Nations Organization, in its task of preserving the peace of the world. Finally, Japan should be removed from the list of contracting powers, while the United States of America should be a signatory in the revised text. It is within this framework that the Government of the Republic would envisage an eventual revision of the Montreux Convention and if, deferring to the requests which have been addressed to it, it has been able to give its consent to be represented at a conference charged with the revision of the dispositions regarding passage through the Straits, one should see in this gesture only the manifestation of a laudable spirit of international cooperation in regard to any initiative which could reconcile the rights of sovereignty and the exigencies of the security of Turkey with the general interest. In consequence, and basing itself on the explanations and the reasoning formulated in the two Notes mentioned above, the Government of the Republic reiterates once more its intention to make no difficulty for the application, with the consent of the Contracting Powers of the Montreux Convention and of the United States of America, and at an international conference uniting the said Powers, of any request for revision specified by the Convention. But it can not admit unfounded complaints tending to justify this revision on the basis of an alleged responsibility on its part, born of pretended violations of the regime of the Straits in the course of the Second World War.

The Turkish Government has also studied with the greatest interest the complementary explanations furnished on the subject of point four of the Soviet Note. It thanks the Government of the U.S.S.R. for the kindness shown in this respect, with the object of assuring a perfect understanding of this point whose delicate character can not escape attention.

It results from these explanations that, in the opinion of

the Soviet Government, the establishment of the regime of the Straits should for the following reasons fall within the exclusive competence of Turkey and of the other riverain Powers of the Black Sea:

1. The Black Sea, as a closed sea, is said to have a special situation. The Straits are said to represent, because of this, a maritime route leading only to the coasts of a limited number of Powers in the Black Sea and to differ in consequence from the maritime routes of world importance such as Gibraltar and the Suez Canal. It is therefore natural that the riverain States of this sea are those most interested in the regulation of the regime of the Straits.

2. The Montreux Conference has already established a preferential regime in favor of the riverain Powers. In addition, in accepting the three first points of the Soviet proposal as basis of discussion, Turkey has recognized for the Black Sea Powers "a much more definitive preferential regime."

3. The special situation of the Black Sea was also recognized by Turkey in Article 5 of the Turco-Soviet Treaty dated March 16, 1921, which establishes the agreement of the two Contracting Parties to entrust the elaboration of the international statute of the Black Sea and of the Straits, on the basis of the principle of free navigation, to a conference uniting the representatives of the riverain countries of the Black Sea. Invoking the authority of this Article, the Soviet Note declares that the regulatory procedure thus envisaged, which meets the legitimate interests of the riverain Powers of the Black Sea without being inconsistent in any way with the interests of other countries, should be applied without further delay.

The Government of the Republic permits itself to develop below the replies which are called forth by the points summarized above:

1. In the opinion of the Soviet Government the Black Sea, as a closed sea, is said to have a special situation which limits interest in it to the riverain Powers alone.

Without wishing to introduce into this debate the authority of the doctrine which, moreover, seems to be unanimous in considering the Black Sea as an open sea, the Turkish Government limits itself simply to the observation that all the regulations of an international character which have appeared thus far, in each case with the participation of Russia, on the subject of the Straits have admitted more or less severe restrictions on the freedom of passage of riverain and non-riverain states only as exceptions freely agreed to by Turkey, in common accord with the other interested powers, in the general interest. It is the exceptional character of the closure which explains the efforts made towards the middle of the 19th century by the Government of the Czar to have this same rule set up as a general principle of European public law. To cite only examples from the most recent conventions, in support of the point of view developed above, it suffices to refer to the acts of Lausanne and Montreux which, breaking with the ancient rule of the Ottoman Empire sanctioned by international treaties, a rule in virtue of which it was forbidden at all times for foreign powers to enter the Straits while the Porte was at peace, having admitted the principle of the freedom of passage through the Straits, which includes equally the freedom of navigation in the Black Sea. The exceptions made by the conventions mentioned above to the principle of freedom in favor of the riverain powers of the Black Sea prove, not the possibility of excluding the non-riverain powers from negotiations looking toward the amendment of certain provisions of the regime at present in force, but the necessity of basing the revision on the agreement and the consent of all the powers interested in a reasonable regulation of this problem. To depart from these general limits of competence would mean nothing less than the negation of the fundamental principle of the law of nations, according to which a Power can be released from the obligations of a treaty, or modify its stipulations only by the assent of the contracting parties. In consequence, since the point under discussion has reference to the regime of passage through the Turkish Straits and since the Montreux Convention places upon the signatory Powers the obligation of proceeding to a modification of the provisions of this document only in an international conference uniting the contracting States and in accordance with a procedure foreseen by the text of the convention itself, it follows that the Soviet point of view is difficult to reconcile with the principles of international public law.

Without doubt Turkey is the first power to recognize the vital interest which free navigation through the Straits has for the riverain countries of the Black Sea. This is, moreover, the reason why she has without difficulty consented to be represented at a conference of revision. But she can not fail to recognize the interest which the other Powers also have in an equitable regulation of the same problem. Turkey has a clear consciousness of her status as a Power of the Black Sea. But she cannot forget that she is also a Mediterranean country. Charged by a particularly delicate geographic situation, with assuring the liaison between two worlds separated by the restricted space of the Straits, she is conscious of the obligation which this situation imposes on her with respect to the two seas which bathe her. The Turkish Government can therefore not consider the question of the Black Sea and of the Straits as a problem interesting the riverain Powers of this sea alone.

2. The Turkish Government agrees with the Government of the U.S.S.R. that the Montreux Convention, going still further than the Lausanne Convention concerning the regime of the Straits, has established for the benefit of the riverain states of the Black Sea a sharply defined system of preference. It is equally clear that in adopting as a basis of discussion at the international conference foreseen for the revision of the Montreux Convention, the three principles suggested by the Government of the United States of America, and taken up again later by the Soviet Government, the Turkish, British, and American Governments in a spirit of conciliation

have consented to take into consideration the possibilities of giving greater satisfaction to the Soviet desiderata. It seems to the Turkish Government that, in these conditions, the argument advanced in the Soviet Note serves rather to emphasize the complete good will with which the requests of the U.S.S.R. have been received by the Governments principally interested in the revision of the regime of the Straits; but it in no way removes the right and the interest which the same Powers as well as the other signatories of the Montreux Convention can have in seeing the procedure of revision begin and end under the happiest auspices, in the interest naturally not only of the Black Sea Powers, destined to derive a considerable profit from the new concessions foreseen in their favor, but also of all the States entitled to make their voices heard and to defend their interests in the course of the important meetings in prospect.

3. Considered from the strictly legal point of view, Article 5 of the Turco-Soviet Treaty signed at Moscow on March 16, 1921 expresses an undertaking. In actual fact, the two Contracting Parties disposed of it otherwise, and manifested their act of will in an absolutely opposite sense, in the first place, by their effective participation in the negotiations undertaken at Lausanne on the subject of the regime of the Straits within a considerably enlarged international framework. It is true that in the course of the discussion engaged in on this subject, Mr. Chicherin, First Soviet Delegate, who defended with ardor and eloquence the system of closure of the Straits, did not hesitate to announce its intention of "proposing to the Black Sea Powers the calling of a conference to establish the reciprocal conditions of an effective security of the shores of this sea." This project nevertheless, encountered the almost unanimous objection of the Delegations present at the Conference. It results from the declarations made on this subject that the Soviet point of view appeared not to take into account the views of the other riverain Powers, whose representatives in effect denied to the U.S.S.R. the right to

speak in their name and added that their ideas on the main-tenance of the peace of the world and the security of their territories on the shores of the Black Sea differed substantial-ly from those of the Soviet Government. Moreover, the same declaration made it apparent that the Soviet proposal exclud-ed the principle of international law according to which the passage between two seas should be considered as an inter-national route; that it would give to the U.S.S.R. if it were adopted by the Conference, an exceptional and unjustly ad-vantageous position in the Black Sea; and that the Soviet argument according to which the opening of the Straits to warships would be to the advantage of the strongest naval power lost all its force and value in the presence of the con-trary argument according to which the closing of the Black Sea would put the other riverain states at the mercy of the maritime power which possessed the strongest land forces, in other words, at the mercy of the U.S.S.R. itself.

The same change in the attitude of Turkey and of the U.S.S.R. toward the subject of the framework of elaboration of the regime of the Straits appeared, in the second place, in the participation of authorized representatives of the two countries in the conference which established the Montreux regime, the fruit of long and laborious discussions in the course of which the eminent Soviet Delegate, Mr. Maxim Litvinov, distinguished himself by the great competency with which he defended and carried to victory the points of view of his Government. It is not in vain that at the last plenary session of the Conference, he rejoiced in the excellent results obtained. It is also not in vain that in speaking at the closing session of the Conference, he addressed to his audience this moving appeal: "The Conference has had to understand that in place of the old imperialist Russia which sought to use the Black Sea as a base for its participation in the imperialist struggle of the great Powers and for the realization of new territorial conquests, there is today a new Soviet and socialist state which occupies the largest part of the Black Sea and one of whose first acts was to renounce completely all imperialist objectives, and which subsequently has invariably and systematically pursued a policy of peace, jealous not only of its own security, but also of that of all states near or far. . . . All those who have participated in the Conference will go away satisified there will be no one discontented."

These words, just as well as realistic, which do honor to the Government from which they emanate, words which the Government of the Republic is glad to recall and which still sound in the ears of those who had the privilege of hearing them, have moreover the merit of proving that the Government of the Turkish Republic, initiator of the meeting at Montreux, and the Soviet Government were in 1936 no longer at the point where, in 1921, they envisaged for the regulation of the question of the Straits a conference limited to the Black Sea Powers only. There is no doubt that the terms on which an understanding between states is based cease to be in force from the day when a subsequent accord of the parties replaces the former undertaking by new arrangements duly signed and ratified. This is the case, especially, with relation to the framework of elaboration of the regime of the Straits. The preceding explanations and the citations demonstrate clearly that the controversy that the Soviet note has raised by invoking Article 5 of the Treaty of Moscow has today only a historic character. In any case, the facts set forth above are there to prove that the historic argument advanced by the Government of the U.S.S.R. no longer appears of a nature to serve as a solid base for the thesis which it maintains.

The same explanations and citations also prove the fact that the Soviet formula directed toward the elaboration of a regime of the Straits by the riverains of the Black Sea alone does not seem, contrary to the opinion expressed in the Note of September 24, to satisfy any of the non-riverain countries whose interests in the Straits are involved.

The same reasoning and the same conclusions are equally valid in refuting the Soviet demonstration based on the authority of an article, drafted in the same manner as the said Article 5 and appearing in the treaty of October 13, 1921, concluded between Turkey and the Transcaucasian Republics, as well as in the treaty of January 21, 1922 concluded between Turkey and the Ukrainian Soviet Socialist Republic.

In its Note dated August 22, the Turkish Government was intent on setting forth the reasons of a contractual character which were opposed to the revision of the regime of the Straits except within the framework and according to the procedure foreseen by the Montreux Convention. In the presence of the complementary explanations obligingly advanced in the Soviet Note of September 24 on the subject of point four, the Turkish Government has felt bound to develop, in its turn, the manner in which it views the new commentaries furnished by the above-mentioned Note. The Government of the Republic would consequently be grateful to the Government of the U.S.S.R. if it would consider the explanations of the present note as supplementing those furnished on the same subject in the previous Note.

With regard to point five of the Soviet Note of August 7, which recommends a mixed system of Turco-Soviet defense in the Straits, the Government of the U.S.S.R. states that the Turkish Government considers this proposition as incompatible with the rights of sovereignty and the security of Turkey and that it arrives at this conclusion without having previously examined the concrete considerations of the Soviet Government on this subject. In doing this, the Note adds, and in formulating suspicions which are baseless and incompatible with the dignity of the Soviet Union, the Turkish Government finds itself in full contradiction with its own declarations concerning the restoration of friendly relations, marked by mutual confidence with the U.S.S.R. The Soviet Government believes that the application of its proposal could be realized not only without the slightest prejudice to the sovereignty of Turkey, but with an appreciable augmentation of its security.

The Turkish Government cannot share the opinion according to which it has opposed the discussion of point five, which it regards as incompatible with the rights of sovereignty and the security of Turkey, without previously having examined the concrete suggestions of the Soviet Government on this subject. It is first of all necessary to underline here that the Government of the Republic has never failed to receive with interest and good will the démarches of foreign powers with which it has relations. In this connection, the Turkish Government wishes particularly to recall that, raised for the first time at Moscow in 1939, in the course of the Saracoglu-Molotov conversations, the question of a joint defense of the Straits by the Turkish and Soviet Governments was also taken up, later, by the Government of the U.S.S.R. in an aggravated form, in the course of a conversation with the Turkish representative at Moscow. It is because this subject has been justly considered as injuring the rights, through the respect of which a nation is and remains independent, that it has encountered the opposition of Turkey. The entire question of the Straits has continued likewise to be, by means of the extensive correspondence recently exchanged on this subject between Ankara and Moscow, the subject of a substantial examination of the respective positions of Turkey and the U.S.S.R. It is therefore unjust to accuse the Turkish Government of avoiding the opening of friendly conversations with the U.S.S.R. with the object of clarifying point 5. The principle of freedom of passage through the Straits is, according to principles universally recognized, limited by the right of the riverain State to guard the security and defense of its territory, and can not in any way diminish the right and duty that State has to see to its preservation. The right to defend itself against all aggression is, beyond denial, for an independent State which respects itself the most essential attribute of its sovereignty. The acceptance by Turkey of a joint defense of the Straits would mean no less than the sharing of her sovereignty with a foreign power. The Government of the Republic, in its note of August 22, has given to the Soviet Government all the necessary assurances with regard to its firm intention to defend, as in the past, Turkish territory against all aggression and had indicated to it its desire to see established between Turkey and the U.S.S.R. cordial and confident relations. It is happy to repeat again the same assurances. It does not lose sight of the fact that the Soviet coasts on the Black Sea have a length of 2100 kilometers, but it also does not forget that the Turkish coasts of the Black Sea are almost as long. If the principle of the closing of the Straits to the powers non-riverain of the Black Sea, a principle which, in itself, already constitutes a very important guarantee for the security of the U.S.S.R. is not sufficient to eliminate Soviet apprehensions completely, it is in order for that country to have recourse, in the event of an attack against the Black Sea, to the most perfect solution which mankind has yet found to repel aggression, that is the joint defense by national forces and the forces of the United Nations Organization charged with preventing all aggression, from wherever it comes.

Apart from these reflections, the Turkish Government cannot understand how the right of defense of the Soviet Union can be exercised in Turkey, in defiance of the rights of sovereignty of this country. The Turkish Government cannot resist recalling here the vehement terms in which Mr. Chicherin protested at the Lausanne Conference, against the proposal to take from Turkey the control of the passage of the Straits and opposed what he rightly called "a flagrant violation of the sovereignty and independence of Turkey." It cannot conceive that the rejection by Turkey of this same demand for control now proposed by the Soviet Union should be considered by that Power as incompatible with its dignity, since, in the opinion of the Government of the Republic, it is on the contrary to the honor, the dignity and the very existence of Turkey, as an independent nation, which are involved.

The Soviet note recalls, in support of its thesis, the passage of the German cruisers *Goeben* and *Breslau* through the Straits in 1914. This reference to two vessels purchased by the Ottoman Government has no relation either to the subject under discussion or to the enforcement of the Montreux Convention and seems rather a question of international law relating to the propriety of the acquisition by neutrals of belligerent vessels taking refuge in their territorial waters.

In the same way, the allusion made in the Soviet note to the subject of the adoption of supposed military measures in the Straits by joint accord with certain powers non-riverain of the Black Sea is not understood in Turkey, since it relates to facts lacking any foundation. In consequence it is outside this discussion.

In its note of August 22, the Turkish Government, after having emphasized that the most certain guarantee of the security of the U.S.S.R. in the Black Sea rested not in the seeking of a privileged strategic position in the Straits, a position incompatible with the dignity and the sovereignty of an independent country, but in the restoration of relations of trust with a strong Turkey, ardently desirous of contributing to that healthy task, but whose activity in this respect has unfortunately been restricted by lack of efforts on a parallel plane, added that in addition to this first class guarantee furnished by Turkey, the U.S.S.R. should, in the wholly improbable case of an attack in the Straits, also count upon the efficacy of the United Nations Organization of which she as well as Turkey is a member.

After having recalled this reference the Soviet Government states in its note that its proposal No. 5 is entirely in conformity with the principles and objectives of the said Organization. In emphasizing the importance of the United Nations Organization in a question which is properly of the utmost interest to the U.S.S.R. the Turkish Government precisely wished to refer to the First Article of the Charter, relative to objectives and to principles, an article according to the terms of which the new international organization should, henceforth, answer for the security of everyone, placed under the guarantee of the international forces put at the service of the Organization. It also wished to allude to the undertaking solemnly assumed by the members of the Organization, by virtue of Article 2 of the said Charter relative to principles "to refrain in their international relations, from the threat or use of force, against either the territorial integrity or the political independence of any State, or in any other manner inconsistent with the purposes of the United Nations."

Putting aside any considerations as to the necessity of allowing every country to defend itself in its own way against outside aggression, the Government of the Republic has difficulty in understanding how, in an age when all the peoples avid for tranquility and peace are in the position of having placed their hopes in the guarantees of security flowing from the work of San Francisco, a proposal disregarding the existence of the new Organization and the guarantees of collective security which it provides can be compatible with the objectives and the principles thereof. It also asks itself how this same proposal which, to establish security at home, believes it possible to wipe out the security and sovereignty of a neighbor can be reconciled with the obligation to respect the territorial integrity and political independence of others. The Government of the Republic is thus obliged to repeat again that point 5 of the Soviet note of August 7 is incompatible with the inalienable rights of sovereignty of Turkey and with her security which permits of no restriction.

Basing itself upon the long explanations furnished above, the Turkish Government is convinced that it has established tangible proof of its good will and of its spirit of conciliation in agreeing to participate in a conference for the revision of the Montreux Convention. It appeals to the Soviet Government to ask it to study, in its turn, the reflections which its proposals evoke, with the same objectivity and the same good will.

Finally, to reply briefly to the Soviet reproach to the Turkish Government that it confines itself to conditions of admissibility of the procedure for the revision of the Montreux

Convention, without taking the Potsdam decisions into account, this Government must first of all state that the decisions in question, which by a free manifestation of its will it has consented to take into consideration, contemplated only the attempting by means of conversations of an endeavor at conciliation of the respective points of view of the three Powers represented at the said conference, within the framework of the rights of sovereignty of Turkey, in a manner to prepare the ground for the convocation of the conference for revision. They are symptomatic of the interest which these same Powers attach to the question of the Straits, but they cannot replace the Montreux Convention which, alone, binds the signatory states. Moreover, the Government of the Republic believes it useful to point out that, to its knowledge, the decision to which the Soviet note refers envisaged direct conversations between the Turkish Government, on the one hand, and each of the three Powers represented at Potsdam on the other hand, on the subject of the eventual revision of the Montreux Convention. Now, in the opinion of the Turkish Government, the preliminary preparatory work desired by the Potsdam conference is now virtually completed, thanks, in the first place, to the communications made by the Governments of the United States of America and of Great Britain to Ankara and, then, to the exchange of notes which has taken place concerning the same subject between Turkey and the Soviet Union. The Government of the Republic consequently believes that the contacts thus accomplished have definitely and sufficiently clarified the respective positions of Turkey and of the three Powers concerned with respect to the question of the Straits. Under these circumstances, the Turkish Government cannot avoid expressing its doubts as to the usefulness and the advisability of continuing to follow, in the future, the same procedure of exchange of views by means of correspondence. It considers the ground sufficiently prepared in order that the procedure of revision can be usefully begun (*déclenchés*). The Turkish Government, insofar as it is concerned, while maintaining its attitude defined in the present note as well as in that of August 22, concerning points 4 and 5 of the Soviet demands, declares itself ready to attend a conference at which are assembled the Soviet Union, the United States of America, the United Kingdom, and France as well as the other states signatories of the Montreux Convention, except Japan, in order to proceed with negotiations for the revision of the above-mentioned convention.

This note would certainly be incomplete if it closed without a fervent homage rendered to the organism which crystallizes all the hopes of peoples towards a future of peace. The Government of the Republic wishes, once more, to express its profound faith in the future of the United Nations Organization, the support of the universal order based on concord, equity and mutual respect, framework of efficacious institutions in the service of living cooperation. It bases the greatest hopes on this constellation which has assumed the task of inculcating in everyone the necessity of collaboration between the peoples and of a law which governs them, and of orienting the community of nations towards a rich development of solidarity and interdependence, thus creating a work of high civilization, regenerator of stability and general prosperity. The Government of the Republic firmly hopes to find itself with its great neighbor of the North in this field of serenity, in the effulgence and radiance of international collaboration, dispenser of benefits for all the peoples of good will.

A copy of the Soviet note of September 24 has been transmitted by the Turkish Government to the Governments of Great Britain and of the United States of America.

A copy of the present note has been sent to the signatories of the Montreux Convention—except Japan—and to the Government of the United States of America.*

---

*Source: United States, Department of State, *The Problem of the Turkish Straits* (Washington, D.C.: U.S. Government Printing Office, 1947), pp. 60-68.

APPENDIX 27

Note from the Soviet Ministry of Foreign Affairs to the Turkish Ambassador in Moscow

July 20, 1953

[complete text]

The U.S.S.R. Ministry of Foreign Affairs has the honor of giving the following message to the Embassy of the Turkish Republic.

The Turkish Ministry of Foreign Affairs has reported to the Soviet Embassy in Ankara that from July 22 to 27 a formation of U.S. naval vessels composed of 10 ships, including two cruisers, three destroyers, four mine sweepers and one landing ship, will be in the port of Istanbul. After this, from July 27 to August 3, a formation of British naval vessels composed of 22 ships, including three cruisers, four destroyers, six mine sweepers and four landing ships, will be in the port of Istanbul.

In connection with this report by the Turkish Foreign Ministry, it is impossible not to note the fact that recently the touching of foreign naval formations, including large naval vessels, in ports of the Black Sea straits has become more frequent and the above-mentioned visits to the port of Istanbul by 10 American and 22 British naval vessels may be viewed as a kind of military demonstration.

In view of the circumstances, the Soviet government hopes for further information from the Turkish government.*

---

*Source: J. C. Hurewitz, *Diplomacy in the Near and Middle East: A Documentary Record, 1914-1956*, Vol. II (Princeton, N.J.: D. Van Nostrand, 1956), p. 343.

APPENDIX 28

Note from the Turkish Foreign Ministry to the Soviet Ambassador in Ankara

July 24, 1953

[complete text]

On July 20, 1953, his Excellency Mr. Zorin, Deputy Foreign Minister of the U.S.S.R., gave the Turkish Ambassador in Moscow a verbal note, the text of which was immediately published by the Soviet government, in which the Foreign Ministry, making a pretext of calls at Istanbul to be made in the immediate future by the American fleet and later by the British fleet, states that it cannot refrain from calling attention to the fact that recently visits to the straits ports by foreign naval formations, including large vessels, are becoming more frequent, that the two visits under discussion can be viewed as a kind of military demonstration and expresses hope of additional information from the Turkish government.

In answer to this note the Foreign Ministry of the Turkish Republic has the honor of requesting the U.S.S.R. embassy to be so kind as to report the following to its government:

The government of the U.S.S.R., being regularly informed under Art. 24 of the Montreux Convention on the straits regime, cannot but know that the visits referred to in the above-mentioned note are courtesy visits.

Since Arts. 14 (paragraph three) and 17 of the Montreux Convention grant naval forces on courtesy visits to the straits complete freedom as to tonnage and since the visits under discussion are being made in full conformity with these articles, their frequent repetition cannot be interpreted other than as happy evidence of the friendly ties uniting Turkey with the countries to which the invited fleets belong.

In view of what is set forth above and taking into account that all data and information concerning the two visits, to which the Soviet government deemed it necessary to call special attention, were reported to it in the necessary manner and in due form, the Turkish government cannot conceal its surprise at the fact that the Soviet government deemed it necessary to demand additional information, which could be viewed as a kind of intervention on a question which is left by international custom to the discretion of the countries concerned.*

---

*Source: J. C. Hurewitz, *Diplomacy in the Near and Middle East: A Documentary Record, 1914-1956*, Vol. II (Princeton, N.J.: D. Van Nostrand, 1956), pp. 343-44.

APPENDIX 29

Note from the Soviet Ministry of Foreign Affairs to the Turkish Ambassador in Moscow

July 31, 1953

[complete text]

In connection with the Turkish Foreign Ministry's note of July 24, the U.S.S.R. Foreign Ministry has the honor of making the following statement to the embassy of the Turkish Republic:

In its note of July 20 the U.S.S.R. Foreign Ministry, referring to a report by the Turkish Foreign Ministry on a visit to the port of Istanbul this July by U.S. naval units comprising

10 ships and of British naval units comprising 22 ships, called attention to the fact that recent calls at ports on the Black Sea straits by foreign naval formations including large vessels, have become more frequent. The Ministry also stated that the visits by 10 American and 22 British naval vessels, mentioned in the note, to the port of Istanbul may be viewed as a kind of military demonstration.

Having studied the Turkish Foreign Ministry's answer to this note July 24, the U.S.S.R. Foreign Ministry deems it necessary to add that in recent years the number of visits to the Black Sea straits by large foreign naval vessels has increased considerably. The following official data prove this:

The Black Sea straits have been visited by:

In 1950—33 foreign naval vessels with a displacement of 197,800 tons.

In 1951—49 foreign naval vessels with a displacement of 378,800 tons.

In 1952—69 foreign naval vessels with a displacement of 587,727 tons.

In seven months of 1953—60 foreign naval vessels with a displacement of more than 300,000 tons.

In view of this, when visits to the Black Sea straits by foreign naval vessels have reached the above-mentioned large dimensions, the request by the U.S.S.R. Foreign Ministry for additional information from the Turkish Foreign Ministry concerning the increasing frequency of visits to the Black Sea straits by large foreign naval formations could not come as a surprise.

Yet the Turkish Foreign Ministry, in its answering note of July 24, deemed it possible to reduce this whole question to its narrowly formal aspect which, in the given instance, has no real significance. As for the Soviet side's above-mentioned request for additional information on a matter of importance to the Soviet Union and quite natural in normal relations between two neighboring states, the Turkish Foreign Ministry found it possible to view this request as a kind of intervention in a question within Turkey's competence, although there was no foundation at all for such a conclusion.

The U.S.S.R. Foreign Ministry is sending this reply to the Turkish Foreign Ministry's note of July 24 to confirm the importance of the question raised in the Ministry's note of July 20, 1953.*

---

*Source: J. C. Hurewitz, *Diplomacy in the Near and Middle East: A Documentary Record, 1914-1956*, Vol. II (Princeton, N.J.: D. Van Nostrand, 1956), pp. 344-45.

APPENDIX 30

Letter from N. S. Khrushchev, Chairman of the U.S.S.R. Council of Ministers to General Cemal Gürsel, Prime Minister of Turkey

June 28, 1960

[complete text]

Mr. Prime Minister,

With great satisfaction I and my colleagues in the Soviet Government have made ourselves familiar with your latest pronouncements about Turkey's relations with the Soviet Union, made during the talk with our Ambassador in Ankara on June 14 of this year. I should like to note, above all, our agreement with you that both Turkey and the Soviet Union have a common desire to make our relations good. We also note and, for our part, ardently welcome the fact that you do not have any objections of principle to the subsequent turning of Soviet-Turkish relations into close co-operation. Since your and our goals will coincide in this respect, this will then be what we must work on in the interests of the peoples of our two countries.

Of course, we are to solve several questions on this road, questions requiring settlement. We understand your consider-ations about the complexity of the situation in which Turkey has landed after 10 years of the policy of participation in military blocs with the western powers, which egged Turkey on to steps which were in no way compatible with the tradi-tional good-neighbourly relations between Turkey and the Soviet Union.

You are well aware of our attitude to military blocs, and also our views on participation in them on the part of our neighbours, and I would not be frank if I did not state this now, too.

Of course, I shall say this frankly—it is our deep conviction that the most sincere relations between our two neighbour countries would develop if Turkey embarked upon the road of neutrality. This would only benefit the country. Turkey would receive an opportunity to use her resources, not for war preparations, on which huge funds have so far been squandered, but for raising the level of the country's national economy and the wellbeing of its people. Military expendi-tures, Mr. Prime Minister, are a bottomless pit and not every country can endure the burden of them and develop its econ-omy at the same time.

As for Turkey, you, of course, know better than I that this is so.

I have expressed to you my frank opinion. This, of course, is not a condition for beginning the improvement of our relations. We believe that this should be started and any step in this direction, let alone the achievement of this goal, will be greeted by us as by sincere and true friends of the Turkish people and the independent Turkish state. Nor are we striving to worsen Turkey's relations with America or other western powers. Such a desire is alien to us. Moreover, we ourselves are striving to have good relations with the western powers, including the United States. If we are unable to establish such relations with some of them, or, moreover, unable to make them good and lasting, that is no fault of ours.

We agree with you that there is no need to postpone the improvement of Soviet-Turkish relations until all the major problems of those relations can be fully resolved, and that we should at least avoid such actions in the immediate future as could further worsen Soviet-Turkish relations, which under the previous Turkish Government were brought to a state which could not and cannot satisfy either the Soviet Union or Turkey.

I consider it necessary, Mr. Prime Minister, to stress once again that the statement of the new Government of Turkey that it intends to abide by the principles of the policy formulated by the founder of the Turkish Republic and fighter for Turkey's independence Kemal Atatürk, with whose name friendly and even fraternal realtions between our two neighbour countries are associated in our minds, has been received with a feeling of satisfaction in Moscow. We remember Atatürk's words that Soviet-Turkish friendship has so far only benefited international peace and that this friendship would be beneficial and fruitful in the future.

If the new Turkish Government really abides by the policy of Atatürk, we shall all see Soviet-Turkish relations return to the high level of the true good-neighbourliness and genuine friendship at which they were in the days of the great founder of the Soviet Union and friend of the eastern peoples, V. I. Lenin, and the leader of the new Turkey, Atatürk.

Your desire that Turkey, in spite of the binding nature of the existing commitments and alliances, should pursue an independent policy, meets with the understanding of the Soviet Government. We in the Soviet Union want most of all to see our neighbour countries prosper and pursue an independent foreign policy.

Being desirous of improving its relations with neighbouring Turkey, the Soviet Government pointed out in its well-known statement of May 30, 1953, that the policy of the U.S.S.R. is based on the Leninist principles of complete respect for the territorial integrity, sovereignty and independence of the Turkish state, on the principles of equality of large and small nations, on the principles of peaceful coexistence and co-operation between states with different social and economic systems. Now, too, we abide by this position and believe it is necessary and useful to confirm this once again.

The Soviet Government presumes that Turkey, as a state, can in no way benefit from such relations with its northern neighbour as developed and were maintained for several years under the previous Turkish Government.

Irrespective of the past, the time has now come to start ridding our relations of the burden of prejudices of various kinds and to start restoring, step by step, the confidence which formerly existed in the relations between our two countries.

It is absolutely clear that the main thing now is not to search for questions on which we disagree. On the contrary, we must search for points on which our views coincide so as to advance along the road to *rapprochement*.

The Soviet Government hopes that the government of which you are the head will view in a positive way the considerations put forward in this letter—considerations which, so it seems to us, coincide on the whole with your pronouncements on the questions of Soviet-Turkish relations.

Permit me to express the sincere hope that with your direct participation a start will be made on the resumption of the earlier existing friendship and mutual co-operation in the relations between Turkey and the Soviet Union.

N. KHRUSHCHEV*

---

*Source: *Documents on International Affairs, 1960* (London: Oxford University Press [for the Royal Institute of International Affairs], 1964), pp. 419-21.

APPENDIX 31

**Letter from General Cemal Gürsel, Turkish Prime Minister,
to N. S. Khrushchev, Chairman of the U.S.S.R. Council of
Ministers**

July 8, 1960

[complete text]

Mr. Chairman,

I have studied with keen interest and very great attention
your message of June 28, 1960, which was handed to me by
the Soviet Ambassador in Ankara. I note with satisfaction the
desire expressed in your message to arrive at better relations
between our two countries and I can sincerely assure you
that I fully share this wish.

However, guided by the desire to leave no doubts concerning the position of the Turkish Government on certain points
of your message, I should like in this connection to give Your
Excellency the following explanations. I wish to add that this
clarification in no way reduces the prospects for improving
relations between our two countries, but is proof that Turkey's commitments under the defensive alliances to which
she belongs leave her enough leeway for arriving at the desired improvement.

The government which I head was set up as a result of the
movement for national reforms, started on May 27 of this
year. This movement, in conformity with its very first statement, did not fail to declare with ample clarity that Turkey
would remain loyal to her international commitments and, in
particular, to those of them which arise from the existence of
her alliances, such as NATO and CENTO.

These alliances were concluded in conformity with the decisions of the United Nations Charter. They pursue purely

defensive purposes and are a consequence of a lawful and imperative need which Turkey cannot overlook, lest she should prejudice her independence and security.

This policy of alliances, pursued by Turkey, has nothing incompatible with good-neighbourly relations between our two countries. As I have already pointed out, the alliances to which Turkey belongs are of an exclusively defensive nature and are not directed against any country, only against a potential aggressor.

Allow me, Mr. Chairman, to dwell on the thought which occurred to me when I was reading your message. I do not think that the pursuance of a neutral policy can free the government from military expenditures. If that were so, then such countries as Sweden, Switzerland, or India for that matter would have no military budgets. However, these countries, as you certainly know, maintain considerable means of defence pressing as a heavy burden on their budgets. They do so because they feel it necessary in spite of their neutralist policies.

In reality, liquidation or at least reduction of military expenditures can be made possible, not by neutrality, but by the establishment of a system of universal disarmament with an effective control mechanism, which would ensure the security of all the countries of the world, whether large or small, against any aggression on the part of any state. Until the creation of such a system of international disarmament, towards which Turkey is striving just as passionately as any other country sincerely desiring peace, no state can renounce the means of ensuring its security. Turkey, prompted by this lawful concern, remains loyal to its policy of membership in collective security systems.

I am happy to learn that the establishment of a new regime in Turkey was favourably received in Moscow. I can confirm to you that in the sphere of international relations, too, my government will abide by the principles of Atatürk.

Let me emphasize in this connection that far from ever

contradicting the pursuance by Turkey of a policy of multilateral cooperation with a view to securing peace and the
independence of nations, these principles, on the contrary,
are a logical foundation of this policy. Proof of this is the
fact that already in 1934 and 1937 Turkey was successfully
working in accordance with these principles to create the
Balkan and Saadbad pacts, the purpose of which was to preserve the independence of their members and the peace of
the area in question.

I note with great satisfaction, Mr. Chairman, that the Soviet Government desires to confirm its statement of May 30,
1953; I, like you, really believe that the genuine improvement of relations between our countries is possible within the
framework of the principles put forward in this statement—
principles which Turkey, for her part, has never rejected.

In conclusion I would like again to express the hope that
the considerations I have set forth above will convince Your
Excellency that nothing in Turkish policy obstructs the improvement of relations between our two countries. It suffices
for this policy to meet with the same good will on the part of
our Soviet neighbour. Your Excellency's letter, and particularly the part of it mentioning the need, throwing aside any
prejudiced views whatsoever, to direct our joint efforts
towards the solution of those problems on which our viewpoints coincide, gives me hope that a similar desire also exists
on the Soviet side.

Please accept, Mr. Chairman, this expression of my deep
respect.

CEMAL GÜRSEL*

*Source: Documents on International Affairs, 1960 (London: Ox-
ford University Press [for the Royal Institute of International Affairs],
1964), pp. 421-22.

APPENDIX 32

Letter from President Lyndon B. Johnson to Prime Minister Ismet Inönü of Turkey

June 5, 1964

[complete text]

Dear Mr. Prime Minister:

I am gravely concerned by the information which I have had through Ambassador Hare from you and your Foreign Minister that the Turkish Government is contemplating a decision to intervene by military force to occupy a portion of Cyprus. I wish to emphasize, in the fullest friendship and frankness, that I do not consider that such a course of action by Turkey, fraught with such far-reaching consequences, is consistent with the commitment of your Government to consult fully in advance with us. Ambassador Hare has indicated that you have postponed your decision for a few hours in order to obtain my views. I put to you personally whether you really believe that it is appropriate for your Government to present a unilateral decision of such consequence to an ally who has demonstrated such staunch support over the years as has the United States for Turkey. I must, therefore, first urge you to accept the responsibility for complete consultation with the United States before any such action is taken.

It is my impression that you believe that such intervention by Turkey is permissible under the provisions of the Treaty of Guarantee of 1960. I must call your attention, however, to our understanding that the proposed intervention by Turkey would be for the purpose of effecting a form of partition of the island, a solution which is specifically excluded by the Treaty of Guarantee. Further, that Treaty requires consultation among the Guarantor Powers. It is the view of the United States that the possibilities of such consultation have by no means been exhausted in this situation and that, therefore, the reservation of the right to take unilateral action is not yet applicable.

I must call to your attention also, Mr. Prime Minister, the obligations of NATO. There can be no question in your mind that a Turkish intervention in Cyprus would lead to a military engagement between Turkish and Greek forces. Secretary of State Rusk declared at the recent meeting of the Ministerial Council of NATO in the Hague that war between Turkey and Greece must be considered as "literally unthinkable." Adhesion to NATO, in its very essence, means that NATO countries will not wage war on each other. Germany and France have buried centuries of animosity and hostility in becoming NATO allies; nothing less can be expected from Greece and Turkey. Furthermore, a military intervention in Cyprus by Turkey could lead to a direct involvement by the Soviet Union. I hope you will understand that your NATO allies have not had a chance to consider whether they have an obligation to protect Turkey against the Soviet Union if Turkey takes a step which results in Soviet intervention without the full consent and understanding of its NATO Allies.

Further, Mr. Prime Minister, I am concerned about the obligations of Turkey as a member of the United Nations. The United Nations has provided forces on the Island to keep the peace. Their task has been difficult but, during the past several weeks, they have been progressively successful in reducing the incidents of violence on that Island. The United Nations mediator has not yet completed his work. I have no doubt that the general membership of the United Nations would react in the strongest terms to unilateral action by Turkey which would contravene the efforts of the United Nations and destroy any prospect that the United Nations could assist in obtaining a reasonable and peaceful settlement of this difficult problem.

I wish also, Mr. Prime Minister, to call your attention to the bilateral agreement between the United States and Turkey in the field of military assistance. Under Article IV of the Agreement with Turkey of July 1947, your government is required to obtain United States consent for the use of military assistance for purposes other than those for which such assistance was furnished. Your Government has on several occasions acknowledged to the United States that you fully understand this condition. I must tell you in all candor that the United States cannot agree to the use of any United States supplied military equipment for a Turkish intervention in Cyprus under present circumstances.

Moving to the practical results of the contemplated Turkish move, I feel obligated to call to your attention in the most friendly fashion the fact that such a Turkish move could lead to the slaughter of tens of thousands of Turkish Cypriots on the Island of Cyprus. Such an action on your part would unleash the Furies and there is no way by which military action on your part could be sufficiently effective to prevent such a catastrophe.

You may consider that what I have said is much too severe and that we are disregardful of Turkish interest in the Cyprus situation. I should like to assure you that this is not the case. We have exerted ourselves both publicly and privately to assure the safety of Turkish Cypriots and to insist that a final solution of the Cyprus problem should rest upon the consent of the parties most directly concerned. It is possible that you feel in Ankara that the United States has not been sufficiently active in your behalf. But surely you know that our policy has caused the liveliest resentments in Athens (where demonstrations have been aimed against us) and has led to a basic alienation between the United States and Archbishop Makarios. As I said to your Foreign Minister in our conversation just a few weeks ago, we value very highly our relations with Turkey. We have considered you as a great ally with fundamental common interests. Your security and prosperity have been a deep concern of the American people and we have expressed that concern in the most practical terms. You and we have fought together to resist the ambitions of the communist world revolution. This solidarity has meant a great deal to us and I would hope that it means a great deal to your Government and to your people. We have no intention of lending any support to any solution of Cyprus which endangers the Turkish Cypriot community. We have not been able to find a final solution because this is, admittedly, one of the most complex problems on earth. But I wish to assure you that we have been deeply concerned about the interests of Turkey and of the Turkish Cypriots and will remain so.

Finally, Mr. Prime Minister, I must tell you that you have posed the gravest issues of war and peace. These are issues which go far beyond the bilateral relations between Turkey and the United States. They not only will certainly involve war between Turkey and Greece but could involve wider hostilities because of the unpredictable consequences which a unilateral intervention in Cyprus could produce. You have your responsibilities as Chief of the Government of Turkey; I also have mine as President of the United States. I must, therefore, inform you in the deepest friendship that unless I can have your assurance that you will not take such action without further and fullest consultation I cannot accept your injunction to Ambassador Hare of secrecy and must immediately ask for emergency meetings of the NATO Council and of the United Nations Security Council.

I wish it were possible for us to have a personal discussion of this situation. Unfortunately, because of the special circumstances of our present constitutional position, I am not able to leave the United States. If you could come here for a full discussion, I would welcome it. I do feel that you and I carry a very heavy responsibility for the general peace and for the possibilities of a sane and peaceful resolution of the Cyprus problem. I ask you, therefore, to delay any decisions

which you and your colleagues might have in mind until you
and I have had the fullest and frankest consultation.

Sincerely,

Lyndon B. Johnson*

---

*Source: United States Embassy in Ankara. The letter was also pub-
lished in the *Middle East Journal*, Summer 1966, pp. 386-389.

APPENDIX 33

Letter from Turkish Prime Minister Ismet Inönü
to President Lyndon B. Johnson

June 14, 1964

[complete text]

SECRET

Dear Mr. President:

I have received your message of June 5, 1964 through
Ambassador Hare. We have, upon your request, postponed
our decision to exercise our right of unilateral action in
Cyprus conferred to us by the Treaty of Guarantee. With due
regard to the spirit of candour and friendship in which your
message is meant to be written, I will, in my reply, try also to
explain to you in full frankness my views about the situation.
Mr. President:
Your message, both in wording and content, has been dis-
appointing for an ally like Turkey who has always been giving
the most serious attention to its relations of alliance with the

United States and has brought to the fore substantial divergences of opinion in various fundamental matters pertaining to these relations.

It is my sincere hope that both these divergences and the general tone of your message are due to the haste in which a representation made in good-will was, under pressure of time, based on data hurriedly collected.

In the first place, it is being emphasized in your message that we have failed to consult with the United States when a military intervention in Cyprus was deemed indispensable by virtue of the Treaty of Guarantee. The necessity of a military intervention in Cyprus has been felt four times since the closing days of 1963. From the outset we have taken a special care to consult the United States on this matter. Soon after the outbreak of the crisis, on December 25, 1963 we have immediately informed the United States of our contacts with the other Guaranteeing Powers only to be answered that the United States was not a party to this issue. We then negotiated with the United Kingdom and Greece for intervention and, as you know, a tri-partite military administration under British command was set-up on December 26, 1963. Upon the failure of the London Conference and of the joint Anglo-American proposals, due to the attitude of Makarios and in the face of continuing assaults in the Island against Turkish Cypriots, we lived through very critical days in February and taking advantage of the visit of Mr. George Ball to Ankara, we informed again the United States of the gravity of the situation. We tried to explain to you that the necessity of intervention to restore order in the Island might arise in view of the vacuum caused by the rejection of the Anglo-American proposals and we informed you that we might have to intervene at any time. We even requested guarantees from you on specific issues and your answers were in the affirmative. However, you asked us not to intervene and assured us that Makarios would get at the United Nations a severe lesson while all the Turkish rights and interests would be preserved.

We complied with your request without any satisfactory result being secured at the United Nations. Moreover the creation of the United Nations Force, decided upon by the Security Council, became a problem. The necessity for intervention was felt for the third time to protect the Turkish community against the assaults of the terrorists in Cyprus who were encouraged by the doubts as to whether the United Nations Forces would be set up immediately after the adoption of the Security Council Resolution of March 4, 1964. But assuring us that the Force would be set up very shortly, you insisted again that we refrain from intervening. Thereupon we postponed our intervention once again, awaiting the United Nations Forces to assume their duty.

Dear Mr. President,

The era of terror in Cyprus has a particular character which rendered ineffective all measures taken so far. From the very outset, the negotiations held to restore security and the temporary set-ups have all helped only to increase the aggressiveness and the destructiveness of the Makarios administration. The Greek Cypriots have lately started to arm themselves overtly and considered the United Nations as an additional instrument to back up their ruthless and unconstitutional rule. It has become quite obvious that the United Nations have neither the authority nor the intention to intervene for the restoration of constitutional order and to put an end to aggressions. You are well aware of the instigative attitude of the Greek Government towards the Greek Cypriots. During the talks held in your office, in the United States, we informed you that under the circumstances we would eventually be compelled to intervene in order to put an end to the atrocities in Cyprus. We also asked your Secretary of State at the Hague whether the United States would support us in such an eventuality and we received no answer. I think I have thus reminded you how many times and under what circumstances we informed you of the necessity for intervention in Cyprus. I do remember having emphasized to your high level

officials our due appreciation of the special responsibilities
incumbent upon the United States within the Alliance and of
the necessity to be particularly careful and helpful to enable
her to maintain solidarity within the Alliance. As you see, we
never had the intention to confront you with a unilateral
decision on our part. Our grievance stems from our inability
to explain to you a problem which caused us for months
utmost distress and from your refusal to take a frank and
firm stand on the issue as to which party is on the right side
in the dispute between two Allies, namely Turkey and
Greece.

Mr. President,

In your message you further emphasize the obligation of
Turkey, under the provisions of the Treaty, to consult with
the other two Guaranteeing Powers, before taking any unilateral action. Turkey is fully aware of this obligation. For
the past six months we have indeed complied with the requirements of this obligation. But Greece has not only
thwarted all the attempts made by Turkey to seek jointly the
ways and means to stop Greek Cypriots from repudiating
international treaties, but has also supported their unlawful
and inhuman acts and has even encouraged them.

The Greek Government itself has not hesitated to declare
publicly that the international agreements it signed with us
were no longer in force. Various examples to that effect
were, in due course, communicted in detail, orally and in
writing, to your State Department.

We have likewise fulfilled our obligation of constant consultation with the Government of the United Kingdom, the
other Guaranteeing Power.

In several instances we have, jointly with the Government
of the United Kingdom, made representations to the Greek
Cypriots with a view to restoring constitutional order. But
unfortunately, these representations were of no avail due to
the negative attitude of the Greek Cypriot authorities.

As you see, Turkey has earnestly explored every avenue of

consulting continuously and acting jointly with the other two Guaranteeing Powers. This being the fact, it can not be asserted that Turkey has failed to abide by her obligation of consulting with the other two Guaranteeing Powers before taking unilateral action.

I put it to you, Mr. President, whether the United States Government which has felt the need to draw the attention of Turkey to her obligation of consultation, yet earnestly and faithfully fulfilled by the latter, should not have reminded Greece, who repudiates treaties signed by herself, of the necessity to abide by the precept "Pacta sunt servanda" which is the fundamental rule of international law. This precept which, only a fortnight ago, was most eloquently characterized as "the basis of survival" by your Secretary of State himself in his speech at the "American Law Institute," is now being completely and contemptuously ignored by Greece, our NATO ally, and by the Greek Cypriots.

Dear Mr. President,

As implied in your message, by virtue of the provisions of Article 4 of the Treaty of Guarantee, the three Guaranteeing Powers have, in the event of a breach of the provisions of that Treaty, the right to take concerted action and, if that proves impossible, unilateral action with the sole aim of reestablishing the state of affairs created by the said Treaty. The Treaty of Guarantee was signed with this understanding being shared by all parties thereto. The "Gentlemen's Agreement," signed on February 19, 1959, by the Foreign Ministers of Turkey and Greece, is an evidence of that common understanding.

On the other hand, at the time of the admission of the Republic of Cyprus to the United Nations, the members of the Organization were fully acquainted with all the international commitments and obligations of the said Republic and no objections were raised in this respect.

Furthermore, in the course of the discussions on Cyprus leading to the resolution adopted on March 4, 1964, by the

Security Council, the United States delegate, among others, explicitly declared that the United Nations had no power to annul or amend international treaties.

The understanding expressed in your message that the intervention by Turkey in Cyprus would be for the purpose of effecting the partition of the Island has caused me great surprise and profound sorrow. My surprise stems from the fact that the data furnished to you about the intentions of Turkey could be so remote from the realities repeatedly proclaimed by us. The reason of my sorrow is that our ally, the Government of the United States, could think that Turkey might lay aside the principle constituting the foundation of her foreign policy, i.e., absolute loyalty to international law, commitments and obligations, as factually evidenced in many circumstances well known to the United States.

I would like to assure you most categorically and most sincerely that if ever Turkey finds herself forced to intervene militarily in Cyprus this will be done in full conformity with the provisions and aims of international agreements.

In this connection, allow me to stress, Mr. President, that the postponement of our decision does naturally, in no way affect the rights conferred to Turkey by Article 4 of the Treaty of Guarantee.

Mr. President,

Referring to NATO obligations, you state in your message that the very essence of NATO requires that allies should not wage war on each other and that a Turkish intervention in Cyprus would lead to a military engagement between Turkish and Greek forces.

I am in full agreement with the first part of your statement. But the obligation for the NATO allies to respect international agreements concluded among themselves as well as their mutual treaty rights and commitments is an equally vital requisite of the Alliance. An alliance among states which ignore their mutual contractual obligations and commitments is unthinkable.

As to the concern you expressed over the outbreak of a Turco-Greek war in case of Turkey's intervention in Cyprus in conformity with her rights and obligations stipulated in International Agreements, I would like to stress that Turkey would undertake a "military operation" in Cyprus exclusively under the conditions and for the purpose set forth in the agreements. Therefore, a Turco-Greek war so properly described as "literally unthinkable" by the Honorable Dean Rusk could only occur in case of Greece's aggression against Turkey. Our view, in case of such an intervention is to invite to an effective collaboration, with the aim of restoring the constitutional order in Cyprus, both Greece and the United Kingdom in their capacity as Guaranteeing Powers. If despite this invitation and its contractual obligations Greece were to attack Turkey, we could in no way be held responsible of the consequences of such an action. I would like to hope that you have already seriously drawn the Greek Government's attention on these matters.

The part of your message expressing doubts as to the obligation of the NATO allies to protect Turkey in case she becomes directly involved with the U.S.S.R. as a result of an action initiated in Cyprus, gives me the impression that there exists between us wide divergence of views as to the nature and basic principles of the North Atlantic Alliance. I must confess that this has been to us the source of great sorrow and grave concern. Any aggression against a member of NATO will naturally call from the aggressor an effort of justification. If NATO's structure is so weak as to give credit to the aggressor's allegations then it means that this defect of NATO needs really to be remedied.

Our understanding is that the North Atlantic Treaty imposes upon all member states the obligation to come forthwith to the assistance of any member victim of an aggression. The only point left to the discretion of the member states is the nature and the scale of this assistance. If NATO members should start discussing the right and wrong of the situation of their fellow-member victim of a Soviet aggression, whether this aggression was provoked or not and if the decision on whether they have an obligation to assist this member should be made to depend on the issue of such a discussion, the very foundations of the Alliance would be shaken and it would lose its meaning. An obligation of assistance, if it is to carry any weight, should come into being immediately upon the occurrence of aggression. That is why, Article 5 of the North Atlantic Treaty considers an attack against one of the member states as an attack against them all and makes it imperative for them to assist the party so attacked by taking forthwith such action as they deem necessary.

In this connection I would like to further point out that the agreements on Cyprus have met with the approval of the North Atlantic Council, as early as the stage of the United Nations debate on the problem, i.e., even prior to the establishment of the Republic of Cyprus, hence long before the occurrence of the events of December, 1963.

As you will recall, at the meeting of the NATO Ministerial Council held three weeks ago at the Hague, it was acknowledged that the Treaties continued to be the basis for legality as regards the situation in the Island and the status of Cyprus. The fact that these agreements have been violated as a result of the flagrantly unlawful acts of one of the parties on the Island should in no way mean that the said agreements are no longer in force and that the rights and obligations of Turkey by virtue of these agreements should be ignored. Such an understanding would mean that as long as no difficulties arise, the agreements are considered as valid and they are no longer in force when difficulties occur. I am sure you will agree with me that such an understanding of law cannot be accepted. I am equally convinced that there could be no shadow of doubt about the obligation to protect Turkey within the NATO Alliance in a situation that can by no means be attributed to an arbitrary act of Turkey. An opposite way of thinking would lead to the repudiation and denial of the concept of law and of Article 51 of the United Nations Charter.

In your message, concern has been expressed about the commitments of Turkey as a member of the United Nations. I am sure, Mr. President, you will agree with me if I say that such a concern, which I do not share, is groundless especially for the following reasons: Turkey has distinguished herself as one of the most loyal members of the United Nations ever since its foundation. The Turkish people has spared no effort to safeguard the principles of the United Nations Charter, and has even sacrificed her sons for this cause. Turkey has never failed in supporting this Organization and, in order to secure its proper functioning, has borne great moral and material sacrifices even when she had most pressing financial difficulties. Despite the explicit rights conferred to Turkey by the Treaty of Guarantee, my Government's respect for and adherence to the United Nations have recently been demonstrated once more by its acceptance of the Security Council Resolution of March 4, 1964 as well as by the priority it has given to the said Resolution.

Should the United Nations have been progressively successful in carrying out their task as pointed out in your message, a situation which is of such grave concern for both you and me would never have arisen. It is a fact that the United Nations' operations in the Island have proved unable to put an end to the oppression. The relative calm which has apparently prevailed in the Island for the past few weeks marks the beginning of preparations of the Greek Cypriots for further tyranny. Villages are still under siege. The United Nations Forces, assuaging Tukish Cypriots, enable the Greeks to gather their crops; but they do not try to stop the Greeks when the crops of Turks are at stake and they act as mere spectators to Greek assaults. These vitally important details may not well reach you, whereas we live in the atmosphere created by the daily reports of such tragic events.

The report of the Secretary-General will be submitted to

the United Nations on June 15, 1964. I am seriously concerned that we may face yet another defeat similar to the one
we all suffered on March 4, 1964. The session of March 4th
had further convinced Makarios that the Treaty of Guarantee
did not exist for him and thereupon he took the liberty of
actually placing the United Nations Forces under his control
and direction. From then on the assassination of hostages and
the besieging of villages have considerably increased.

(ed that we may face yet another defeat similar to the one we
all suffered on March 4, 1964. The session of March 4th had
further convinced Makarios that the Treaty of Guarantee did
not exist for him and thereupon he took the liberty of actually placing the United Nations Forces under his control and
direction. From then on the assassination of hostages and the
besieging of villages have considerably increased.)

Dear Mr. President,

Our allies who are in a position to arbiter in the Cyprus
issue and to orient it in the right direction have so far been
unable to disentangle the problem from a substantial error.
The Cyprus tragedy has been engendered by the deliberate
policy of the Republic of Cyprus aimed at annulling the
Treaties and abrogating the Constitution. Security can be established in the Island only through the proper functioning
of an authority above the Government of Cyprus. Yet only
the measures acceptable to the Cypriot Government are being
sought to restore security in Cyprus. The British administration set up following the December events, the Anglo-
American proposals, and finally the United Nations Command have all been founded on this unsound basis and consequently every measure acceptable to Makarios has proved
futile and has, in general, encouraged oppression and aggression.

Dear Mr. President,

You put forward in your message the resentment caused in
Greece by the policy pursued by your Government. Within
the context of the Cyprus issue, the nature of the Greek

policy and the course of action undertaken by Greece indicate that she is apt to resort to every means within her power
to secure the complete annulment of the existing treaties. We
are at pains to make our allies understand the sufferings we
bear in our rightful cause and the irretrievable plight in which
the Turkish Cypriots are living. On the other hand, it is not
the character of our nation to exploit demonstrations of resentment. I assure you that our distress is deeply rooted since
we can not make you understand our rightful position and
convince you of the necessity of spending every effort and
making use of all your authority to avert the perils inherent
in the Cyprus problem by attaching to it the importance it
well deserves.

That France and Germany have buried their animosity is
indeed a good example. However, our nation had already
given such an example forty years ago by establishing friendly relations with Greece, right after the ruthless devastation
of the whole [of] Anatolia by the armies of that country.

Dear Mr. President,

As a member of the Alliance our nation is fully conscious
of her duties and rights. We do not pursue any aim other than
the settlement of the Cyprus problem in compliance with the
provisions of the existing treaties. Such a settlement is likely
to be reached if you lend your support and give effect with
your supreme authority to the sense of justice inherent in the
character of the American nation.

Mr. President,

I thank you for your statements emphasizing the value
attached by the United States to the relations of alliance with
Turkey and for your kind words about the Turkish Nation. I
shall be happy to come to the United States to talk the
Cyprus problem with you. The United Nations Security
Council will meet on June the 17th. In the meantime, Mr.
Dirk Stikker, Secretary General of NATO, will have paid a
visit to Turkey. Furthermore, the United Nations mediator
Mr. Tuomioja will have submitted his report to the Secret-

ary-General. These developments may lead to the emergence of a new situation. It will be possible for me to go ahead to join you, at a date convenient for you, immediately after June 20th.

It will be most helpful for me if you would let me know of any defined views and designs you may have on the Cyprus question so that I am able to study them thoroughly before my departure for Washington.

Finally, I would like to express my satisfaction for the frank, fruitful and promising talks we had with Mr. G. Ball in Ankara just before forwarding this message to you.*

Sincerely,

ISMET INÖNÜ*

---

*Source: United States Embassy in Ankara. The letter was also published in the *Middle East Journal*, Summer 1966, pp. 389-93.

Notes

CHAPTER 1

1. See Arnold J. Toynbee, *A Study of History*, abridgement of Vol. VII-X (New York: Oxford University Press, 1957), pp. 238-40.

2. Herodotus, *The Histories* (Edinburgh: Penguin Classics, 1954), Book Five, p. 270. The distances mentioned in the text are Greek measurements converted into statute miles.

3. The description of the Straits and the Sea of Marmara largely follows the Preparatory Document printed for the United Nations Conference on the Law of the Sea: *A Brief Geographical and Hydrographical Study of Straits Which Constitute Routes for International Traffic* by Commander R. H. Kennedy, U.N. Official Records, Geneva, 1958, Document A/CONF.13/6 and Add. 1, pp. 137-39.

4. See M. S. Anderson, *The Eastern Question, 1774-1923* (London: Macmillan, 1966), pp. 258, 304.

5. Anderson, pp. 326-27; Roderic H. Davison, *Turkey* (Englewood Cliffs, N.J.: Prentice-Hall, 1968), p. 117.

6. Vernon J. Puryear, *Napoleon and the Dardanelles* (Berkeley, Calif.: University of California Press, 1951), p. 144. Admiral Duckworth called the Dardanelles "that infernal strait."

7. See Jean Gottman, *A Geography of Europe* (3rd ed., New York: Holt, Rhinehart & Winston, 1962), p. 636.

8. Lewis V. Thomas and Richard N. Frye, *The United States and Turkey and Iran* (Cambridge, Mass.: Harvard University Press, 1951), p. 5.

9. Puryear, pp. 325-26.

10. Adolphe Thiers, *Histoire du Consulat et de l'Empire*, Vol. VII (Paris: Paulin, 1847), p. 654.

11. See Felix Sartiaux, *La Question de Troie et les origines préhistoriques de la Question d'Orient* (Paris: Hachette, 1915).

12. For the history of the Straits in antiquity and the Middle Ages, see N. Dascovici, *La Question du Bosphore et des Dardanelles* (Geneva: Georg and Company, 1915), pp. 1-34.

CHAPTER 2

1. See B. H. Sumner, *Peter the Great and the Ottoman Empire* (Oxford: Basil Blackwell, 1949).

2. See M. S. Anderson, *The Eastern Question, 1774-1923* (London: Macmillan, 1966), pp. 29, 34-35.

3. See Coleman Phillipson and Noel Buxton, *The Question of the Bosphorus and Dardanelles* (London: Stevens & Haynes, 1917), pp. 43-45; Vernon J. Puryear, *Napoleon and the Dardanelles* (Berkeley, Calif.: University of California Press, 1951), *passim*.

4. See Philip E. Mosely, *Russian Diplomacy and the Opening of the Eastern Question in 1838 and 1839* (Cambridge, Mass.: Harvard University Press, 1934).

5. See U.S. Department of State, *Foreign Relations of the United States. Diplomatic Papers: The Conference of Berlin (The Potsdam Conference), 1945* (Washington, D.C.: U.S.Government Printing Office, 1961), Vol. I, p. 1035.

6. For the individual cases when warships were permitted to pass the Straits, see Phillipson and Buxton, *op. cit.* n. 3, pp. 150-70.

7. For the adventures of the *Goeben* and the *Breslau*, see the masterly description by Barbara W. Tuchman, *The Guns of August* (New York: Macmillan, 1962), pp. 137-62.

8. See Feridun Cemal Erkin, *Les Relations Turco-Soviétiques et la Question des Détroits* (Ankara: Basnur Matbaasi, 1968), pp. 51-52.

9. Before World War I, 54 per cent of Russia's maritime exports originated in Black Sea ports; Jacques Grosbois, *La Turquie et les Détroits* (Paris: Editions du Chêne, 1945), p. 12.

10. See Ahmet Emin Yalman, *Turkey in the World War* (New Haven, Conn.: Yale University Press, 1930), pp. 276-77.

11. For the text of the abortive Treaty of Sèvres, see J. C. Hurowitz, *Diplomacy in the Near and Middle East* (Princeton, N.J.: D. Van Nostrand, 1956), Vol. II, pp. 81-89.

CHAPTER 3

1. The proceedings of the conference are recorded in the following publication *Actes de la Conférence de Montreux, 22 juin-20 juillet 1936*. Compte rendu des séances plénières et procès-verbal des débats du Comité technique (Liège [Belgium]: H. Vaillant-Carmanne s.a., October 1936). For a detailed analysis of the positions taken by the various delegations at Montreux and their deliberations, see D. A. Routh, "The Montreux Convention Regarding the Regime of the Black Sea Straits (20th July, 1936)" in *Survey of International Affairs, 1936* (London: Oxford University Press, 1937), pp. 584-661. See also U.S., Department of State, *The Problem of the Turkish Straits* (Washington, D.C.: U.S. Government Printing Office, 1947), pp. 1-12.

2. See Juliette Abrévaya, *La Conférence de Montreux et le régime des Détroits* (Paris: Éditions Internationales, 1938), p. 101.

3. *Actes de la Conférence, op. cit.* n. 1, p. 15.

4. *Ibid.*, p. 43.

5. *Ibid.*, pp. 84-85.

6. *Ibid.*, pp. 90-97, 110-14.

7. See *Survey of International Affairs, 1938*, Vol. III (London: Oxford University Press, 1953), pp. 444-45.

8. See Harry N. Howard, "The Straits After the Montreux Conference," *Foreign Affairs*, October 1936, pp. 199-202.

CHAPTER 4

1. For a detailed narrative of the visit of Foreign Minister Saracoğlu in Moscow in September-October 1939, see Feridun Cemal Erkin, *Les Relations Turco-Soviétiques et la Question des Détroits* (Ankara: Başnur Matbaası, 1968), pp. 154-79. The author was at that time general director of the Political Section in the Turkish Ministry of Foreign Affairs and accompanied Saracoğlu to Moscow. See also Michael Sokolnicki, *The Turkish Straits* (Beirut: American Press, 1950), pp. 17-19.

2. See Alvin Z. Rubinstein (ed.), *The Foreign Policy of the Soviet Union* (2d ed., New York: Random House, 1966), pp. 160-62.

3. For the negotiations between Molotov and the German leaders in November 1940 in Berlin, see Necmeddin Sadak, "Turkey Faces the Soviets," *Foreign Affairs*, April 1949, pp. 449-61.

4. See Ferenc A. Váli, *Bridge Across the Bosporus* (Baltimore: Johns Hopkins Press, 1971), pp. 31-33, 189-90.

5. See Feridun Cemal Erkin, *op. cit.* n. 1, pp. 295-96.

6. Winston S. Churchill, *Triumph and Tragedy; The Second World War*, Vol. 6 (Boston: Houghton Mifflin, 1953), p. 572.

7. See United States, Department of State, *The Problem of the Turkish Straits* (Washington, D.C.: U.S. Government Printing Office, 1947), pp. 36-37.

8. For the text of the treaty, see J. C. Hurewitz, *Diplomacy in the Near and Middle East*, Vol. I. (Princeton, N.J.: D. Van Nostrand, 1956), pp. 102-5.

9. See Harry N. Howard, "The United States and the Problem of the Turkish Straits," *Middle East Journal*, January 1947, pp. 59-72.

10. Feridun Cemal Erkin, *op. cit.* n. 1, pp. 315-17.

11. See Altemur Kiliç, *Turkey and the World* (Washington, D.C.: Public Affairs Press, 1959), pp. 125-26.

12. *The Problem of the Turkish Straits*, p. 37.

13. For the wartime precedents, see Cemil Bilsel, "The Turkish Straits in the Light of Recent Turkish-Soviet Russian Correspondence," *American Journal of International Law*, October 1947, pp. 727-47.

14. For Soviet threats against Turkey, see Walter Laqueur, *The Soviet Union and the Middle East* (New York: Frederick A. Praeger, 1959), pp. 143-45; *Survey of International Affairs, 1951* (London: Oxford University Press, 1954), p. 36. For the Turkish note, see *Documents on International Affairs, 1951* (London: Oxford University Press, 1954), p. 69.

15. *Documents on International Affairs, 1953* (London: Oxford University Press, 1956), pp. 277-78.

16. *Ibid.*, p. 278.

17. For an analysis of the new trend in the foreign policy of Turkey, see Ferenc A. Váli, *op. cit.* n. 4, pp. 133-37.

CHAPTER 5

1. For the text of the North Atlantic Treaty see TIAS (Treaties and Other International Agreements), 1964; *United States Statutes at Large*, 81st Congress, 1st Sess., 1949, LXIII, Part II, 2242. For the Protocol of Accession of Greece and Turkey see TIAS 2390, *United States Treaties and Other International Agreements*, Part 1, 43.

2. See *Survey of International Affairs, 1951* (London: Oxford University Press, 1954), pp. 33-34.

3. See further Ferenc A. Váli, *Bridge Across the Bosporus—The Foreign Policy of Turkey* (Baltimore: Johns Hopkins Press, 1971), pp. 119-20.

4. See Sir Knox Helm, "Turkey and Her Defence Problems," *International Affairs* Vol. XXX, No. 4 (October 1954), 434-39.

5. For complaints concerning the lack of sufficient modernization of the army and navy, see the articles in the Turkish newspapers *Milliyet* (July 3, 1967) and *Tercüman* (December 12, 1967).

6. See Jean Labayle, "La Marine turque," *Revue de Défense Nationale,* June 1970, pp. 1042-44.

7. Hanson W. Baldwin, "Strategy of the Middle East," *Foreign Affairs,* July 1957, pp. 655-65. The reference in the text is from p. 660.

8. See Dankwart A. Rustow, "Defense of the Near East," *Foreign Affairs,* January 1956, pp. 271-86; see also Timothy W. Stanley, *NATO*

in Transition: The Future of the Atlantic Alliance (New York: Praeger, 1965), pp. 298-99.

9. See the declaration of Defense Minister Ahmet Topaloğlu during the defense budget debate in the Turkish Senate; *Cumhuriyet*, February 2, 1969.

10. See E. Hinterhoff, "Les flancs de l'OTAN," *Revue de Défense Nationale*, January 1960, pp. 124-36. For the northern flank of NATO, see Nils Örvik, *Europe's Northern Cap and the Soviet Union* (Cambridge: Harvard University, Center for International Affairs, 1963), Occasional Papers No. 6.

11. See *New York Times*, April 6, 1967; *Milliyet*, September 26, 1967; *Tercüman*, September 29, 1967; *Cumhuriyet*, December 12, 1967.

12. See Fred S. Hoffman, "NATO's Mobile Forces," *Atlantic Community Quarterly*, Vol. IV, No. 2 (Summer 1966), 242-48.

13. See, particularly, the article by Turkish Rear Admiral (retired) Sezai Orkunt in *Cumhuriyet*, October 30, 1967.

14. See *New York Times*, November 21, 1952. See also George C. McGhee, "Turkey Joins the West," *Foreign Affairs*, July 1954, pp. 617-30.

15. For further details see Váli, *op. cit.*, n. 3, pp. 125-46.

16. See *New York Times*, June 15 and August 5, 1970.

17. For the Sixth Fleet, see *New York Times*, July 23, 1968, and December 24, 1970; *Cumhuriyet*, February 11, 1969.

18. *New York Times*, December 7, 1968; *Milliyet*, November 19, 1968; *Hurriyet*, March 26, 1969.

19. See *Cumhuriyet*, February 5, 1969.

20. *New York Times*, December 7, 9, 10, and 11, 1968.

21. *Akşam*, December 10 and 13, 1968; defending American rights, see *Yeni Gazete* and *Son Havadis*, December 13, 1968.

22. *Milliyet*, December 7, 1968.

23. *Yeni Gazete*, December 11, 1968.

24. *Cumhuriyet*, December 9, 1968.

25. *Yeni Gazete*, November 10, 1970.

26. See *New York Times*, February 8, 1969; *Milliyet*, February 11, 1969. This writer was assured by officials of the Turkish Ministry of Foreign Affairs that no Soviet submarine is permitted to pass the Straits.

CHAPTER 6

1. See Robert J. Kerner, "Russian Naval Aims," *Foreign Affairs*, January 1946, pp. 290-99.

2. See Robert Waring Herrick, *Soviet Naval Strategy* (Annapolis, Md.: United States Naval Institute, 1968), pp. 134-35.

3. See Martin Edmonds and John Skitt, "Current Soviet Maritime Strategy and NATO," *International Affairs* (London), January 1969, p. 30. Data on Soviet naval strength are also taken from *Jane's Fighting Ships, 1969-1970* (London: Sampson Low, Marston & Company, 1969).

4. See Paul Wohl, "Soviet Canals Grow, and Grow," *Christian Science Monitor*, July 18, 1970.

5. Herrick, *op. cit., n. 2;* Henry E. Eccles, "The Russian Maritime Threat: An Approach to the Problem," *Naval War College Review*, Vol. XXI, No. 10 (June 1969), 4-14; Edward L. Beach, "An Appraisal of Soviet Maritime-Naval Capabilities," *Naval War College Review*, Vol. XXI, No. 10 (June 1969), 15-25; Robert A. Kilmarx (ed.), *Soviet Sea Power* (Washington, D.C.: Center for Strategic and International Studies, Georgetown University), Special Report Series, No. 10, 1969.

6. This is the view held by Edmonds and Skitt, *op. cit.* n. 3.

7. See Milovan Djilas, *Conversations with Stalin* (New York: Harcourt, Brace and World, 1962), p. 182.

8. For the description of the *Moskva*-type helicopter carrier, see *Jane's Fighting Ships, 1969-70*, p. 539.

9. See Kilmarx, *op. cit.* n. 5, pp. 56-59; Alec Douglas-Home, "Red Fleet of Suez–Mediterranean Challenge," *Atlantic Community Quarterly*, Vol. 7, No. 1 (Spring 1969), 78-79.

10. Vice Admiral N. Smirnov, "Soviet Ships in the Mediterranean," *Krasnaya Zvezda,* November 12, 1968.

11. See, for instance, Abdı Ipekci in *Milliyet,* July 25, 1967; and Mehmet Barlas in *Cumhuriyet,* October 2, 1970.

12. Captain Carl H. Amme, Jr., "The Soviet Navy in the Mediterranean," *Naval War College Review,* Vol. XXI, No. 10 (June 1969), 155.

13. Douglas-Home, *op. cit.* n. 9, p. 83.

14. Denis Healey, then the British Defense Secretary, said in an interview that in the event of war the Soviet fleet in the Mediterranean would not have time to fire its remote-control missiles and would be sunk within minutes; *New York Times,* February 11, 1969.

15. Douglas-Home, *op. cit.* n. 9, p. 84.

16. Drew Middleton in *New York Times,* November 24, 1968.

17. Drew Middleton in *New York Times,* May 13, 1970.

18. See Hanson W. Baldwin, "Strategy of the Middle East," *Foreign Affairs,* July 1957, p. 659.

19. Statement of Turkish Ambassador to NATO, Muharrem Nuri Birgi; *Yeni Gazete* and *Tercüman,* June 30, 1970.

20. *New York Times,* October 7, 1970.

21. See Aaron S. Klieman, *Soviet Russia and the Middle East* (Baltimore: Johns Hopkins Press, 1970), p. 98.

22. See Bernard Lewis, "The Great Powers, the Arabs, and the Israelis," *Foreign Affairs,* July 1969, p. 645.

23. *Pravda,* November 27, 1968, as reported and commented on by the *New York Times,* November 28, 1968.

24. *Son Havadis,* July 24, 1968.

25. See Ferenc A. Váli, *Bridge Across the Bosporus—The Foreign Policy of Turkey* (Baltimore: Johns Hopkins Press, 1971), pp. 157-64.

26. From an article by Rear Admiral (retired) Sezai Orkunt in *Cumhuriyet,* April 12, 1968.

27. See Váli, *op. cit.* n. 25, pp. 73, 160-61.

28. *Milliyet*, June 24, 1970. Italics added.

29. *Milliyet*, July 10, 1968, quoted *Pravda* after Çaglayangil's meet-ing with Soviet Foreign Minister Gromyko that despite friendly Turk-ish-Soviet relations "the clouds have still not been dispelled."

30. "Our target is to raise our nation to the level of contemporary civilization. This target includes everything." Prime Minister Süleyman Demirel before the General Executive Board of the Justice Party on November 28, 1968; *Milliyet*, November 29, 1968.

CHAPTER 7

1. For the text of the Convention on the Territorial Sea and the Contiguous Zone, see *The American Journal of International Law*, Vol. 52, No. 4 (October 1958), 834-42.

2. See R. R. Baxter, *The Law of International Waterways* (Cam-bridge, Mass.: Harvard University Press, 1964), pp. 165-68.

3. Document No. 1366, U.S. Department of State, Foreign Rela-tions of the United States, Diplomatic Papers, *The Conference of Berlin (The Potsdam Conference), 1945*, Vol. II (Washington, D.C.: U.S. Gov-ernment Printing Office, 1960), pp. 1425-26.

4. See Stévan Tchirkovitch, "La Question de la révision de la Con-vention de Montreux concernant le régime des Détroits Turcs: Bosphore et Dardanelles," *Revue Générale de Droit International Pub-lic*, Vol. 56 (1952), 189-222.

5. See Fred S. Hoffman, "NATO's Mobile Forces," *Atlantic Com-munity Quarterly*, Vol. 4, No. 2 (Summer 1966), 248; *Cumhuriyet*, October 11, 1970.

6. See, for instance, the articles in *Milliyet* and *Cumhuriyet* (No-vember 7-8, 1970) based on reports by their correspondents writing from Brussels.

7. See Ferenc A. Váli, *Bridge Across the Bosporus—The Foreign Policy of Turkey* (Baltimore, Md.: Johns Hopkins Press, 1971), pp. 369-85.

8. Drew Middleton in the *New York Times*, November 2, 1970.

9. See Paul Cohen, "The Erosion of Naval Surface Power," *Foreign Affairs*, January 1971, pp. 330-41.

10. *New York Times*, September 18, 1970.

11. Admiral Thomas H. Moorer, Chief of Naval Operations, in testimony before Congress; *New York Times,* April 23, 1970.

12. See article by Neil Sheehan, "Navy, Pointing to Soviet, Seeks 4th Atomic Carrier," *New York Times*, August 22, 1970.

13. See Drew Middleton in the *New York Times*, December 26, 1970.

14. See Robert E. Hunter, *The Soviet Dilemma in the Middle East, Part I: Problems of Commitments*, Adelphi Papers No. 59 (London: Institute for Strategic Studies, 1969), pp. 24-25.

15. The story was told by Foreign Minister Çaglayangil who, as a member of the Turkish parliament, was also present at this incident; *Cumhuriyet*, May 22, 1970.

Bibliography

DOCUMENTS, OFFICIAL PUBLICATIONS, REFERENCE BOOKS

Actes de la Conférence de Montreux, 22 juin-20 juillet 1936. Compte rendu des séances plénières et procès-verbal des débats du Comité technique. Liège (Belgium): H. Vaillant-Carmanne s.a., 1936.

Bilsel, Cemil. *Türk Boğazları* (The Turkish Straits). Istanbul: Ismail Akgün, 1948. (Documents and texts of Soviet and Turkish diplomatic notes relative to the Straits.)

Documents on International Affairs, 1936. London: Oxford University Press (for the Royal Institute of International Affairs), 1937.

Documents on International Affairs, 1951. London: Oxford University Press (for the Royal Institute of International Affairs), 1954.

Documents on International Affairs, 1953. London: Oxford University Press (for the Royal Institute of International Affairs), 1956.

Documents on International Affairs, 1960. London: Oxford University Press (for the Royal Institute of International Affairs), 1964.

Hurewitz, J. C. *Diplomacy in the Near and Middle East: A Documentary Record.* Vols. I and II. Princeton, N.J.: D. Van Nostrand, 1956.

Jane's Fighting Ships, 1969-1970. London: Sampson Low, Marston and Company, 1969.

Kennedy, R. H. *A Brief Geographical and Hydrological Study of Straits Which Constitute Routes for International Traffic.* Preparatory Document No. 6. I. *United Nations Conference on the Law of the Sea.* Off. Rec. 114 (U.N. Doc. No. A/CONF. 13/38) (1958).

Lawson, Ruth C. (ed.). *International Regional Organizations.* New York: Praeger, 1962.

League of Nations Treaty Series. Vol. XXVIII (1924), pp. 115-137. (Convention Regarding the Regime of the Straits. Signed at Lausanne, July 24, 1923.)

League of Nations Treaty Series. Vol. CLXXIII (1936), pp. 215-241. (Convention Regarding the Regime of the Straits. Signed at Montreux, July 20, 1936.)

NATO—Facts About the North Atlantic Treaty Organization. Paris: NATO Information Service, 1965.

Rubinstein, Alvin Z. (ed.). *The Foreign Policy of the Soviet Union.* 2d ed. New York: Random House, 1966.

Survey of International Affairs, 1936. London: Oxford University Press, 1937.

Survey of International Affairs, 1951. London: Oxford University Press, 1954.

United States. Department of State. *The Problem of the Turkish Straits.* Washington, D.C.: U.S. Government Printing Office, 1947.

The Conferences of Malta and Yalta, 1945. Foreign Relations of the United States, Diplomatic Papers. Washington, D.C.: U.S. Government Printing Office, 1955.

The Conference of Berlin (The Potsdam Conference), 1945. Foreign Relations of the United States, Diplomatic Papers. Washington, D.C.: U.S. Government Printing Office, 1960, Vols. I and II.

HISTORICAL AND BACKGROUND BOOKS

Ancel, Jacques. *Géopolitique.* Paris: Librairie Delagrave, 1936.

Anderson, M. S. *The Eastern Question, 1774-1923.* London: Macmillan, 1966.

Anshen, Ruth Anda (ed.). *Mid-East: World-Center, Yesterday, Today, and Tomorrow*. New York: Harper and Brothers, 1956.

Churchill, Winston S. *The Second World War: Triumph and Tragedy*. Boston: Houghton Mifflin, 1953.

Davison, Roderic H. *Turkey*. Englewood Cliffs, N.J.: Prentice-Hall, 1968.

Djilas, Milovan. *Conversations with Stalin*. New York: Harcourt, Brace and World, 1962.

Gottmann, Jean. *La Politique des Etats et leur géographie*. Paris: A. Colin, 1952.

―――. *A Geography of Europe*. 3d ed. New York: Holt, Rinehart and Winston, 1962.

Herodotus. *The Histories*. Edinburgh: Penguin Classics, 1954.

Marriott, J. A. R. *The Eastern Question*. 4th ed. Oxford: Clarendon Press, 1947.

Puryear, Vernon J. *Napoleon and the Dardanelles*. Berkeley, Calif.: University of California Press, 1951.

Sartiaux, Félix. *La Guerre de Troie et les origines préhistoriques de la Question d'Orient*. Paris: Hachette, 1915.

Sumner, B. H. *Peter the Great and the Ottoman Empire*. Oxford: Basil Blackwell, 1949.

Thiers, Adolphe. *Histoire du Consulat et de l'Empire*. Vol. VII. Paris: Paulin, 1847.

Toynbee, Arnold J. *A Study of History*. New York: Oxford University Press. (Abridgment of Vols. I-VI [1947] and Vols. VII-X [1957].)

BOOKS

Abrévaya, Juliette. *La Conférence de Montreux et le régime des Détroits*. Paris: Editions Internationales, 1938.

Baldwin, Hanson W. *Strategy for Tomorrow*. New York: Harper and Row, 1970.

Baxter, R. R. *The Law of International Waterways*. Cambridge, Mass.: Harvard University Press, 1964.

Buchan, Alastair. *NATO in the 1960's: The Implication of Interdependence*. New York: Praeger (for the Institute for Strategic Studies), 1960.

Campbell, John C. *Defense of the Middle East: Problems of American Policy*. New York: Harper, 1958.

Dascovici, N. *La Question du Bosphore et des Dardanelles*. Geneva: Georg and Company, 1915.

Erkin, Feridun Cemal. *Les Relations Turco-Soviétiques et la Question des Détroits*. Ankara: Başnur Matbaasi, 1968.

Gasteyger, Curt. *Conflict and Tension in the Mediterranean*. Adelphi Papers No. 51. London: Institute for Strategic Studies, September 1968.

Goriainov, Serge M. *Le Bosphore et les Dardanelles*. Paris: Plan-Nourrit, 1910.

Graves, Philip Perceval. *The Question of the Straits*. London: E. Benn, 1931.

Grosbois, Jacques. *La Turquie et les Détroits*. Paris: Editions du Chêne, 1945.

Gullion, Edmund A. (ed.). *Uses of the Seas*. Englewood Cliffs, N.J.: Prentice-Hall, 1968.

Harari, Maurice. *Government and Politics of the Middle East*. Englewood Cliffs, N.J.: Prentice-Hall, 1962.

Herrick, Robert Waring. *Soviet Naval Strategy*. Annapolis, Md.: U.S. Naval Institute, 1968.

Hoskins, Halford L. *The Middle East: Problem Area in World Politics*. New York: Macmillan, 1954.

Howard, Harry N. *The Partition of Turkey: A Diplomatic History, 1913-1923*. New York: Howard Ferig, 1966.

Hunter, Robert E. *The Soviet Dilemma in the Middle East*. Part I: *Problems of Commitment*. Adelphi Papers No. 59. London: Institute for Strategic Studies, 1969.

Hurewitz, J. C. *Middle East Politics: The Military Dimension.* New York: Praeger (for the Council of Foreign Relations), 1969.

–––. (ed.). *Soviet-American Rivalry in the Middle East.* New York: Academy of Political Science, Columbia University, 1969.

Imhoff, Christoph von. *Duell im Mittelmeer: Moskau greift nach dem Nahen und Mittleren Osten.* Freiburg i. Br.: Rombach, 1968.

Kennedy, Robert F. *Thirteen Days: A Memoir of the Cuban Missile Crisis.* New York: W. W. Norton and Company, 1969.

Kilmarx, Robert A. (ed.). *Soviet Sea Power.* Special Report Series No. 10. Washington, D.C.: Center for Strategic and International Studies, Georgetown University, 1969.

Klieman, Aaron S. *Soviet Russia and the Middle East.* Baltimore, Md.: Johns Hopkins Press, 1970.

Lacoste, Raymond. *La Russie soviétique et la Question d'Orient; La poussée soviétique vers les mers chaudes, Méditerranée et Golfe persique.* Paris: Editions Internationales, 1946.

Laqueur, Walter Z. *The Soviet Union and the Middle East.* New York: Praeger, 1959.

Lewis, Bernard. *The Middle East and the West.* Bloomington, Ind.: Indiana University Press, 1964.

Mischef, P. H. *La Mer Noire et les Détroits de Constantinople.* Paris: Arthur Rousseau, 1899.

Mosely, Philip W. *Russian Diplomacy and the Opening of the Eastern Question in 1838 and 1839.* Cambridge, Mass.: Harvard University Press, 1934.

Örvik, Nils. *Europe's Northern Cap and the Soviet Union.* Occasional Papers No. 6. Cambridge, Mass.: Center for International Affairs, Harvard University, 1963.

Phillipson, Coleman, and Noel Buxton. *The Question of the Bosphorus and Dardanelles.* London: Stevens and Haynes, 1917.

Reitzel, William. *The Mediterranean: Its Role in America's Foreign Policy.* New York: Harcourt, Brace and Company, 1948.

Shotwell, James T., and Francis Deak. *Turkey at the Straits: A Short History.* New York: Macmillan, 1940.

Sokolnicki, Michael. *The Turkish Straits*. Beirut: American Press, 1950.

Stanley, Timothy W. *NATO in Transition: The Future of the Atlantic Alliance*. New York: Praeger, 1965.

Stevens, Georgiana G. (ed.). *The United States and the Middle East*. Englewood Cliffs, N.J.: Prentice-Hall, 1964.

Thomas, Lewis V., and Richard N. Frye. *The United States and Turkey and Iran*. Cambridge, Mass.: Harvard University Press, 1951.

Tuchman, Barbara W. *The Guns of August*. New York: Macmillan, 1962.

Tukin, Cemal. *Osmanlı Imperatorluğu devrinde boğazlar meselesi* (The Problem of the Straits in the Epoch of the Ottoman Empire). Istanbul:Üniversite Matbaacilik Kommandit Şirketi, 1947.

Váli, Ferenc A. *Bridge Across the Bosporus–The Foreign Policy of Turkey*. Baltimore, Md.: Johns Hopkins Press, 1971.

Yalman, Ahmet Emin. *Turkey in the World War*. New Haven, Conn.: Yale University Press, 1930.

ARTICLES

Amme, Captain Carl H. "Seapower and the Superpowers," *United States Naval Institute Proceedings*, Vol. 94, No. 10 (October 1968), 27-35.

–––. "The Soviet Navy in the Mediterranean," *Naval War College Review*, Vol. XXI, No. 10 (June 1969), 154-59.

Baldwin, Hanson W. "Strategy of the Middle East," *Foreign Affairs*, July 1957, pp. 655-65.

Beach, Edward L. "An Appraisal of Soviet Maritime–Naval Capabilities," *Naval War College Review*, Vol. XXI, No. 10 (June 1969), 15-25.

Bilsel, Cemil. "International Law in Turkey," *American Journal of International Law*, October 1944, pp. 546-56.

–––. "The Turkish Straits in the Light of Recent Turkish-Soviet Correspondence," *American Journal of International Law*, October 1947, pp. 727-47.

Douglas-Home, Alec. "Red Fleet off Suez–Mediterranean Challenge," *Atlantic Community Quarterly*, Vol. 7, No. 1 (Spring 1969), 78-89.

Eccles, Henry E. "The Russian Maritime Threat: An Approach to the Problem," *Naval War College Review*, Vol. XXI, No. 10 (June 1969), 4–14.

Edmonds, Martin, and John Skitt. "Current Soviet Maritime Strategy and NATO," *International Affairs* (London), January 1969, pp. 28-43.

Esmer, Ahmed Sükrü. "The Straits: Crux of World Politics," *Foreign Affairs*, January 1947, pp. 290-302.

Helm, Sir Knox. "Turkey and Her Defence Problems," *International Affairs* (London), October 1954, pp. 434-39.

Hinterhoff, E. "Les flancs de l'OTAN," *Revue de Défense Nationale*, January 1960, pp. 124-36.

Hoffman, Fred S. "NATO's Mobile Forces," *Atlantic Community Quarterly*, Vol. 4, No. 2 (Summer 1966), 242-48.

Howard, Harry N. "The Straits After the Montreux Conference," *Foreign Affairs*, October 1936, pp. 199-202.

–––. "The United States and the Problem of the Turkish Straits," *Middle East Journal*, January 1947, pp. 59-72.

Hurewitz, J. C. "Russia and the Turkish Straits," *World Politics*, July 1962, pp. 605-32.

Kerner, Robert J. "Russian Naval Aims," *Foreign Affairs*, January 1946, pp. 290-99.

Labayle, Jean. "La Marine turque," *Revue de Défense Nationale*, June 1970, pp. 1042-44.

Lewis, Bernard. "The Great Powers, the Arabs, and Israelis," *Foreign Affairs*, July 1969, pp. 642-52.

Padelford, Norman J. "Solutions to the Problem of the Turkish Straits: A Brief Appraisal," *Middle East Journal*, April 1948, pp. 175-90.

Radek, Karl. "The Bases of Soviet Foreign Policy," *Foreign Affairs*, January 1934, pp. 193-206.

Routh, D. A. "The Montreux Convention Regarding the Regime of the Black Sea Straits," in *Survey of International Affairs, 1936*. London: Oxford University Press, 1937.

Rustow, Dankwart A. "Defense of the Near East," *Foreign Affairs*, January 1956, pp. 271-86.

Sadak, Necmeddin. "Turkey Faces the Soviets," *Foreign Affairs*, April 1949, pp. 449-61.

Smirnov, Vice Admiral N. "Soviet Ships in the Mediterranean," *Krasnaya Zvezda*, November 12, 1968.

Tchirkovitch, Stévan. "La Question de la revision de la Convention de Montreux concernant le régime des Détroits turcs: Bosphore et Dardanelles," *Revue Générale de Droit International Public*, Vol. 56 (1952), 189-222.

Thomas, Lewis V. "Turkey: Guardian of the Straits," *Current History*, July 1951, pp. 8-11.

Van Alstyne, Richard W. "The Question of the Turkish Straits," *Current History*, August 1947, pp. 65-70.

TURKISH PERIODICALS AND DAILY PAPERS

Akşam (Ankara)

Cumhuriyet (Istanbul)

Milliyet (Istanbul)

Pulse (English review of the Turkish press)

Son Havadis (Istanbul)

Tercüman (Istanbul)

Turkish Yearbook of International Relations. Published by the Institute of International Relations, University of Ankara.

Ulus (Ankara)

Index